PRAISE FOR PHIL GAIMON

"[A] wickedly funny and insightful cycling book that unmasks the mundane and hilarious truths behind a too-often mythologized sport. Much of *Pro Cycling on $10 a Day* spins as pure pleasure—an inside account of what it's really like to race for a living and occasionally be among the sport's elite. Anyone who loves the sport will enjoy Gaimon's self-flagellating accounts of races and the hidden codes of the roadway. (In one race, he finds himself repeatedly flicked toward the dirt by Armstrong's teammates for daring to challenge their authority.) The best parts read like an unpretentious insider's diary, full of the kind of wisecracks, gossip and advice traded on memorable long rides."

—Jason Gay, *The Wall Street Journal*

"At a time when pro cycling has struggled with its image, Phil Gaimon has emerged as a refreshing voice—intelligent, humorous, articulate, and above all, transparent. As a college-educated latecomer to the sport, as an outsider who struggled to be given a chance, and as someone with the perspective to laugh at the absurdity of being paid to ride a bicycle for a living, Gaimon's insights into the pro cycling world resonate with a wide audience. He's a rider you want to hear from, and know more about, win or lose."

—*Velo* magazine

"Having watched Phil race over the past few years, we know he is a great, versatile rider with a huge amount of talent. Beyond that, he is also funny, smart, and a unique addition to the team."

—Jonathan Vaughters, CEO, Team Garmin-Sharp

"An outspoken proponent of clean competition, Gaimon sports a tattoo of a bar of soap with the word 'clean' on his right bicep, and he was attracted to Garmin-Sharp for its ethical code."

—CyclingNews.com

"Phil Gaimon embodies what every aspiring cyclist wants to be: skinny, fast, and clean. He attacked his dream of going pro so hard he ended up in a nightmare with me. Read his book and you'll realize that Phil speaks the truth: Bike racing is hard, but becoming a pro is even harder."

—Brad Huff, professional cyclist for Optum presented by Kelly Benefit Strategies

"*Pro Cycling on $10 a Day* is the story we all want to hear: A regular guy who rides from overweight amateur to European pro in a short time, finding his way and making the best decisions from the resources he had. Phil's story inspires hope in up-and-comers about what hard work can produce. If you listen, pay attention, and surround yourself with the best people you can, then no dream is out of reach."

—Jeremy Powers, professional cyclist for Jelly Belly Cycling Team and Team Rapha-Focus, and two-time U.S. Cyclocross National Champion

PRO CYCLING ON $10 A DAY

PRO CYCLING ON $10 A DAY

FROM FAT KID TO EURO PRO

PHIL GAIMON

Boulder, Colorado

▼ velopress®

3002 Sterling Circle, Suite 100
Boulder, Colorado 80301-2338 USA
velopress@competitorgroup.com

Distributed in the United States and Canada by Ingram Publisher Services

Library of Congress Cataloging-in-Publication Data
Gaimon, Phil.
  Pro cycling on $10 a day: from fat kid to Euro pro / Phil Gaimon.
    pages cm
  ISBN 978-1-937715-24-3 (paperback)
1. Cyclists—United States—Biography. 2. Bicycle racing. 3. Cycling. I. Title.
GV1051.G35 2014
796.6092—dc23
[B]
            2014004498

For information on purchasing VeloPress books, please visit www.velopress.com.

Cover design by Charles Chamberlin
Interior design and composition by Andy Omel
Front cover photograph by Brad Hines
Back cover photograph by Lyne Lamoureux
Interior photographs courtesy of the author, with the exception of the following:
p. 4, Kimberly Filipek; p. 9, Ryan Fisher; p. 22, Matthew Koschara; p. 37, Marco
Quezada; p. 57, Casey B. Gibson; p. 68, Al Hospers, neclimbs.com; p. 166, Michelle
Blake; p. 228, Danny Munson; pp. 230 and 234, Jonathan Devich/epicimages.us;
p. 257, Deborah Ball McGeorge; p. 259, Gil Dupuy; p. 265, Kristy Morrow;
p. 295, Brad Hines.

Text set in Amasis

16 / 10   9   8   7   6   5   4

When Tyler Hamilton tested positive for a blood transfusion,
he claimed that he had a twin who died in utero,
and some of those blood cells remained in his body.

I'd like to dedicate this work to the memory of Tyler's
tragically "vanishing" chimeric twin sibling
and to Lance Armstrong's famous missing testicle.

May they rest in peace.

CONTENTS

CONFESSION

I've been holding this in for too long. Now that all the other cyclists are admitting it, it's my turn to get some things off my chest, so I can finally start to let it go and move on. I was pressured into it by my team, doctors, and competition, and I had no choice. Even though it wasn't my fault at all (so I definitely shouldn't be punished in any way), I deeply regret the decisions I made and how they affected those around me.

I confess: I often left the plastic clip thing off the bread bag. A couple times, I started to cross the street when the red hand was already flashing; and once, the clerk at Whole Foods mistook the $14 fresh almond butter for $5 peanut butter, and I didn't correct her. Everyone else was doing it, and going along with them was the only way I could keep up. I stopped in 2006, and I never did it again.

The truth is that I'm sick of all the scandals, sick of all the stories about the dirty side of the sport, sick of guys writing tell-all books so they can cash in again on the same crimes. I get why they did it, but as juicy and entertaining as it may be, that doesn't have to be the story of pro cycling anymore. I think you're sick of it, too, but I have good news! There'd be no such thing as a fake Rolex if there wasn't a real one out there somewhere, and in just the same way, there is a real pro cycling, every bit as pure and beautiful as the first time you took off your training wheels and felt the wind in your face.

PREFACE

I spent the first month of 2013 at the vacation home of Billy Jones, a former team sponsor in Tucson, Arizona. He also organized a junior development team, and some of the riders flew in for a long weekend to train in the warm weather and, Billy hoped, to learn a thing or two from a real pro cyclist.

One evening I was sitting on the sofa, minding my own business, when Billy's son asked what he should do if he wanted to be a pro someday. His younger teammate chimed in. "Yeah, and what's it like once you've made it?"

I stared back at the two teenagers, trying to think of a good response. I could tell them about the intervals I'd been doing, or what to eat before a race, but that would be irresponsible, because I knew that those little pointers were meaningless. Top cyclists have individual training plans and diets, but they get to the Tour de France and finish seconds apart. What they have in common is attitude, lifestyle, work ethic, how they learn from setbacks, and not giving up.

Maybe I should have taken the boys on a grand tour of my dust-covered Toyota Matrix parked in the driveway, filled with everything I owned, with gas receipts stuffed in the console and 200,000 miles on the odometer. I could show them the scars, and list the nine states and three different countries where I'd left my skin on the pavement. That's what it's fucking like when you're a pro cyclist, kids! But I didn't want to scare them.

What I wanted to do was get one of those memory erasers that Will Smith had in *Men in Black,* or shake their heads like an Etch A Sketch, to remove everything they thought they knew about pro cycling. Then I'd sit them down for a lecture. I would start by explaining how hard it's going to be, how many years of solitude and poverty they'll have to push through, and how many opportunities and relationships they'll have to sacrifice. Only after the young riders grasped the downside would I feel comfortable explaining the beauty of the sport, what I've taken away from it, and why I wouldn't trade it for anything.

As I tried to think of an answer, the pizza man rang the doorbell, rescuing me for the night. But I can't shirk my responsibilities to the youth of my beloved sport. I hope they can find an answer in here somewhere. Maybe I can share what I've learned, so they'll have an easier time of it than I did. Along the way, I'll try to paint a picture of pro cycling, or at least my corner of it, so if scandal burns down the sport, they can use this as a blueprint to help resurrect it.

I didn't use a ghost writer, either. These words are mine.

INTRODUCTION: IT'S PRECARIOUS

When I was a kid, my father took me grocery shopping every Saturday morning. Perched on the thin wire seat in the top of the cart, munching a donut from the bakery aisle, I'd hold the coupons as he filled the cart, grabbing things I wanted for myself when he wasn't looking. If I got lucky, maybe he wouldn't notice the army men, toy dinosaurs, or candy when we arrived at the checkout.

The highlight was when my dad left me at the end of an aisle while he went to look for something. Once he was gone, I had a chance to play an impromptu game of hide-and-seek: I'd reach out of the cart and push off of a shelf or anything solid I could reach, propelling the cart away from where he'd left me. He usually caught me in the act and grabbed the handle before I made any ground, but once in a while I'd make it around a corner and out of sight.

One morning, it must have been early in the trip when I saw my chance for escape, because the cart was still light. I moved parallel to the dairy fridge, facing backward like a rower and launching off of each door handle I passed for an extra boost of speed. I'd gained a lot of momentum when I cleared the frozen fish, but I had no means to brake or turn when I saw the display of Old El Paso Chunky Salsa rapidly approaching. I ducked and covered, already crying as the jars came crashing down around me.

My father returned to a bawling 4-year-old and a red, chunky mess at the end of the aisle. "I'm sorry!" I wailed, now adding the inevitable time-out to the tally of horrors. To my great relief, I wasn't punished at all. My dad wiped salsa off my face and said, "It's okay, Phillip. Those jars were precarious. Do you know what that means?"

It must have meant that things could be stacked up in such a way that there's little chance for a positive outcome, so it's not necessarily my fault if I find myself in a mess. *Precarious* has been my favorite word ever since.

1
TAKE WHAT YOU CAN GET

I never asked to be a professional cyclist. I feel like it just happened to me, and before I realized it, I was chasing something. I guess that means my path was unorthodox compared to most guys who race bikes for a living. No one in my family ever raced a bike. None of my friends raced bikes. In fact, I can't think of anyone I grew up around who was particularly athletic or competitive, or even watched a lot of sports on TV. Somehow, I found bikes, and pro cycling sucked me in. I still haven't caught the something that I'm chasing. In fact, I'm not completely sure what it is. But I'm not complaining.

I n 10th-grade technology class, everyone took a career aptitude survey. We input our interests, preferences, and abilities, and the computer suggested professions accordingly. Mine said "Pro Athlete, or Agriculture/Forestry." I lived in a suburb in Atlanta, nowhere near any agriculture, and I'd never planted a tree or set foot on a farm, so that was out. I was also five foot nine, obese, and

Me in eighth grade. If I wore a baggy shirt and held a bunch of binders and books, maybe no one would notice that I was a fatty.

exhausted by physical activity. I laughed at the test and made fun of the teacher, but I suppose I owe Mr. Beck an apology.

My older sister was a star student. Teachers recognized my last name and always had high hopes for me, but sooner or later I wouldn't live up to Valerie's legacy. Junior year, I was the first to arrive in English class, so I walked straight to the back of the empty rows.

"The back, huh? You know I notice that sort of thing," said the teacher.

"You'd have figured it out anyway," I told her.

By sophomore year, bad diet and lack of physical activity had built up a spare tire and stretch marks on my belly, while puberty and teenage angst had caused my grades to slip and my teachers to call my parents, complaining that I was being a disruptive smart-aleck in class. Who, me? I hadn't gotten into any real trouble yet, but it was probably coming. And then I found bikes.

When I bought a used Trek hybrid, I didn't think of it as a poten-tial profession. It was a mode of transportation. On weekends and after school, I'd ride around Atlanta to friends' houses, where we played video games, copied each other's homework, and killed time. On the way, I found that riding was a way to relieve some of my anger and get out of the house for a while, away from concerns about college, life, and the future. I discovered and experienced a whole new world outside of the suburbs, from the woods to the inner city. As a bonus, after a couple months of getting around by bike, I noticed that my size 36 pants needed a belt to stay up.

My parents bought me a car when I was 18, but it was too late to stop my bike addiction. Riding had become its own purpose rather than a means to hang out with my friends, and it was all I wanted to do. It gave me a goal, and it formed the basis of a healthy routine. I took the same route every day, exactly 10 miles from the top of our driveway—through busy streets (riding on sidewalks), over the hiking trails in a park near my friend Kalin's house, and around the mall on the other side of the neighborhood. I rode as hard as I could every day, wearing jeans and a T-shirt, trying to cross my finish line at the top of the driveway in under 30 minutes.

I enjoyed the equipment side of it, too. I was constantly buying and selling used bikes from yard sales and web sites, making a small profit each time and coming out with a cooler bike.

I never achieved the elusive 20 mph average speed I was shooting for, but the attempt helped to solve a lot of my problems. Spending all that time outdoors cleared up my allergies, I lost 40 pounds, and my waist size dropped to 30 inches. By the time I finished high school my grades had improved, and I was less moody, more confident, more social, and happier in general. It was nice to be able to lift things or run up the stairs when I needed to. Best of all, when I looked down, I didn't see a big roll of fat anymore. I felt okay about myself.

One of my first races was a time trial in Florida for my university team. My arm warmers never fit right.

BIKES ARE A GREAT WAY TO GET THROUGH COLLEGE

I didn't know anyone at the University of Florida (UF) when I started school there in the fall of 2004, but I liked riding bikes, so I joined the collegiate cycling club. The coach, Dan Larson, was a strong racer, and he was working on a master's degree in sports management. Dan e-mailed a training plan each week, and with no friends other than the guys I met on the team, and nothing to do but show up for my entry-level classes, I did every workout, often adding a little extra. I still wore a T-shirt and shorts, and I didn't have a road bike yet, but I'd upgraded to a Specialized Stumpjumper mountain bike with slick tires. Gainesville, Florida, is a great place to start riding, with flat roads, warm weather year-round, and lots of open countryside and nature to explore.

When Dan and his wife, Rebecca, convinced me to get a road bike, shave my legs, and order a set of UF tights for the 2005 season, I won my first few time trials and a few criteriums (flat courses with lots of short laps and full of corners—very hazardous to a beginner). I upgraded from the Category V races, which were for riders just starting out, to Cat. IV, for riders still likely to crash but at slightly higher speeds. For collegiate racing, the packs were smaller and safer than the open amateur races, and I was strong enough, so Dan threw me into the A class, which was intended to be for elite-level racers. I wasn't experienced enough to contribute much, but I climbed well, and I was always on the podium in the time trials. We drove to races throughout the Southeast most weekends during the spring semester, crammed into the cheapest hotels we could find. I slept on a sofa at a Howard Johnson one weekend—and scored a free room when I found a used condom in the cushions.

For the rest of my time at UF, most of my friends, roommates, girlfriends, and social activities stemmed from the cycling team. I didn't go to a lot of college parties, and I never saw a football game, but I was happy. Dan and Rebecca became my parents away from home, and I'd often be the third wheel when they went out to dinner. Unlike in high school, I found myself sitting in the front of the classroom and acing my exams.

EAT AND DRINK

My first road race was hosted by Georgia Tech. It was hilly, and twice as long as anything I'd done so far. Dan pointed out when to use the little chainring (I hadn't needed it in Florida), and when I finished, with my legs cramping after 75 miles with just water in my bottles, Rebecca gave me some Gatorade and energy bars for the next time.

Thanks to the fuel and the use of my bike's shifters, my legs were much better the day after, and I made the breakaway with three of the best guys in the conference. I didn't know much about being in a break or how team tactics worked, but I knew I wanted to win, so I took long pulls, and we got a huge lead on the field. Near the finish, the star rider from Cumberland College attacked, the group shattered, and I came in alone for fourth. It seemed like a good result to me, but UF had the strongest team in the race, so fourth was a disappointment to the team. Dan patiently explained that I shouldn't have worked so hard; if I had taken shorter pulls, I would have had a better chance of winning. Or, if the break had been caught, someone else on our team would have won, or at least done better than fourth. I realized that I'd raced selfishly, but I was thankful that nobody held it against me. I hadn't learned all the tactical nuances of the sport, but I wouldn't make that mistake again.

IF YOU WIN, YOUR TACTICS WERE RIGHT

The next weekend was another collegiate road race, this time in Auburn, Alabama. The man to watch was a 31-year-old Cat. I road racer (the top level you can achieve as an amateur) who'd won a number of pro races, and a national championship the year before. He was finishing a degree at Georgia State, presumably racing collegiate for fun and training. When he attacked early in the 61-mile road race, the field hesitated, and Dan told me what to do.

"Phil! Go with him, but don't pull through."

I did what I was told. When my companion flicked his elbow, indicating it was my turn to take a pull in the wind, I shook my head. He pulled another few miles and looked back again.

"Pull!" he demanded.

2005 collegiate team photo. Back row (*left to right*): Coach Dan Larson, my roommate Brad Davis, me (with the horrible bowl cut), Jared Fullerton, Ryan Fisher, Gabe Altman, Marco Verwijs. Front row: Rebecca Larson, Teresa Garcia, Anton Tupa, David Guttenplan, Damon Sununtnasuk, Rob Newsom.

"Sorry, I can't. Dan told me not to."

The Georgia State rider was angry. He called me a faggot and slapped the top of my helmet. It was pretty clear that I'd done something wrong, but I wasn't sure what, and I was positive that Dan had told me not to pull, so I listened to my coach. We'd been out there for over an hour when my new enemy gave up and stopped to pee, rejoining the group. I attacked.

An hour later I won my first A race, solo. When I mentioned that I had been hit on my helmet, I saw Dan angry for the first time. He confronted the bully, who accused our team of "Cat. V tactics" but eventually apologized. I was almost a Cat. III by then, after all, and I proved it was no fluke when I won the crit the next day, launching myself into the lead in the South Eastern Conference overall standings. No one hit my helmet again.

Dan was turning into a close friend, and I admired his morality and sense of sportsmanship. He was the only Cat. I rider I knew, so I always kept an eye on him to see what I could learn. He never talked about the doping problem in cycling, but while his competitors took caffeine pills before time trials, he'd have an energy bar. When stuck behind a pileup in a crit, most guys would take a free lap whether they crashed or not, but Dan would dutifully chase back on, and he often won anyway.

Collegiate racing is based on total points, so the overall competition rewards attendance over placing. Because most of the A racers had commitments to amateur or professional teams, they all missed a few collegiate events.

"Where's Holt this weekend?" I asked, noticing that Florida State University's top rider was absent.

"He's at Redlands with his team," someone explained.

I didn't know what Redlands was, but I was glad I had no such stupid obligations. I was better off going to places like Lees McRae College in North Carolina for a mountainous road race than I would have been in a Cat. IV criterium in Florida. I had to do the local races occasionally, since it was the only way to move up to a higher category, but it wasn't any fun to beat up on weaker guys. My only advantage was that I had more time to train, but I didn't feel like celebrating when I won, because I knew I belonged in a harder race. It was a feeling I later got about doping: Wouldn't winning that way be a hollow, meaningless victory?

BE CAREFUL WITH NAILS

The only real sponsor of the UF team was a local bike shop, and it was clear that the owner was only using the sponsorship to rip off dumb college students like me. With no price tags in the shop, he could charge as much as he thought he could get away with. The secret store motto was, "In a college town, you get a whole new batch of suckers every four years." On my first set of clipless pedals, the receipt indicated I was charged 20 percent sales tax.

A nicer guy eventually bought the shop, and the previous owner put his money into renovations on his house, which was featured in a local magazine, rewarding him for his ill-gotten fortune. That issue was still on the shelves when he pulled a nail out of the wall and right into his eye socket, a fittingly biblical punishment. Now he walks around with an eye patch. Cheating is no way to get rich. One way or another, you get what's coming.

IF YOU'RE NICE TO EVERYONE, IT MIGHT PAY OFF SOMEDAY

I ended my collegiate season at nationals with a big DNF ("Did Not Finish" in the official results) in the crit and road race, and began to focus more on noncollegiate races and category upgrades. By April I had moved up to Cat. II, and I joined A.G. Edwards, an amateur team based in Atlanta, thanks to my collegiate teammate, David Guttenplan (known as "the Gutt"). He was glad to have a strong teammate but was even more excited that he'd have someone to split gas with on the long drives from Florida. I spent most of the summer and fall racing with David in the Southeast. A.G. Edwards had a strong team, but Jittery Joe's was the team to watch. When its pros showed up in their team-provided H2 Hummer or Mini Cooper, with all the stickers and fancy bikes on the roof, the rest of us were racing for second. I stared in admiration when they walked by.

Jittery Joe's got to race in the Tour de Georgia, the biggest event in the United States at the time. One of the stages came within a half-mile of my parents' house, and I watched the finish in a park where I often trained. Some guy named Tom Danielson won the yellow jersey.

That summer I also watched Lance Armstrong win his seventh Tour de France. When they gave him the microphone on the final podium, I thought it was strange that he decided to address his skeptics. "I'm sorry you can't dream big, and I'm sorry you don't believe in miracles," he said. And I'm sorry I believed him.

It was time for me to stop watching big races and try doing one myself, so I signed up for the Under-23 national championships in Park City, Utah. I finished 37th in the time trial (a few seconds ahead of future Olympic champion Kristin Armstrong, who won the women's pro race). I DNFed the road race and watched Ian McGregor win, riding for TIAA-CREF, a professional development team started by former pro Jonathan Vaughters. That looked like a good team to be on. Tyler Farrar was second; he would later become one of the best sprinters in the world. I was so new to the sport that I didn't consider any of these names to be my peers, potential friends, teammates, or even competition. They lived on a plane far above all that, mingling with the gods.

Although I wasn't yet seeing good results in the local pro fields, my debut in track racing went well. It was my third time on a fixed-gear bike when I lined up next to Bobby Lea and Mike Friedman at the collegiate nationals points race. They were teammates at Penn State, and both were selected for the next Olympics. It was intimidating, but I remembered one of my mom's favorite stories about my first visit to the ocean at the age of 4: My older sister was afraid of the wind and the waves. But I took one look, removed my imaginary sword from my imaginary scabbard, and ran toward the water, yelling "CHARGE!"

I applied the same strategy (minus the yelling) in the points race, attacking from the gun. I led the points count for more than half the race, but Bobby and Mike finally bridged up and beat me into oblivion. Third was still pretty damn good, though. By October of my first season I'd won 20 races and had four national championships medals.

At a race in Florida at the end of 2005, Dan Larson noticed a stranger who'd flatted his tire just as his category was about to start. Always the nice guy, Coach Dan lent the man a wheel. When they talked later, the stranger turned out to be an employee and close friend of the Bahamian billionaire investor and avid cyclist Mark Holowesko. When Mark later decided to start a pro cycling team, Dan was the only guy he knew with a sports management degree, so by an absurd coincidence, the one man on the planet who might think I deserved a shot at a pro team was hired to manage one.

The budget was modest, and by the time the decision was made to start a team for 2006, it was too late for Dan to find any good equipment sponsors. Even the roster was reminiscent of *The Bad News Bears* since most of the top-tier young riders were already signed to other teams. Not me, though. I still hadn't figured out how to corner or finish a criterium, but I was on a pro team. The team was called VMG, which stands for "velocity made good," a term that sailors use when a boat is pushing into a headwind. I appreciated the symbolism but got tired of explaining it, and we heard a lot of creative guesses from other teams (Very Many Gays was common).

PRACTICE YOUR ACCENTS

My initial salary was $2,000 and two bikes, and the season started with a training camp in the Bahamas. Due to heavy traffic on the main road, our training started at sunrise and was usually over by 10 a.m.

That gave us plenty of time during the day to tour the island, gamble at the casinos, and wine and dine.

Everywhere we went that week was a don't-even-think-about-opening-your-wallet event, with great food and open bars. We took private jets to another island for one ride, and a yacht to dinner a night later. Mark had to work pretty hard to get those things, but I got to share the experience just for riding a bike. Being a pro cyclist had its perks. Still, I knew I was lucky to be on the team. I couldn't shake the feeling that it was all temporary, that a rude awakening was on the way.

DOPING WORKS

Our first race was the Tour of the Bahamas, a three-day stage race sponsored by (guess who?) VMG. We started our entire pro roster, plus a few VMG triathletes and team sponsors, against a field of mostly Florida-based elite amateurs and one small pro team. I finished second in the prologue, and after cramping out of the breakaway in a 120-mile road race in pouring rain, was still the best-placed finisher on the team, in fifth overall. That was also the first time I raced against a doper. Ricardo Hernandez, of the JC Investors team from Miami, also made the break. We were moving fast when he attacked us on the last lap, but he rode away at twice our speed. I remember thinking I could cut his head off and he would still win. Ricardo later served a two-year suspension for human growth hormone (HGH).

Holowesko noticed me, and based on my performance at this regional race in February, my salary was quadrupled to $8,000, which probably made me the highest-paid Cat. II in the history of pro cycling. It was confusing to get a raise out of the blue, but David Guttenplan gave me some good advice.

"Take what you can get," he said. "And save your money." David had been at it awhile and had never earned more than free bikes and clothing.

We flew to Orlando after the stage, and then drove the two hours back to Gainesville. I was sick from the cold rain, dehydration, and fumes from the new pavement, but I hunkered down on the flight to study for a 9:30 a.m. exam in my advertising class. With only four hours of sleep, I limped my sore, feverish body to the back row of the auditorium and pulled out the Scantron sheet and the number-two pencil I'd stolen from the lottery display at a gas station on the way to class. The girls in front of me in matching sorority T-shirts were complaining that they had barely had time to study after a tailgate party for the football game. They were glad "we won," as if they were on the field making tackles. I liked having cycling to escape the college atmosphere. I was a superhero, and "Phil the student" was merely my alter ego. It was funny how much easier school was after a weekend of hard competition. The real world didn't stand a chance.

I'd entered college with a decent amount of credit, so my class load wasn't too difficult, but I had to carefully budget my absences. The English Department had a rule that you could only miss three days of any class or you'd automatically lose half a letter grade, so I'd usually leave for a race on a Friday afternoon and drive back in the wee hours on Monday mornings.

YOU RACE HARDER WHEN YOU NEED THE PRIZE MONEY

During spring break I met my teammates in California for two races, where I earned some points toward my Cat. I upgrade. In between races, we went on a hike through the redwood trees. I don't remember if it was intended for "team building," or even whose idea it was, but I do remember that I had horrible gas. Alex Boyd was walking behind me, trying to figure out where it was coming from. At the time, I had to bite my tongue to keep from laughing, but I'll admit it now. It was me, Alex.

I went back to Florida to finish the spring semester, and it was more than a month before I saw the team again at a house we had for the summer in Kutztown, a city in eastern Pennsylvania Amish country. On the way there, I took a detour to a four-day stage race in Tennessee. The prize money was good, and attendance was low (always a great combination). My reservation at a cheap motel never went through, so I had to book three nights at more expensive places. (Back then, $99 per night qualified as expensive. Actually, it still does.) I didn't know how I would pay. That pressure may have helped me force a breakaway on the final stage, which moved me up from 11th to 2nd overall. I won $850 in prize money, with no team-mates to share with. Not bad for a weekend.

I left the race on a high and arrived in Kutztown at a two-story, no-A/C, stink bug–infested house on White Oak Street. The team was paying for it, and any form of lodging was more than we deserved

VMG team photo in Sequoia National Park. *From left*: Alex Boyd (this must have been pre-farts), Rudy Robaina, me, Peter Simms (team mechanic and my roommate in Florida at the time), Todd Henriksen, Dan Larson, Zach Bolian on the bottom.

given our results, but it was a far cry from the mojitos and conch fritters we'd feasted on in the Bahamas. It was tight quarters at the house, and the retired couple across the street eyed us suspiciously through drawn curtains. I'm sure they were wondering how many kids in tights could live in the same dwelling. Several of the riders whined to Dan, blaming their poor results on air mattresses and low-class living conditions, and a photo circulated of the exterior of the house with prison bars drawn over our faces in the windows. Beds and better housing might have helped our results, but I'm sure they would have been second-rate either way, and Dan was doing the best he could with his budget.

It was good to live with the team. Most of us had different training schedules, but there was always someone to ride with, and we kept each other honest and motivated. If a guy said he was leaving for a five-hour ride but came back four hours later, we'd block the door so he couldn't get in.

On Tuesday and Friday nights we'd race at the velodrome in nearby Trexlertown. Track racing was great practice for tactics, with four races in an evening. It gave me an opportunity to screw up in every possible way, and I learned a lot about how hard to work in a breakaway, when to attack, and when to be patient.

In July we gathered around the television every morning to watch the Tour de France. We cheered when Floyd Landis won his stage and fought his way back into yellow from an eight-minute deficit, and we took that motivation into our training ride that afternoon, the hardest we rode all summer. Weeks later, we were in the midst of a five-day race in Pennsylvania when a rumor spread that someone from the Tour had tested positive for drugs. Around the halfway point, word came over the radios that it was indeed Floyd, and he'd be stripped of his win. News spread through the field like wildfire, and the pace slowed down for a few miles, because nobody felt like racing. The older guys probably weren't too surprised, many of them having lived through it or raced in Europe, but for us, a hero had fallen.

RACE WITH A $5 BILL IN YOUR POCKET

After a few DNFs and mediocre results at Under-23 nationals, only two races remained on the calendar. At USPro Nationals in Greenville, South Carolina, I made the front selection of 40 riders over Paris Mountain, but I was so cross-eyed from the effort that I crashed on a sharp corner at the base.

My day was even worse at the Univest Grand Prix. We lined up on a hot, humid morning at the start in Souderton, Pennsylvania, the gun went off, and I stood up and shifted my derailleur into my spokes, tearing apart my derailleur and half my wheel. I hadn't even made it to the actual start line, and my day was over. I spent the morning sitting on the curb, watching my teammates suffer on the Jumbotron. With no cash for lunch, I had to snack on packets of energy gel.

I do my own stunts.

KEEP AN EYE ON THE BIG PICTURE

I'd finished my first season as a professional, and my mind turned to the next year. I didn't have much of a résumé, so my calls weren't returned when VMG shifted its sponsor money to the U.S. National Team program. I sent e-mails to all the pro teams, but the only reply I got was from the manager of the Georgia-based Jittery Joe's team. "Do more NRC races," was all it said, referring to the series of pro races that make up the National Racing Calendar. It might as well have said "Fuck you."

At the time, I thought I was ready, that I deserved to be a pro, and I was angry that the teams didn't see it. Looking back now, that's pretty funny. My teammates didn't have much luck either. They were all stars in the junior circuit, but two years later, not one of them was still racing. Maybe they didn't have it and I did. Or maybe they figured something out that's taking me a little longer. The truth is, the biggest factor in who made it to the next level wasn't talent or work ethic. It was a willingness to keep plugging away through all the hard times.

I had never set out to be a pro cyclist. Doors had opened, and I went through them. Now I'd been kicked out, and I had to decide: Did I want to try racing as an amateur and pay my dues? Would pro cycling be worth it if I would have to earn it like everyone else? Was it worth the crashing, the time away from home, and the long rides in the rain?

Thanks to bike racing, I spent most of my days doing what others did for fun on the weekends. Halfway through a training ride, I could sit on the bench at the Pearl Country Store in Micanopy, Florida, with a Styrofoam cup full of iced tea, sharing boiled peanuts with David Guttenplan, and I could honestly say I was working.

I was only starting to understand the beauty of the sport, but I could tell there was a lot more there. Planning a route through the countryside was an art form, even though I was the only one to experience it. For the first time in my life, my deep, primitive urge to compete was satisfied, and I saw my body and myself as a work in progress. I loved the moment on long rides when I was tired and sore, 50 miles from town, and all I could do was keep pushing, left foot right foot, with the faith that it would take me home.

During finals week, I set up a trainer in my room and improvised a table over my handlebars so I could study while I rode. I'd been to so many new places and experienced them in a unique and intimate way. How would I be able to see the coral reef in the Bahamas or the redwoods in California again without bike racing? How many great places and experiences would I miss out on if I went back to the life of the average college student? Of course it was worth it.

I would have to be an amateur for a while, but I decided that I would be a pro cyclist again, and I'd shoot to race at the highest level. I heard rumors that doping was a problem in Europe, but I'd do it clean or not at all. Maybe I wouldn't get to win those big races like the dopers, but a win wasn't worth it if you couldn't hold your head up high. I never wanted to let down the people who believed in me. I had no idea that the drug problem was so rampant, or that scandal would soon have the sport teetering on the edge of a cliff.

When I set my goal I knew of a lot of talented guys who'd tried to make it as bike racers and had failed or given up, and I'd gotten a later start than most of them. How could I succeed where they hadn't? Simple. I'd have to outwork everyone around me. I'd have to be more focused, more dedicated, and more disciplined than they were. The plan was so distant it was almost abstract, but I thought I was up to it. Sometimes, I wish I could go back in time and slap myself.

2

GET IN YOUR FUCKING CAR

I took the only offer I had for 2007, from an Under-25 amateur squad out of New York City called Sakonnet (it rhymes with bonnet, but everyone called us "team suck on it"). The team was hoping to mimic VMG's program on a smaller budget, so it offered no salary but took care of bikes and travel. It also had a house in Kutztown and signed David Guttenplan. It was nice to be reunited. Basil Moutsopoulos was the team manager. He lived in New York but had attended the University of Florida, so training camp was right at home in Gainesville.

Sakonnet was a software company in New York City. Apparently, you can take watts that haven't been generated yet and sell them on the commodities market (you could probably trade in used watts, too, for all I know). Sakonnet made software for this type of trading, and it did very well. Did an amateur cycling team help the company advertise its products? No, but two of the three founders

Wieners at the Tour of Virginia. *From left:* **Guy East, Gavi Epstein, Basil Moutsopoulos, me, Andy Cornelison, Rob Giannini, Chris Kuhl.**

of Sakonnet were cyclists, and that was a good enough reason to throw away $100,000.

One of the founders, Thurston Bannister, came to training camp. He was pale and slightly overweight, with a strong British accent, stereotypical British teeth, and a type of ease and humor that you only find in the wealthy. When Thurston showed up at the start of our training ride with no food and only one bottle of water, we were all a bit worried that he wouldn't be able to keep up, but he rode over a hundred miles without complaint. That night, we learned that he was the son of Roger Bannister, the first runner to break the four-minute mile. Genetics.

As an amateur, you race mostly in your own region, so I didn't know anything about my new teammates except that some had awesome Hollywood-style names, like Chris Kuhl, Johnny Hayes, and Guy East. Most of the guys on Sakonnet hadn't come straight from five years of top-level junior racing, so they were a little less injured, burned out, and entitled than my previous teammates. We meshed well, but there was still a *Bad News Bears* element to the team.

Sakonnet had started out as an Under-23 development team, for kids to spend a couple years with good support. After that, they would either move on to the pros or give up and get a job. It made sense in theory, but in practice, Basil had a huge heart, and when some of the guys got too old, Sakonnet aged into an Under-25 team instead of kicking out the older guys, which gave some people the impression that results and training weren't all that important. If the sponsor money hadn't dried up, it's entirely possible that Sakonnet would be a masters team now, with much the same roster.

CLIMBING IS NOTHING LIKE RACING A CRIT

Our first team race was the Tour of Virginia, where we met our new director, Matt Koschara. He was hired soon after training camp to run the day-to-day operations of the team, from travel logistics to driving the team car behind the race. Matt was an ex-racer who talked a lot about how bad doping was in his era, how he never did it, and how hard he had to work for what he had, implying that we were spoiled by our sponsors. When I mentioned that my previous team reimbursed our bike fees on flights, Matt rolled his eyes.

"Well, this team isn't a fucking candy shop," he said. "It's time to pay your dues." Matt didn't seem to care if we liked him or not.

The Tour of Virginia was an eight-day NRC race, featuring tons of climbing and long stages. Most of the bigger pro teams were elsewhere, but there was no drug testing, and Matt insisted that some of the teams were doped to the gills. I was skeptical until I noticed that most of the Colombian National Team riders had bandages on their arms, right below their elbows. Rock Racing's star sprinter was also in attendance. He was huge, covered in tattoos, and wore a stars-and-stripes jersey from his national criterium championship. I wasn't ready to call him a doper until he made the front group on a mountaintop stage.

As I cramped at the finish line, I overheard Rock's sprinter being interviewed on the stage. The announcer pointed out how impressive it was for a sprinter to climb so well. "You know, climbing is just like racing a crit," he explained. Interesting. He eventually served a two-year ban from racing, rumored to be an EPO supplier for his teammates and much of the domestic peloton.

Dopers had only deprived me of a couple results, but that type of defeat was hard to swallow. When I thought about going through a decade of it, I started to understand why Matt Koschara was bitter.

SHORTCUTS DON'T WORK

A few weeks later, with our college semester over, David and I piled our bags into my car and drove nonstop to Kansas for collegiate nationals. Well, we did stop at least once, because we ate something bad somewhere on the way and spent the weekend glued to the toilets at a motel instead of winning national championships. During the Division I crit (nationals was divided into two categories based on the size of the schools), I went to the ER for fluids, returning to the course just in time to watch Jared Faciszewski win the Division II race. I had shared the low spot on the totem pole with him when we were teammates on VMG, so it was great to see Jared climb up a few notches while other guys were quitting.

David started the crit, but he was out of shape. His coach had instructed him to do his winter training by heart rate, with a certain number of hours to complete each week. The plan was reasonable, except that David found a loophole: If he drank enough coffee, he could raise his heart rate without pedaling harder.

"Dude, if I have three cups, I'm almost in zone two just sitting on the sofa!" he explained. Guess what, dude? It took David months to race into fitness.

GOOD TEAMMATES ARE HARD TO COME BY

We left Kansas for the Tripeaks Challenge, a well-attended NRC stage race in Arkansas. David and I didn't have a full team, but thanks to hard training in Virginia, combined with the forced rest of illness, I finally had good legs. In the road race, I made the break with all the big pro teams represented: Toyota-United, Healthnet, Jelly Belly. I hadn't raced these guys much before, so I didn't recognize anyone when I was pulling through. I learned later that all my work in the break that day was a waste of energy because I was the only amateur with all the best climbers and general classification (GC) guys in the country. There was no way that break was coming back.

I didn't have any responsibility to push the pace, but I felt that it was more important to impress the pros by working than to sit on the back and try to beat them. I rotated all day and then cramped at the base of the finishing climb, going right off the back with Justin England, who'd been working for his teammate. Nine guys were battling it out for the stage win up ahead, and Justin started to cruise in toward the finish, job done, with me suffering next to him.

"I just want a top 10," I begged, knowing that a real pro wouldn't care about his result. To Justin's credit, he tried hard to not drop me, but he got sick of waiting, and I finished 11th on the stage.

I was still pretty well-placed in the GC, so David put himself on domestique duty for the rest of the stages, protecting me during the crit (where he could have had a good result if he'd raced for himself) and leading me into the climbs at the front of the field. When teammates are close friends, you actually feel glory when the other guy gets the result, so my friendship with David made us both able to ride harder than we could have independently. After his effort to get me to the front when the climb started on the final stage, I climbed faster and dug deeper, because I couldn't let him down.

I came in 12th overall at the end of the stage race, a great result for a young amateur; it was my first hint that I might actually be pretty good someday. It was also the first time that any pros noticed me or bothered to learn my name.

ALWAYS CARRY DUCT TAPE

I moved back to Kutztown that summer; this time my team lived in two connected apartments on Main Street. When you drive into Kutztown from Reading, Main Street starts at the top of a steep hill on U.S. Route 222, with a traffic light at the bottom, so vehicles have to stop just as they've picked up speed. We spent most of the summer shouting over the noise of trucks squealing to a sudden halt and then shifting for the green light. We didn't have enough bedrooms to go around, so David chose the privacy of a small closet, which fit only his suitcase and a twin-sized air mattress. His head rested about six feet from the trucks' exhaust pipes.

The upside was that our apartment was right above Salon Joey, so we got discounts on haircuts. Joey even told me the best style for a guy who's too lazy for brushes, combs, or hair product (number four on the sides, scissors on the top).

Now that I had some experience in Kutztown, I made a couple investments to improve my summer. First, I bought a double-height, queen-sized air mattress with a removable foam top, and I slept like a baby. Next I got a town bike. Because street parking was limited to two hours, we had to park our cars in a public lot that was 10 minutes away by foot—much too far for a cyclist. Instead of walking, I purchased a beat-up steel bike at an Amish yard sale for $25. The wheels were out of true, the saddle was rusted into the seatpost, and I had to drag my feet to compensate for weak brakes, but it got me to my car and back.

Sakonnet didn't have the budget for a team car, so our teammate Guy East's father lent us his diesel-powered Dodge Sprinter for the summer, with his business's name and logos all over it. "U-Built-It Homes" wasn't technically a team sponsor, but the van made travel much easier.

I always volunteered to drive. I would use the size of the van to my advantage, changing lanes on a whim and turning right from the left lane. We wove through New York City and laughed at all the suckers caught in traffic. It was a game to see how many angry drivers would flip us the bird, or how they'd react to a naked ass in the window. I was well into the double digits on middle fingers one day when Guy's phone rang. It was his dad. The phone number for his company was on the back of the van, and he'd been getting a lot of angry calls. We jumped out and covered the number with duct tape so we could safely resume our shenanigans.

After one race, we took a detour to Hershey Park to try the amusement rides. I was terrified of roller coasters as a kid, but after bumping shoulders in crits all summer and diving into turns with nothing but colorful stretchy pants between me and the pavement, I wasn't scared anymore.

Only a few days later, I had noticed another indirect benefit from racing. It was pouring rain as I drove my car back from the grocery store on Route 222, and the corn had grown so high that you couldn't see the cars around the next bend anymore, so I had to hit the brakes pretty hard to avoid rear-ending an SUV stopped at a red light. I took a deep breath and then saw in my rearview mirror an 18-wheeler barreling toward me. I twisted the wheel as hard as I could to the right and floored it into a cornfield, watching as the truck slammed into the SUV that was just in front of me. The domino effect soon had five cars trading insurance information with the truck driver. Everyone was okay, but the SUV was totaled, which meant that my Toyota would have been squashed like a bug. I didn't remember having reflexes like that before I started racing.

SET YOUR ALARM

David Guttenplan had been my teammate and best friend for a few years. I'd never met anyone with a better heart, but he did have his flaws. For example, David was always late. We would set a time to be out the door for a race, and we'd all get up early, make oatmeal, load our bikes into the van, and slide into our usual seats at exactly the agreed-upon time. Then we'd notice that someone was missing, and I'd go upstairs to find David sitting alone at the kitchen table, hair disheveled, eating cereal in nothing but boxer shorts, and squinting from the lights in the kitchen. We would roll our eyes and jump in the van to take off without him, amid protests that we should just "hold on for a second" as the Gutt scrambled through his suitcase.

YOU CAN LIE YOUR WAY ONTO A TEAM, AND COASTING MAKES YOU GO FASTER

Sakonnet's base in New York made the Harlem Skyscraper Classic criterium a big target for the team. David and I went to the city a few days early and stayed at Matt Koschara's apartment. Matt had trouble adjusting to young bike racer houseguests, especially after David knocked over a piece of art that Matt had been working on for six months. Our host sprinted across the room and did a full-speed baseball slide to keep his painting from hitting the floor.

It was tight quarters in Manhattan, which made for a long week for all of us. The day before the race, Matt, David, and I drove to the Sakonnet offices to have lunch with a man named Kyoo, one of the founders of the company. Matt was in a strange (bad) mood, and we later learned that he had a history with Kyoo. They grew up racing together as juniors, but Kyoo decided to give up on bikes and go to college. Matt had stuck it out and been pretty successful as a pro, but 20 years later he found himself begging his old training partner for a fraction of their marketing budget. Matt was on edge from being stuck with me and David all week, and this sudden reversal of winner/quitter in his relationship with Kyoo sent him over the edge. He walked out of the restaurant and took the train home, leaving David and me to find our way back through the city.

I could understand Matt's frustration when he explained it later. Pro cycling has a very high prestige-to-salary ratio. Kyoo failed at racing and quit, while Matt persevered and succeeded, but Kyoo became a millionaire and Matt didn't. Matt had made it in a much more competitive field, but he didn't realize until then who the long-term winner was, and it was too late for him to turn the tables.

The race in Harlem was the debut of Sakonnet's first guest rider, a 23-year-old from Australia. He'd apparently lied on his résumé, fooling Basil with a photo of a field sprint that showed him finishing just behind pro star sprinter Robbie McEwen; he neglected to mention that he'd been lapped. He was given an air mattress at the team house for a couple weeks, and we took him to Harlem as a tryout. We didn't see him in the race at Harlem or in the races the weeks after. Finally, Matt convinced Basil to send him home. Our guest rider did leave a pair of board shorts in his closet, which I still wear, so I can't say he didn't contribute. Several girlfriends have begged me to throw them away. Also, come to think of it, the board shorts may have belonged to someone else.

TAKE AS MANY FREE LAPS AS YOU CAN

I'd struggled in crits since I started racing, and Harlem was no exception. I'd brake before each corner, take the turn too slow, and waste energy sprinting back to the wheel in the straightaway. When I found myself too far back, the only recourse was to wait for a straight section and move up in the wind, a huge waste of energy. I was usually able to get through the races, but only in the way that a large sea mammal is transported to an aquarium by truck, sprayed with water every few minutes: I was surviving, but minimally. I didn't know what I was doing wrong or how to fix it, but I knew it was holding me back.

When I asked for advice about criteriums, all I'd ever get was "stay at the front" or "save your energy." Gee, thanks. And then I can win if I just go faster than the other guys, right? Finally, I was approached by Jason Snow, a friend from Florida and an old teammate of Dan Larson's who usually spent the summers in Kutztown to race at the velodrome. Jason had always been a cagey crit specialist, and he was sick of getting stuck behind me in corners. He explained how to race crits in a way that no coach or director ever did.

"When the race is hard and all strung out, as you're approaching the corner, you start to coast," he said. "So you leave a small gap to the guy in front of you. When you get to the corner, you can use that space to take the turn at full speed. If you have to touch the brakes, you didn't open a big enough gap."

His advice clicked, and just like that, I became a halfway decent crit racer (okay, two-fifths of a decent crit racer). By opening a few bike lengths to the guy in front of me, I had room to fly through the turn at full speed instead of braking, and I came out with more momentum than the riders in front of me, which I could use to move up in the field. Suddenly, I was improving my position through every turn, just by coasting! After a little practice over a few weeks, I went from suffering at the back of the field to attacking off the front.

SPITE COSTS EVERYONE

Cable TV was $40/month in Kutztown: too much to spring for lightly, even though it would have been split among eight of us. We decided to sign up just for July to watch the Tour de France, but Guy said he didn't want it, refusing to pay a $5 share. He'd resolved to read more and didn't want the distraction. The team agreed to split the bill seven ways, but only if Guy promised he wouldn't watch when the Tour came on. He wouldn't agree to that, either, so just to spite him, our house was TV-free for the summer. I wonder if Guy ever finished *War and Peace*.

DON'T BASE YOUR PLAN ON ANOTHER TEAM

The team had two major races left. National championships was the first, once again in Seven Springs, Pennsylvania. I was stronger this time and was a team leader with a chance for a decent placing, but the end result wouldn't be much different.

In the Under-23 road race, our plan was to cue off of the Slipstream development team, which had eleven of the strongest guys in the race. Hoping to conserve energy, we were certain that we didn't need to cover a breakaway they'd missed, because they'd easily have the manpower to chase it down.

Unfortunately, Slipstream messed it up. A break went away early, with a bunch of riders we'd never heard of. Since there was so much time left, and since Slipstream had missed it, we stayed in the field, expecting an eight-man chase to organize at any moment. That moment never came, and we lost the race along with the favorites.

Elite nationals was the next day, and we signed up for that, too, since amateur riders of any age were eligible. We knew we'd be tired from the Under-23 event, but with no racing for a couple weeks, there was no harm in overdoing it. This was my chance to salvage nationals, but I had to start at a disadvantage: The evening before the race, when I was cleaning and tuning my bike, I found a hole in the carbon frame right under the cranks. I couldn't tell where it came from or how long it had been there, but I could fit my pinky into the hole without touching the sides. The course had several fast, dangerous downhills (we'd hit 60 mph on one descent, where several juniors had been airlifted to the hospital after a crash), so rather than ride a frame that might fall apart on me, I chose to borrow a bike from Shimano Neutral Support.

The neutral bike was an old Litespeed titanium frame. I put my carbon wheels on it, but it was still six pounds heavier than the bike I was used to. The titanium flexed at high speeds, so the bike would shake on descents, and I had trouble controlling it. My legs felt good, though, and I'd resolved to not miss the break for a third time on this course, so I followed all the big attacks, wasting energy, but refusing to miss a move.

The race blew apart on the last climb. I was cramping, which made it hard to bend my right leg, so I took my foot out of the pedal and finished the race one-legged. I still passed a few guys at the top and came in a respectable 14th. I think someone at the United States Anti-Doping Agency (USADA) was impressed, because I earned (and passed) my first-ever drug test that day.

With my time in Kutztown winding down, I had to part with my Amish town bike. I'd left it outside all summer, locked to a railing behind Salon Joey. The brakes had gotten worse, and I didn't even try to shift it anymore. I wrote FREE on a sheet of notebook paper, taped it to the handlebars, and parked the bike at the top of the hill on Main Street. For the rest of the afternoon, every time I looked, the bike had moved another 20 feet downhill, only to be abandoned by each successive owner. No one dared take it uphill, but it slowly worked its way out of town.

SARAN WRAP MAKES A GOOD BANDAGE

With my form finally coming around, I lined up with my teammates for the last race of the summer—the Tour de Toona in Altoona, Pennsylvania. Toona was one of the most prestigious NRC races at the time, and its hard climbs suited me well. Plus, the race was at low altitude, so the Colorado-based climbers didn't have their usual advantage.

We members of the Sakonnet team were true amateurs, and Toona was no exception for us. We washed and repaired our own bikes, and we never had massage or paid feeders like the spoiled pro teams. Instead, we had Barb and Tom, a couple from Florida who were friends of Basil. They were in the area on vacation and had volunteered to drive us around and hand out bottles in the feed zone. Some vacation, huh?

Not that the team had many bottles to hand out in the first place. After each stage, we'd sneak over to the other teams' trailers and steal the empties from their trash. They threw them out after one use, so we washed out their leftovers. No big deal, but I couldn't imagine that happening with some of the spoiled kids on VMG the previous year.

We lost almost two minutes in the opening team time trial, but I rode well after that, the only amateur or Under 23 making small selections over the climbs. With no mountaintop finishes that year, chase groups always made it back to us, and we'd race for the stage win from groups of 30. Healthnet's sprinter, Karl Menzies, barely made it over the climbs, but he had enough left to kill everyone at the finish.

I started at the back of the field for the Blue Knob climb on the last road race stage but flew through the peloton into a front group of 10 riders. It looked like the climbers would finally stay away, and I'd get my long-awaited top 10.

My group rode hard on the descent, trying to stay away from Karl and the other sprinters, and I was pegged at the back when the rider in front of me panicked in a fast corner and overcorrected. We were down before we knew it, sliding on gravel for what seemed like hours, until we finally tumbled into the guardrail. My bike's frame was cracked into pieces, and the right side of my body was chewed to shreds.

My race was over, but the worst was yet to come. The ambulance pulled to a quick stop to check us out, and the drivers parked in the middle of the dangerous corner. When another group flew through the bend a few minutes later, three riders slammed into the back of the ambulance. Koschara had pulled over, and after begging the EMT to move, he ran up the hill to warn the next groups to slow down. There were tears in his eyes. Matt had been the man on the ground plenty of times when he was racing, but he found the helpless bystander role harder to handle.

I limped to Barb and Tom's minivan and bled all over their seats on the way to our extended-stay hotel. By the time my teammates returned, I'd scraped the gravel out of my elbow and thigh, grimaced through a shower, and disinfected my wounds with various stinging chemicals. No amount of bandages in the world would have covered all the square footage I needed, so Matt helped me wrap myself in cellophane, which at least kept everything moist. When I packed my car, I grabbed close to a hundred of the team's supply of lightly used water bottles. They wouldn't need them for the crit the next day, and I had to go home with something.

I drove all the way back to Florida that night, 15 hours straight. Apart from gas, I stopped only once, at a Wal-Mart Supercenter for a cookie. You know how when you go to Wal-Mart, there's always some lowlife with fresh stitches, black eyes, or facial wounds, and you try not to stare? That night, I was the guy with the limp and a right leg that looked like roadkill wrapped in plastic. Everyone stared.

YOU CAN MAKE LEMONADE OUT OF ROAD RASH

It was humid and over a hundred degrees in Florida that August, but I wore pants for a few weeks to keep my wounds covered. The crash took me off the bike for a while, forcing me to recover from the missing skin, a hard stage race, and a long summer. When I showed up at a small stage race in north Georgia the next month, my climbing legs from Toona were back with a vengeance. I was second overall going into the last stage, with two 40-mile laps and three long climbs each. I was only down by two seconds overall, but I attacked from the gun and stayed away to win by four minutes, despite a full Jittery Joe's pro team chasing me all day. A year before, I'd begged that team for a contract, and their manager told me to do more

NRCs. On the third lap, I saw an awful lot of guys in orange Jittery Joe's jerseys on the side of the road, dropped from trying to catch me. I guess they hadn't done enough NRC races.

YELLING IS A TACTIC

It was a good sign for the legs to come back around, because the next weekend was Univest, the last race of the year. I expected to improve on my DNF record, until I woke up weak and nauseous the morning of the race, with a bad headache and phlegm everywhere. I knew from experience that even minor illnesses sap your fitness, so my heart sank as my hopes for the race went into the toilet, along with my dinner from the night before.

Not wanting to wake my teammates, I snuck outside and around the corner to a gas station, where I bought two sausage breakfast biscuits and a Coke, and walked around part of the finishing circuits for the stage. If we were still in the group after all the climbs, we'd get to race five 4-mile laps around town to the finish. When I got back to the house, the guys were up, so I joined them for oatmeal, and we headed out to the staging area.

Basil and Thurston had driven in from New York to watch the race from the team car. They were disappointed to see me coughing and pale, but they were glad I still wanted to start. My secret plan was to attack from the gun, make the early break, which usually got caught on the second of three climbs, and then hop into the car early when my job was done.

My first attack looked promising, and we had 20 seconds on the group when I went through the rotation behind Jonny Sundt, riding for Kelly Benefits. As we both drifted to the back, Timmy Duggan from Slipstream flew by with 10 guys behind him. We'd been caught

The lead group in the finishing circuits at Univest, with Frischkorn at the front.

and countered, and the new break was going away. With Sundt behind me, I sprinted ahead of the break we were in, trying to grab onto the back of Duggan's group, but the two of us found ourselves in no-man's-land between the break and the peloton.

I took a hard pull and flicked my elbow, asking Jonny for help.

"Fuck you! You pull us back there!" he replied. I kept pulling and didn't say a word, but Jonny kept a constant barrage of insults coming, lashing me like a whip.

"Don't you get us dropped from the break, you fucking idiot!"

I figured I must have messed up somehow for him to yell like that, so I managed to drag us across without Jonny's help. After a little more reshuffling, the break of 11 was established with me, Jonny, Stefano Barberi from Toyota-United, John Fredy Parra from Tecos, Timmy Duggan and Will Frischkorn from Slipstream, and a handful of European riders.

The course was mostly flat at first, with lots of tight turns through Pennsylvania's countryside, interrupted by three progressively harder King of the Mountain climbs (KOMs). As the rest of us kept the pace, Jonny and one of the Germans were battling for the sprinter jersey. The German was leading in the points, but he came off the pace on the first climb, and it looked like he held onto his team car to catch up to us.

On the second climb Sundt's rival came off again, but this time, once Jonny had chased back, his director stopped the car and waited for the Germans to approach. He knew that if someone was watching, they wouldn't hold onto the car again. The German didn't finish the race, and Jonny got the green jersey.

After a couple hours in the wind, it was time for the field to bring us back for their sprinters. The lead moto approached with a time gap, and I was looking forward to hearing that we were almost caught so I could call it a day.

"Your lead is nine minutes," he said.

My heart sank. The plan to make the early break and quit had backfired. The field had given up, and I was in for a long day.

Duggan went to the front on the third climb, shedding everyone but me, his teammate Frischkorn, and Parra. The four of us entered the finishing circuits with a massive lead, and when we made the first turn on the second lap, the whole peloton was standing there, pulled from the race, wondering who the skinny Sakonnet kid was. I made sure not to acknowledge them, to act like I knew what I was doing.

Frischkorn attacked and easily stayed away for the win, and I was dropped on the final lap, cruising in alone for fourth and the Best Young Rider award. I was sure I'd get a pro contract from that effort.

After the stage, my result got me more chamois time at the press conference. I sat reluctantly beside Jonny Sundt, afraid to make eye contact after our interaction early in the race, but he was fine. Jonny's rudeness wasn't because he was actually angry, or even a bad guy. It was a tactic, and it earned him a free ride across to the break. He felt bad that I'd fallen for it, and he explained that I, too, could yell at less-experienced riders (he might have said "suckers") to make them do my bidding. I've always appreciated the lesson. I woke up the next morning too weak to move, hit hard by the illness and the effort from the day before, but I knew that from then on, no matter how sick I felt, I'd always at least start the race.

Frischkorn's Team Slipstream was the continuation of the TIAA-CREF development team, still run by Jonathan Vaughters and moving up the ranks fast. Vaughters was the first director to figure out that the doping era was over—he saw that teams with scandal and questionable riders were having trouble finding new sponsors—so he designed and marketed Slipstream around the idea of clean racing and internal testing. Other teams quickly followed suit, and in a way, pro cycling was rescued. I watched Frischkorn finish second (by a tire width) on a stage at the Tour de France the next summer.

PRO ISN'T ALWAYS WHAT YOU WANT

With the racing season over, I turned my focus back to college. I was on track to finish my English degree in the spring but had no plans or prospects beyond that. Racing had been a good way to improve myself and kill time between classes, but until Univest I had never

One of the many bedrooms I'd bummed from strangers that year. I'd have to get used to it.

seen it as a potential livelihood. Now, though, with a good season behind me, racing for a living suddenly looked like a viable option, far more appealing than law school. If I could score a decent contract, I could skip the spring semester and go back to finish in the fall.

I contacted all the teams I could, confident that I could land an offer or two. I'd climbed with the best in the country for most of the year and gotten a few decent results. But the only pro offer I got was from a newer team, Time Pro Cycling. It offered $5,000 for the year and a room at its team house in Winston-Salem, North Carolina, but its race schedule would be mostly criteriums. Guttenplan took their offer.

My other option was Fiordifrutta, an amateur team based in Massachusetts and sponsored by an organic jam company. It had a strong squad and was known to place a couple riders on bigger pro teams every year. Fiordifrutta couldn't match the $5,000 I'd been offered by Time, but it would give me two Cannondale bicycles to keep, and $2,000, which was enough to rent an apartment in Massachusetts for the summer. Apart from mandatory training camp in February, the race schedule would be up to me.

Matt Koschara and I had become friends. I think he saw that we were a lot alike, so he knew that I was in for a rough couple of years racing my bike, and we stayed in touch when the season was over. He pointed out that I'd still mostly been doing small local races with amateur fields. If I wanted to be a professional, I needed to do the pro races, every weekend. He said I was good enough, so if I showed up for every big stage race the next year, I'd build enough of a résumé to get a real pro contract for 2009.

"How can I do all those races without a team?" I asked.

"You get in your fucking car," Matt said. "Just like I did when I was your age."

So I signed with Fiordifrutta. For the first time, bike racing was my primary focus. I didn't *want* to be a pro. I *had* to. And I didn't see any other way.

At the velodrome during the summer, I'd met Colby Pearce. He was riding for Slipstream but was looking to retire from pro racing to spend more time at home and wanted to start coaching elite-level riders. I became one of Colby's first clients.

Univest showed me that I also needed to market myself to teams. I could win a hundred races, but I'd never get a contract if no one knew who I was. To raise my profile, I made a web site with a blog and a page to post race results. I named the web site Philthethrill.net (Philthethrill.com was taken by some asshole with a band). I'd come up with Phil "the Thrill" Gaimon ironically in second grade, after I missed a three-pointer on the basketball court, and I'd been trying to get it to stick ever since.

Some people missed the irony of the nickname and thought that I was full of myself, so I added a disclaimer, explaining that even if I win the Tour de France, I recognize that to most people I'm still a weirdo in tights who needs to get the hell out of the road. I posted the definition of *ironic* and promised that it wouldn't happen again. I also don't do sarcasm anymore.

3

PUT IT IN THE 11

M y 2008 season began with a drive north to training camp in Massachusetts with my new teammate Steve Weller, who'd been training in Athens, Georgia, for the winter. We'd never met, but we became quick friends. Steve was a Dartmouth graduate and elite racer working for Cycle Smart, a coaching company for cyclists run by pro racer Adam Myerson. I'd been volunteer coach for UF's cycling team for over a year and was interested in getting some regular clients to help pay the bills. By the end of the drive, I had a job. I built up a decent number of clients over the next few months to whom I gave weekly training and racing advice. The coaching didn't bring in much money, but it fit well with my lifestyle, and it got me by.

That night we arrived at Steve's house in Hadley, Massachusetts. It was a huge, old place with a big, sloping roof (they called it "the Barn") on a one-way road just off the local highway. As we approached the front door, we could hear a powerful drum beat. I followed Steve, who followed the sound to the back of the house, where we found cyclocross racer Jeremy Powers wearing a huge set of headphones, dancing and shaking his fists to the thump of a massive sound system. The bass speaker was faced down, shaking the wide, cracked planks on the old hardwood floor.

He didn't ask my name. "WATCH THIS," Jeremy yelled. He pushed a button, and the sound of a plane flying past boomed over the speakers. The next button was a gunshot. Jeremy had a huge smile on his face, and we left him to his work.

"IS HE SERIOUS?" I asked the other roommates, gesturing to the louder side of the house, hoping they could hear me over the techno.

"NO ONE KNOWS," said Matt White, another new teammate, rolling his eyes.

I tried to look at the bright side. "WELL, AT LEAST YOU GET TO LIVE WITH A FAMOUS PRO CYCLIST."

"THAT GETS OLD PRETTY FAST."

I could see that.

I counted five couples living at the Barn, all racers and their girlfriends. Jeremy took off the headphones to join us for a dinner of homemade chili and cornbread. I felt right at home.

I was in the guest room at the Barn, on my own trusty air mattress. The house was built in the 1920s as two separate units, which meant that if I had to use the bathroom at night, I could either sneak through a room where Jeremy was sleeping or go out the front door of one unit and through a foot of snow to the front door of the other unit. The next door had a sharp, two-foot-high step into a huge, unfinished bike room. My teammates, all cyclocross experts, could hop right into the house, but I had to dismount and carry my bike in. The bike room must have had 20 bikes in various states of assembly, and parts everywhere.

I was equally smitten with the rest of the team the following day, and excited to be part of such a tight group. The only downside of the situation was the snow falling outside, which meant that most of the training took place indoors on stationary bikes hooked up to a computer screen. We went outside just long enough for some of the guys to show off their cyclocross skills, jumping curbs and sliding across a frozen lake on skinny tires.

GET A CAR WITH GOOD GAS MILEAGE

When training camp ended I took Steve back down to Athens and headed west alone to start the first NRC races of the year. On the road, I ate sandwiches out of a cooler and peed into an empty milk jug. My car had a range of 350 to 400 miles on a full tank, which far surpassed the range of my bladder. Each evening my mom would call to find out where I was so my dad could book a hotel room for me. They didn't want me sleeping in the car.

I drove to San Diego in four days, where I stayed with JC, a friend from high school. His apartment was a small studio in Pacific Beach with a rickety Murphy bed that folded out from the wall. He had just enough floor space for my air mattress; my bike and luggage lived on the porch. It wasn't the most comfortable quarters, but that's what friends are for, and the riding and weather made up for it. In the evenings, we played chess using the box from JC's TV set as our table. I almost always lost. JC is one of the smartest people I've ever met, but he always struggled with basic motor skills, so he was held back in kindergarten. JC was reading five grades ahead, but he couldn't color inside the lines.

JC lived just around the corner from SeaWorld. "So, how often do you go see the killer whale show?" I asked. "Two, three times a week?"

"Yeah, that's about right," JC said sarcastically. "They have good funnel cakes."

CHECK YOUR BOTTLE-CAGE BOLTS

The pro field for San Dimas filled up before I had a chance to register, so that race was out of the picture, and getting into Redlands proved to be a tough task. Since Redlands was a team-only race and my teammates were all back East, I'd need to ride for a composite team, which didn't exist. When I e-mailed the promoter, he just added me to a lengthy list on the race web site of all the riders looking for teams.

Looking at the long waiting list, it was hopeless to think that anyone would pick me up as a guest rider, but I'd come all the way to California, so I had to get into the race somehow. I contacted a few of the other names I knew on the waiting list and we started our own team. The entry fee was $1,000, pretty steep for five guys, but one of the riders found a sponsor to pay $500, the race provided host housing, and JC offered to hand out bottles for us. Fiordifrutta was sponsored by Adidas for shoes, and I was able to get the company to send us a pile of blank red jerseys. Our name was "U25 Devo, presented by Philthethrill.net" (compensation to myself for dealing with the logistics). The race accepted our application (as in, they accepted our money and made us feel lucky about it), and I immediately received e-mails from everyone else on the composite team list looking to join my squad instead of burning the calories to start their own. Bike racers are so tired from all that pedaling, they're often too lazy to get anything else done.

We stayed with a host family at Redlands. Organized by the race promoter, host families provide beds for teams. They might have a relationship with a team or a rider from year to year, but for the most part, they let complete strangers into their homes—and their lives— for a few days while the race is in town. It sounds weird, but it works, and host housing saves a ton of money and hassle over hotels. I always tried to maintain a relationship with host families, making sure to stay in touch and remember the names of the kids and pets. After a few years, I have welcoming faces and friends all over the country, and teams know that if they sign Phil Gaimon, that comes with a nice housing hookup in every town.

That week, I was the epitome of pack fodder, but it could have been worse: My teammates all DNFed, standing in the feed zone while I raced the infamous "Sunset circuits," with narrow roads, hard corners, and lots of climbing. I was riding well, and the group was down to about 30 guys when the top bolt of my bottle cage came out and the cage swung sideways into my pedal stroke. The cage was metal, not plastic or carbon fiber, so I couldn't break it off, and we were going uphill, so I had to stop to borrow a tool from the neutral support mechanic, who took his sweet time and sped off without pacing me back to the group. We were at 15 km to go, so I cruised in to finish 35th overall, earning $40 in prize money—just enough for gas back to San Diego.

My next trip was to Boulder, Colorado, to train with my new coach, Colby Pearce, and acclimate for the altitude at the Tour of the Gila. Boulder is a great town, and I understood why cyclists flocked there. The town has wide bike lanes and a network of paths that let you get almost anywhere without fighting car traffic, but some of the hippie element was hard to get used to for a guy from Georgia. Colby recommended a place for dinner that was all kale and tofu. The next day, I told him it was gross. "But it's all natural," was Colby's argument. Well, so is hemlock.

In between my training I found a test proctoring service in Denver and finished off two of the UF online courses I'd been working through. Half a semester down, all in my spare time.

CRAIGSLIST IS A TRASH CAN THAT PAYS YOU

After my tests, I picked up a new bike rack for my car. Roof racks hurt the gas mileage on my little Toyota, so I'd been using a four-bike hitch rack—the expensive kind that holds the bikes from the wheels so they don't swing around. This served me pretty well but it was heavy, so when the car was full, the bottom of the rack would scrape on the ground when I hit a bump or a pothole (I'm not a particularly gentle driver).

I bought a new rack from REI: a cheap, basic one with two arms that hold the bikes by the frame. I assembled it in the parking lot of the shitty Days Inn where I was staying and got to work removing the old one. It was dark when I realized that the steel tongue was bent, seizing it into the hitch. I pulled and pried, but the only thing that budged was my thumbnail, which I managed to peel halfway off. The hotel clerk showed me the utility room, where I borrowed a sledgehammer, to no avail. Standing in a dirty parking lot at 10 p.m., with blood from my thumb all over the assembly instructions, I was ready to return the new rack, but the store was closed and I needed to leave town at 6 a.m. to get to the next race. In desperation, I drove the car to the middle of the lot, then backed the far left side of the rack into a telephone pole, which straightened the tongue and freed it from the hitch. It was midnight.

The only question was what to do with the old rack. True, it had just taken a couple impacts, but it was steel, and I'd paid $400 for it less than a year before. It still had plenty of life left on a bigger car. I took out my combination lock, wrapped it around the rack and the

Skeet shooting with Jared in Garden of the Gods, Colorado Springs.

fence behind the hotel dumpsters, and put an ad on Craigslist with my phone number and the hotel address, offering to sell the combination for $150. It sold the next morning while I was on my way to Colorado Springs. Bike stuff sells fast in Boulder.

STICK WITH YOUR FRIENDS

The races that weekend were hosted by Colorado College. Former teammate Jared Faciszewski was in school there, so I had a sofa to crash on. They held a crit the first day, which was my first time racing against Taylor Phinney. He was all the talk after winning the national pursuit championship the previous year, his first attempt at the event. Taylor and I had teammates in the break, so we worked together to shut down the field, and once the break was gone, we battled it out for the remaining prize money. I attacked with a few laps to go, taking a 30-second lead into the last lap. I was nowhere near the break, but it looked like I had sixth locked up until Taylor went to the front and raced a world-class 4 km just for fun, or maybe out of boredom. The gap closed, and I was caught in the last turn, but only one guy had the energy to come around me after Taylor's effort. (Taylor's dad won Tour de France stages, his mom was world champion, and my parents are college professors.)

The next morning was a road race. I was caught behind a crash early on and had to untangle myself before I was able to chase back to the group. I caught them eventually, but I knew I was too exhausted to win after the effort. A younger, more determined rider would have stuck it out and finished, but sometimes it's better to just admit that your race is over and call it a day. I dropped out and went back to Jared's place, and he took me in his truck to Garden of the Gods Park, where he taught me how to shoot a shotgun. I'd never touched a firearm, and it was great to take out my frustration on clay Frisbees.

Jared was officially retired at 21. He'd been left off of the new VMG team and hadn't gotten any other offers, even after his national championship the year before. We were friends on VMG, but it's weird when someone quits. It's rarely planned, so you usually just hear they didn't find a team, or realize a year later that you haven't seen them in a while, so you never get to shake their hand. Once he's gone, a wall forms around him and he almost stops existing. He goes back to where he came from, and he won't call you because he doesn't feel like you have anything in common anymore. Or he's ashamed of giving up, and you don't call because you don't want to remind him of what he's missing. My friendship with Jared taught me to always fight that instinct. If your teammate is your friend, sometimes you can meet up years later, and he'll show you how to shoot a gun.

SILVER CITY IS NO PLACE FOR AMATEURS

I left Colorado Springs the next morning and got back in the fucking car for another day of driving for the Tour of the Gila. I'd never driven in snow before, but I made it to Santa Fe and then Albuquerque in the afternoon, careful to dodge all the tumbleweeds on the highway in New Mexico. I hadn't known that those existed outside of cartoons.

Already exhausted when I got off the interstate, I was surprised when my GPS said "48 miles remaining, 1.5 hours' drive time"—I was sure that couldn't be right. Then I saw the steep climbs, bumpy cattle guards, and dangerous descents on the road into Silver City. I drove as fast as I could, sliding my poor car around hairpins in the dark. I made it to the host house, fell asleep, and found two flat tires when I went outside to unpack the car in the morning. They probably weren't meant for drifting.

My luck didn't improve when the race started. I got a flat tire when I went off the road to dodge a crash, and I chased for over an hour to get back to the field. Between the dry air and altitude, I got a major nosebleed.

My car was parked at the base of the finishing climb, and I got there several minutes behind the field, my new white Cannondale and all my clothes covered in blood. The course turned right to go up the climb, and I turned left, climbed into my car, and got the hell out of there. I might have made the time cut, but for the second time in two weeks, I opted to climb in the car instead. I got out of that town like I was about to turn into a pumpkin, and made it back to San Diego nine hours later. If there wasn't a Pacific Ocean to stop me, I'd have driven another day, just to get farther from Gila.

I hadn't missed the tight quarters at JC's place in Pacific Beach, but it was nice to train in California again. I would ride in the afternoons and stop at a bench in Torrey Pines to watch the sun set over the ocean.

JC and I often went bowling when I visited. The alley in Kearny Mesa had plaques above the score screens with the names and dates of the best scores over the past decade. We noticed that a man named Chris Glossner had bowled two consecutive games of 299 points. We pictured the crowd gathering after his 11th strike, in the hopes of a perfect score, and their disappointment when he choked and only nine pins fell.

TEAMMATES ARE A GOOD THING

The summer was starting, and it was just warm enough to drive north for the Mount Hood Cycling Classic in Oregon, my first race with a full team. We only had four skinsuits for six riders, so a couple of us changed quickly after we finished the short prologue time trial to let someone else ride in a dirty chamois. Josh Dillon made a face as he put mine on, feeling the crotch sweat. I made fun of him, but I'd have done the same.

Matt White kept talking about how out of shape he was, and the guys confirmed that he hadn't been training or racing. Matt had raced a strong season the previous year but lost his motivation when that success didn't translate into a pro contract. I was bewildered to

Carrying a cooler to the feed zone with teammate Josh Dillon in Hood River, Oregon.

see him place 11th in the prologue, eight spots ahead of me. I asked him how he could do that if he was truly so out of shape.

"I started in the 18 cog, sprinted up to speed, put it in the 11, sprinted up to speed, shifted back to the 18 before the turnaround, got back up to speed, and then back to the 11 'til the finish." Of course! Just put it in the hardest gear and hold it. I don't know why I didn't think of that myself. Matt said he could do that off the couch in the middle of winter.

Another teammate told me that he'd stopped at a coffee shop during a ride and spotted Matt across the street, having lunch alone. He called Matt's cell and watched as Matt looked at the phone, hit "ignore," and put it back in his pocket. What is it about bike racing and loner weirdos?

I spent the second stage in the early break and rode well, attacking some of the better climbers and only getting absorbed into the field in the closing kilometers. It wasn't much, but I finished the stage race 36th overall, and it was good to have some consistency and decent legs after a disappointing spring. Most important, I was riding at the front over the climbs, and somebody must have noticed, because they weren't making me fight for wheels anymore. I always knew I belonged there, and I was finally accepted.

SPEEDING GETS YOU THERE FASTER

The race ended on a Sunday evening. I woke up before sunset and hopped in the car for another cross-country drive, this time diagonally. It was 2,500 miles from Hood River, Oregon, to Atlanta, Georgia, where I was already registered for a time trial two days later. I rarely dipped under 90 mph, peed into a milk jug instead of stopping (you'll be glad to know I had a new milk jug), and only slept for a few hours, in the car with the seat leaned back. I didn't have time to think about how depressing that was.

I went straight to the time trial course in Atlanta and made it just in time to pin on my race number. Somehow, my legs felt great right out of the car, and I placed second. Oh, to be young and limber.

The race continued for the whole weekend, but I skipped it to spend the time with my parents instead. My dad had just been diagnosed with stage 4 throat cancer, and he was leaving soon for the MD Anderson Cancer Center in Houston to start treatment. I had to go back to New England the following week, so this was the last I would see of them for a couple months. For inspiration, my mom was reading Lance's autobiography. She didn't know any better, but it made me nauseous.

THE CHEAPEST PLACE ISN'T NECESSARILY THE BEST

I'd found a summer rental just down the street from the Barn in Hadley, and I arrived in Massachusetts excited to train with all the friendly folks I'd met at camp. After those nights in my car at rest stops, I thought I could live anywhere. The place I found online was cheap enough, and the girl who posted the ad sounded nice, so I didn't bother to ask all the questions I should have. I signed the sublease agreement via fax and got my key through the mail. I realized my error as soon as I walked in the door.

The place looked like it was decorated by a kleptomaniac. To my left was a college student's trophy wall: a bookshelf filled with empty liquor bottles. To the right: an electric guitar and amplifier. The living room contained five items: a threadbare sofa, a coffee table with a bong and a full baggie of marijuana, and an enormous drum set. No one was home, so I dragged my bag upstairs, inflated my air mattress, and went to sleep. I woke up around 2 a.m. when someone got home, used every item in the living room, and then left.

The next morning I called the girl who'd rented me the room.

"I'm not going to live there," I told her. "And you're going to tear up that check."

"But you signed a lease," she argued. She was pre-law at Smith College in Northampton.

"You can tear that up, too. You can't sublease a room in a house with weed sitting around and roommates who play the drums in the middle of the night."

I'm no square, but it was the best argument I could think of. I heard the gears in her head grinding over the phone. "Oh."

Steve was spending most nights at his girlfriend's house, so I took his room down the street while I looked for another place to rent, and spent some quality time with Jeremy Powers and Al Donahue, another Barn resident.

I moved into a studio basement apartment a couple days later. It was in Amherst, a neighboring town (home of UMass Amherst and its mascot, the Minutemen). It cost more than I wanted to pay, but there were no drum sets or roommates to worry about.

I kept busy between races with more distance courses and reading. I'd never lived alone before, and I found that I liked the distraction-free, monkish lifestyle. I had one bowl, one plate, one knife, one spoon, and one fork to my name. I cooked all my meals, and got into a good routine with training, stretching, and core exercise. I made oatmeal and eggs for breakfast every morning and jumped onto my bike at exactly 9:30, exchanging a smile and wave with an old man who must have had an equally strict schedule, since we'd always pass at the same intersection. One day, he could tell I was running 15 seconds late, because he ran into me a block earlier than usual. He shook his head with a "tsk, tsk" gesture. I didn't let him down again.

It was a half-hour ride from Amherst to the Barn to meet up with the guys. Some days I'd grab a carton of milk at a gas station, and then swing by Café Esselon in Hadley for a chocolate-chip peanut butter cookie with powdered sugar sprinkled on top. Jeremy and Al still remember me as the guy who was always drinking milk and eating cookies. I'm off dairy now, but otherwise I haven't changed a whole lot.

I never worried about the isolation until the night that my inflatable sit-up ball popped underneath me, and my butt hit the hardwood floor unexpectedly at very high speed. No one heard the thud, so I army-crawled to the air mattress where I writhed in pain for a while. I wondered how long it would have taken them to find my body if I'd hit my head. It builds character to experience intense, grimacing pain alone and miles from anyone you know, at least a couple times a year. Right?

DON'T MISS THE BREAK

The big target for the season was the Under-25 Tour of Pennsylvania, an International Cycling Union (UCI) race with lots of prize money. It also contained a field of mostly European development teams, so we actually had help for this one. Team manager Curt Davis drove the team car, with feeds from Hayden Brooks's girlfriend and Josh Lipka's dad. The first stage had a prologue in the morning and a crit in the afternoon, which was basically a lap of the prologue course. It was fun racing a crit with all the Under-23 European guys who came over thinking they'd kill us. I thought I was uncomfortable in crits and corners until I heard a Dutch accent ask, "What is this kamikaze American racing?"

Early in the next stage, they had us riding out of town on a twisty golf cart path, and Jamey Driscoll and I were at the back of the field.

Years later, for some odd reason, I still had a reputation for enjoying the occasional cookie.

He looked at a twist in the path coming up, turned into the grass, rode up the sand trap, through the green, hitting the flag with his elbow like a slalom skier, and jumped back onto the course right at the front of the field, looking back to smile at me. We missed the early break that had all the GC riders in it, but I attacked near the end and almost got across. In a strange reunion, the group consisted of me and two former teammates, David Guttenplan and Alex Boyd. We were close but couldn't quite catch the break before the finish, and those 15 seconds took me out of the GC race.

YOU CAN SCREW UP AS LONG AS YOU WIN

The next day finished in Bedford, home of Cannondale, our bike sponsor, and the pressure was on to impress. I attacked on the first climb and rode away from the field, but Peter Stetina came across and dropped me near the top. I figured he just wanted the KOM points, but he decided to go 60 miles solo instead of waiting for someone to work with. My chase group swelled to about 40 guys, and Stetina made me look stupid, almost staying away solo.

When Stetina came back with 800 meters to go, our sprinter was in the third group, so Jamey Driscoll, Toby Marzot, and I decided to lead Toby out in the sprint. I took the front and sprinted as hard as I could to keep Toby in position. Things were looking perfect until Jamey shot out of the field with 500 meters to go, causing a big swarm. I lost sight of Toby, angry that Jamey didn't follow the plan, until I saw him cross the line with his arms up. You can't say he didn't do it right if he held them all off. With all the sponsors at the finish line, that was probably the best race we could have won all year. That night we were treated to the most expensive meal that Bedford, Pennsylvania, had to offer: the Old Country Buffet.

The next two stages were both near-misses for me. Stage 2 was short with some hard climbing, in pouring rain. I made a selection of the seven top GC guys on the climb, sat on the back, and attacked with 2 km to go. I figured that since I was the only non-GC guy left, they'd let me slip away, but Stefano Barberi chased me back in the last 100 meters, and then everyone sprinted around him. David Veilloux won, so Stefano lost time bonuses to three guys he cared about just to keep me from winning. I remembered being jealous of Stefano when he was living in Florida, riding for TIAA-CREF. I guess he didn't like me.

With only a crit remaining, stage 4 was my last chance to get a result, but about halfway through I hit something in the road and did a somersault, tearing up my hands and landing on my back. The bike was all right, and I paced back to the group, recovered from the crash, and attacked with 20 km to go. I wiped sweat from my eyes, and the blood from my hands looked like war paint. I finished third, caught by two guys with 500 meters to go, but at least I looked like a badass.

With a crit the last day, I begged a massage from the soigneur who was working with Time Pro Cycling (that team had barely cracked the top 10 on a stage, by the way), in the hopes that she would help heal some of my wounds and bruises. I forget how it came up, but she guessed my age at 30. I guess I had a thick beard for a 23-year-old.

The final stage was a crit in downtown Pittsburgh, with more crowds and some sort of a festival with all kinds of food in the middle of the course. After four days of nothing but oatmeal, pasta, and Old Country Buffet, the smells were tantalizing as we warmed up in the rain. I started near the back of the field and got a full view of the best race start of all time: Everyone sprinted into turn one, paved with smooth bricks and soaked from the rain, and they all slid into each other, forming a huge pile of bodies and carbon. The race was neutralized, and after much debate, the officials finally decided that the remaining prize money would go to a local charity and the GC of the race would be over, but they'd like us to "still ride around, because it's on TV and that's good for your sponsors." I couldn't believe that anybody actually got back onto that bloodbath course for no prize money, but they did. I went and got a kielbasa from the festival and watched my friends crash in turn one for half an hour. Bike racers can be stupid.

One of the teams put on a party that night at somebody's mansion and invited everyone but Fiordifrutta, so Toby and I climbed into the van with the Time Pro Cycling guys and crashed it. They were all dressed up, with shirts half-unbuttoned and hair gel, competing with 60 guys for the three podium girls, while Toby and I got drunk on wine and played pool in the basement. The owner of the house came down and asked who invited us. I thought that was pretty rude.

When we got back to the dorms where all the riders were staying, Stefano Barberi was also drunk, sitting in the maid's giant cart of sheets in the parking lot, surrounded by other racers, all teasing him. I told Stefano I had his back, mostly joking, but I think he took it seriously. We were friends after that.

DO REST WEEKS RIGHT

The week after the Tour of Pennsylvania was possibly the laziest of my life, and it might rank among the top 10 laziest weeks of all time. I'd been training and racing hard since February, so my coach prescribed four days off the bike and four days with short easy rides. You know how a hot tub feels better if you just come out of an ice bath? Well, a week on a sofa is better if you've been beating yourself up for months.

For the first few days I woke up around 9 a.m., had breakfast, and then went back to bed for a nap. In the afternoons I drove to Cracker Barrel for grits and sweet tea (I was homesick for Georgia) and watched DVDs on my computer, then went to bed early. With no roommates, I didn't have to worry about being neat, organized, or even hygienic. Instead of drawers, I used three 55-gallon tubs to contain my clothing (one for clean, one for dirty, and a third that I privately referred to as "sometimes in life, you have to make sacrifices"). I still hadn't shaved, so I carved out a goatee.

Hayden had been driving a team-provided Ford Focus hatchback (fully wrapped with Fiordifrutta logos) to the races all summer. He took it in to get serviced that week and found that the brake pads were entirely worn off. One of the team managers insisted on having a friend change it, rather than paying full price at the dealership, so Hayden started to leave.

"No! You really shouldn't drive that!" the mechanic insisted, sincerely concerned for Hayden's safety.

"I made it this far," Hayden replied. "I'll make it just fine." He was right. He made it just fine.

At the end of the rest week, I drove to the Fitchburg-Longsjo Classic, but not to race. I just went to hang out. It was weird to sit out an NRC race that was only an hour from where I was spending the summer, but when I peaked for the Tour of Pennsylvania, my coach and I had decided that it was more important to rest, with nationals coming up in a few weeks.

I walked around with the goatee as my disguise and stood holding a rubber chicken in the feed zone between all the soigneurs and their bottles. It was fun watching Healthnet and all the big teams buzz by screaming for Cokes and Gatorade, and then notice the rubber chicken. Maybe it reminded them to stop being so damn serious.

Someone at the back grabbed the chicken, and I was afraid I'd never see my fake pet again, but it came back a few months later.

It was funny that in my time off of bike racing, I still went to a bike race. I'd grown to like the atmosphere, and all my friends were there. Besides, it wouldn't feel like a weekend if I didn't have to wait in line for a port-a-potty.

BE CAREFUL WITH THE INTERNET

My final prep for nationals was a small time trial in upstate New York. It was a long drive for a local race, and the early start meant that I'd need a hotel room for the night before. Registration was $30, and payout was weak (the web site said $150 split among the top three, so $80/$40/$30 or something similar would have been standard), but it was enough that I thought I could cover my expenses and break even on the trip if I won. Polishing off my training with a real race was worth the gamble.

I felt great and won by a good margin, and then packed up my stuff as fast as I could, hoping to beat an approaching summer rainstorm. The organizers were slow to post results, and when I came to claim the prize money, I was handed a plastic trophy and $50 cash, already drenched. The volunteers were rushing around, breaking down the tents and packing up in the rain, so I e-mailed the organizers the next day, expecting a check in the mail for $30 to rectify what must have been an innocent mistake. The response was that the rider turnout wasn't good enough, so they cut the prize money. I recalled at least 80 paying entrants in a race run by volunteers, with $150 total payout (men's pro was the only category with any prize money at all), so it seemed to me that rather than admitting a mistake and coughing up a few dollars, they were trying to justify it.

Looking back, I realize it wasn't much money, but I was frustrated that this was what I worked so hard for, and my only recourse, as a passive-aggressive coward, was to write a blog about it. I chose a humorous angle, making fun of the fact that the organizers invested in a trophy while they cut the prize list. The title of my entry was "Can I have the cash equivalent instead?" I posted a photo of the trophy with the caption "To be fair, nothing holds a door open like a plastic figure screwed into a faux marble base."

The blog was not well received. A popular New York–based cycling forum soon had a thread called "Phil the Douche," with dozens of comments, but they weren't angry at my criticism of the race itself. It was hard to avoid coming off as a braggart writing about a race that I won, so in addition to downplaying the quality of the race, I'd also downplayed the competition, making the point that I was racing against a bunch of doctors, lawyers, and guys with full-time jobs, so I expected to win.

Come to think of it, that is kind of douchey, but it never occurred to me that my competitors wouldn't expect to be beaten by a guy who'd been doing it full-time. Local racers in Florida always handled their losses gracefully. They'd shake my hand after the finish and consider it a point of pride for "Skinny Phil" to beat them again. To the proud New Yorkers, my attempt at modesty was taken as an insult. I removed the blog entry, but the "Phil the Douche" forum lived on for weeks. I was surprised by how painful it was.

DON'T GET TOO EXCITED

Four days before my flight to Los Angeles for nationals, I got a phone call from Jonas Carney, director of Kelly Benefits, one of the top teams in the country. He'd noticed me at the Tour of Pennsylvania and explained that Nick Waite, one of his best climbers, was about to get fired, and they needed someone to take his place at two races in France starting in 10 days. It didn't mean I had a contract for the following year, but it was a chance to try out and prove myself. I already had my flight booked for nationals, but the goal of that trip would be to get a result that might put me on a team like Kelly Benefits, so the decision was a no-brainer. I told Jonas I was in.

I didn't mention that my old passport was expired, and getting one usually takes a couple weeks. It was too late for the standard rush option, but Boston was a two-hour drive away, one of only a handful of places in the country where you can get a passport the same day for the bargain price of $500. I wasn't about to let paperwork stand between me and this great opportunity to race in Europe for a pro team, so I got all the documents I needed, took photos at the post office, and drove out the next morning. It took all day, but I arrived back in Amherst with a brand new passport, still warm from the printer.

I was ready to go, but Jonas didn't return my phone calls after that. I checked the results of the races the team did in France, and Nick Waite seemed to be riding well. To be fair, Jonas didn't know I'd gone to all that trouble.

CHECK YOUR TIRES

I hadn't canceled my ticket for nationals, so I flew to Los Angeles with my team as planned, where I tried to put scathing forum posts and pro teams out of my mind. The time trial was the first race. I nailed my warm-up and my legs were feeling great until my tire popped on the climb about 8-km into a 30 km course. I heard a loud bang from the rear wheel and instinctively got off the bike. Then I realized that I had no follow car, and it was a slow leak, so I kept riding.

In the back of my mind, I knew that my chance for a result was over, but I kept riding hard up the hills, slowing down for the corners and descents in case the tire blew completely. I still caught a few of the guys in front of me as the tire got flatter and flatter, and crossed the finish line riding on the rim. My result was 13th place out of 80 riders. Looking at the file from my power meter that night, I learned that I would have finished second if I hadn't stopped. I started to calculate how much time I lost from braking on the descents and riding the flat, but wisely abandoned the idea. It was better not to know.

We had one day to recover before the road race, and the team made me proud. We hadn't brought nearly enough bottles for the hot conditions, but rather than buy some at a bike shop, we drove to the road race course early in the morning, hiked up to the feed zone during one of the junior races, and grabbed all the discarded bottles we could find. My teammates and I set up an assembly line in the hotel bathroom, unscrewing the lids, scrubbing the insides with a brush, soaking them in the bathtub with a bleach tablet, and then rinsing everything off. I liked how the teamwork continued off the bike. We were family.

We went for a short ride along the Los Angeles River and then jumped into the rented minivan and headed to the beach. Any pro team director would be horrified at the thought of his riders sitting around shirtless getting sunburned the day before a race, but we didn't have a director, and it sure beat spending the day in a cramped motel room.

I'd focused my training on the time trial and didn't think I was prepared for the road race, but I found myself in a huge early break and felt pretty good. I'd never seen a group of that size work so smoothly together, but over 30 hungry Under-23 racers pulled through on those open roads in the heat of the California valleys, and nobody skipped a pull, so the gap went up fast. Guys finally got tired on the long, gradual hills, where after 60 miles, still only halfway through the race, Garmin's development team chose to start attacking. Kirk Carlsen went first. He put a few seconds on us, and the break blew apart.

Of the 11 riders in the chase group behind Carlsen, five were his Garmin teammates. They refused to pull, and cooperation was bad among the six non-Garmins still in contention for the win. We finally started to work together against the dominant team, taking turns attacking them.

With 35 miles to go, the chase group was back together, and I attacked, followed only by Peter Stetina, who refused to pull at first with his teammate up the road. But that far from the finish, I knew I couldn't do it alone.

"I need your help to stay clear of the chase group," I begged.

"Can't. I have Kirk up the road."

"Yeah, but we won't catch him, and even if we do, you guys can attack me later."

Peter wasn't convinced. I promised to take third, and he took his turns at the front. We were soon joined from behind by Tom Peterson, another Garmin rider. I took one look at him and said I'd take fourth and keep working if they'd help me stay away. Podium was top five, after all. I took a long pull to prove that I was sincere, and they attacked me anyway. I didn't blame them.

There was no point trying to respond to Garmin's attacks with 30 miles left. I knew they'd get rid of me eventually, and I might as well save my energy. I let them go, put my head down, and rode as hard as I could, eventually watching Tom and Peter catch their teammate Kirk and cross the line together, an adorable one-two-three finish for their team. I got my podium, staying clear for fourth. The hard effort and the heat had torn me apart, and I felt like car doors had been slammed on all my limbs. I went to the van, took my shoes off, put my feet out the window, and didn't talk for half an hour. Sometimes I think I'm not any stronger or more talented than anyone else. Maybe I'm just better at suffering.

I staggered to the podium presentation in my socks, with the crusty salt visible on my face. It was tough that I did everything right but didn't come out with quite the result I deserved. That's something that Chris Glossner would have done at the bowling alley in San Diego. Still, I considered highest-placed non-Garmin something of a victory and was happy with how I raced. In the bigger races I'd done, it was all about hanging on for dear life, but when you're strong enough to be in the pool of potential winners, the winner is determined by a fast-paced chess game. This was only my second or third time even sitting at the board, and I'd played well.

We flew back to New England the next morning, where I said goodbye to my teammates and packed up the apartment. I was heading home for the fall semester, but with a couple long detours. First, I drove north, just 30 miles from the Canada border, for the Mount Washington Hillclimb. It is a unique event where everyone starts at once, shooting straight up over dirt roads, past the tree line, all the way to an observatory at 6,200 feet. It was a nice summer day at the bottom, but the top could have been another planet, with no vegetation at all, and full of wind and snow. I rode a steady pace and won by over a minute. It was nice to get my name on the front page of all the cycling news sites, but with no pros on the start list, I would have been disappointed with anything less than a win. After the "Phil the Douche" incident in the forum, I didn't mention that last part in my blog.

Mount Washington is a race for some, but it's mostly an adventure, with a family-focused atmosphere and medals for every age

On the way to victory on Mount Washington.

group that are handed out at an awards banquet after the ride. Riders weren't allowed to coast back down the mountain after the race, so I had to bum a ride from a couple who had room in their car. At least it gave me someone to sit with during the banquet, but it was still strange to be there by myself, doing interviews with cycling magazines and local newspapers, feeling like a big shot, when I was about to climb back into my fucking car, heading to yet another shitty motel. I'd spent most of the year alone and focused like never before. It worked, but now that I was reaping the benefits, I recognized the tradeoff, and the victory felt empty.

STAY AWAY FROM HOUSTON

From Mount Washington, I plugged Houston, Texas, into my GPS. My dad was finishing up his cancer treatment and needed me to help out for the last few days while my mom went back to work. I went for one decent training ride while I was there, but I couldn't escape the sprawl of Houston's metro area and did the rest of my Houston rides indoors. The treatment went well, and my mom flew back to take him home while I hopped in the car and headed to Florida. My semester started in 24 hours, and the drive should have been 15. No big deal, except that a Category 2 hurricane was blowing through Louisiana. Somehow, I kept my car on the road, stopping twice to call 911 for flipped SUVs after making sure the folks inside had gotten out. I didn't sleep, but I made it to class on time.

I'd been gone for almost six months, and my room in Florida was alien to me. I couldn't decide if I should unpack or just throw away everything that I'd left there. If I'd gone that long with only the stuff in my car and my suitcase, I obviously didn't need anything else.

Thanks to the distance courses I'd taken, I had an easy fall schedule, with only six credits remaining to finish the requirements for graduation. Both three-credit courses consisted of a long reading list for class discussion, a 12-page midterm paper, and a 15-page final paper. I was so motivated to finish, and so accustomed to non-stop action from my year on the road, that I started reading ahead to the next lessons. Within six weeks I'd finished all the papers for both classes, and all I had to do was sit at my desk and participate in the discussions for the rest of the semester.

Finally settled in one place for more than a few days at a time, I found a girlfriend that fall. She was the roommate of a friend from the cycling team, finishing up a degree in psychology (just what a bike racer needs).

Since it was my final year of collegiate eligibility, I'd planned to race collegiate track nationals that fall. I'd finished second and third in the points race there and wanted to win a national championship, but I found that since I wasn't a full-time student, I wasn't eligible to race. With nothing left to train for, I called it a season, hung up the bike, and started taking daily naps.

I knew, though, that it was time to find a new team. I didn't have a lot of friends in the pro ranks to help me, so I'd gone through the USA Cycling team database to find contacts for all the U.S. pro teams. I had made it a point to stay in touch with them throughout the year and let them know how I was doing. I rarely got a response, other than a brief "Good to hear. Keep in touch."

Now, with my season over, I sent another round of e-mails to all the team directors, summarizing my goals and results for the year: a handful of top-5 and top-10 finishes at bigger races, and eight regional race wins, which made me the top-ranked amateur in the country at age 22. I detailed my NRC experience and my role in team successes to show that I was ready to contribute to a larger team's plan, and I included a link to the blog and articles I'd had published in various cycling magazines, which I hoped would appeal to sponsors. My tone was polite, modest, and friendly, and I made each e-mail specific to the team I was applying for. I thought those details mattered.

I nervously hit the "send" button. This was a moment of truth. I'd been through some rough times before, but after that year on the road, I'd shown I was ready. Racing had come easy at first, with a pro contract and a salary after less than a year of racing, but there were no yachts when I was riding for Sakonnet and Fiordi-frutta, living out of my car, training my ass off (figuratively), and crashing my ass off (literally). I'd put 140,000 miles on my car in three years, sleeping at rest stops, overstaying my welcome with friends, family, and strangers, all while grinding through a college degree. I kept straight As in my classes, because I felt that I owed it to my parents for supporting me.

The offers came flooding in, but it was one of those really slow, gradual floods. Okay, it was a trickle, maybe a thimbleful. After staring at my inbox and phone for weeks, like a schoolgirl hoping to be asked to prom, I had only two responses. One was from a team sponsored by Colavita (of olive oil fame), saying it might have a spot available for me. It would be unpaid, but I would have a good schedule and full support. I was hoping to get at least some salary, but Colavita got invited to all the major stage races and was a good team, so prize money would be decent. The other response was expected: Time Pro Cycling still wanted me, but its offer was the same $500/month that I'd turned down to ride for Fiordifrutta, and its schedule would be mostly crits again. I was desperate for an offer from a team like Kelly Benefits. Everyone raved about Kelly's director, Jonas Carney, one of the few who had raced through the dirty era and never touched a banned substance, so I didn't hold a grudge about missing out on the trip to France. If Jonas had sent me a bar napkin with a picture of a bicycle drawn on it in lipstick, I'd have gladly signed.

I called around to every racer I knew, hoping to hear rumors of new teams coming together. My friends had been contacting directors as well, and at least 10 of them had gotten the same promising e-mail from Colavita, which must have just sent a form response to every young American it heard from. My chances of free olive oil plummeted, and I signed a contract with Time Pro Cycling. It wasn't what I wanted, but I couldn't put off being pro another year and thought I could make it work.

I went on an eBay selling spree that week. Teams like Fiordifrutta's have good relationships with their sponsors, so at the beginning of the year we were given great prices (slightly cheaper than bike shops) on anything we wanted—bikes, wheels, clothing, power meters, and so on. I ordered as much as I could and then put it all in the closet to sell at the end of the year. As long as riders were discreet and didn't abuse their deals, the team and sponsors considered this a roundabout way of paying us.

It had only been a few days since I'd put the bike away, but I was already in full off-season mode, eating pizza, napping, and barely leaving the sofa. On Halloween I had my first taste of alcohol in over a year, and lost a drunken wrestling match with a friend who played football at UF. He didn't want to hurt me, so he put me on the ground in some sort of wrestling hold until I said "Uncle." I got up and dusted myself off. "Who's next?" I yelled.

ALWAYS ANSWER CALLS FROM NUMBERS YOU DON'T RECOGNIZE

I woke up the next morning with a sore back (among other aches and pains, possibly from drunken wrestling), and a coach who suggested I race elite track nationals since collegiate was off the table. It was an Olympic year, so the competition wouldn't be too bad, and the top young rider in each event would be awarded an Under-23 national championship, so I still had a shot at a coveted stars-and-stripes jersey (probably the last chance for the rest of my racing career, or at least until I enter the age-group categories).

"Is it even worth it to go?" I asked. "I mean, I haven't ridden in . . . Sunday, Monday, Tuesday, Wednesday. Oh, that's not so bad."

"No, that's not so bad," Colby confirmed.

"But I should probably ride today."

"Yeah." I didn't mention my hangover, or my wrestling injuries.

I made the finals in the points and scratch races and spent some time attacking, but I didn't win anything. My first track nationals went about as expected, but there was no worse feeling than competing and knowing I hadn't given it my best in practice and preparation. Want to know the best teachers I've ever had? Failure and regret.

As I was packing up after the points race, my phone rang with a number I didn't recognize. It was Danny Van Haute, from Jelly Belly Pro Cycling. Jelly Belly wasn't the best team around, but it was well established, and a handful of Americans who made it to Europe had gone through the program. Jeremy Powers must have mentioned that I was still available. Danny had been a pro in the 1980s and went to the Olympics as a track racer. He'd ignored all my previous attempts to contact him (I wondered if I had the right e-mail address), but before I said a word, Danny offered me a spot on the team and a good race schedule for 2009, but no salary. "Well, that sounds pretty good," I said, "but I already signed to Time Pro Cycling for $500 a month."

"Time Pro Cycling. That's a pro team? Would they let you out?" They'd been a pro team for three years.

"Yeah. I think they'd release me for a team like yours, but it would be hard to explain it to them if I was riding for free. I'm not saying no, but do you think you could match their offer? That would make it much easier."

"We can do $2,000. Take it or leave it."

"Umm, okay. I guess I'll take it—"

"You're a climber, right?" he interrupted.

"Uhh, yeah." Shouldn't he know that already?

And then he hung up. I thought I was the victim of a prank, but sure enough, I got an e-mail from Danny the next morning with a contract for $2,000. Adam Myerson, still employing me as a coach, was running Time Pro Cycling. He said it was a tough call, but ultimately Jelly Belly was the better opportunity. I'd get to develop in bigger races, and if I did well and proved myself, I'd get a reasonable salary as a core rider. It was worth it to get my foot in the door of a team that paid a living wage to its top guys, even if it took another year to make decent money.

There's always talk that third division teams like Time and Jelly Belly should have minimum salaries, but that never made sense to me, because teams, managers, and owners aren't paying themselves much. If someone enforced a minimum salary, it couldn't be more than $5,000/year, or teams like Time would just go back to amateur status, where they'd have even more trouble finding sponsors. But a disparity rule would be nice. For example, no rider on a team should get paid more than three times the salary of any of his teammates. That would at least prevent the common problem of a rookie getting stuck in a no-salary gig, sacrificing his results and development for a guy making $100,000. But that would be a hard rule to enforce, and nobody listens to me, anyway.

Time Pro Cycling dissolved my agreement without complaint, a very generous move. It's frowned-upon to pursue a rider who's already under contract, and rare for a transfer without some money changing hands to the losing team. If the team had insisted that Danny buy out my contract, he would have just hired someone else rather than make a phone call or pay Time on my behalf. I sent both of the team owners $50 gift certificates to Outback Steakhouse to show my appreciation. I was 22, and that was the classiest thing I could think of.

One of my professors wanted me to stay at UF, offering to be my advisor for a fully supported master's program. I declined, explaining that I was going to be a pro cyclist.

She looked at me strangely. "Is that a career?" she asked.

Good question. On the other hand, is English professor a career?

When the dust settled, I had signed to a strong pro team, but I'd still be getting paid less than the team's mechanic, and I'd definitely have to keep up my coaching and writing work. I couldn't decide whether to celebrate my success or print out graduate school applications. I was a pro, but had I made it? How would I know when I did? I had mixed emotions, but I was confident that things would continue in the right direction. I'd paid my dues, so the hard times were over. Right?

Despite my big-picture concerns, I was more motivated than ever to start training again going into 2009. I skipped my college graduation ceremony in favor of a long bike ride, but I did tie a tassel to my helmet for the day.

4

PAY YOUR DUES AGAIN

elly Belly's training camp in February took a lot of adjustment. Danny Van Haute ran everything on the team, from signing riders and sponsors to booking flights, so he didn't have time to coddle me at camp. As a first-year pro, there were a lot of little things I'd never learned—I didn't know that I should bring my own towel for massage, nor that I should ask the mechanics to work on my bike if something wasn't shifting right, rather than try to fix it myself. Camp is especially stressful on staff, and some of them were short with me when I asked dumb questions. John Sessa, one of the mechanics, was from San Antonio, Florida, a spot I'd frequently visited for training. The Florida bond was enough for John to show me the ropes, and he was always there for me when I needed extra tires or a spare chain to take home.

Jeremy Powers was the only teammate I knew, but he skipped camp to finish off his cyclocross season. Most of the guys didn't go out of their way to make me feel at home (in fact, some were down-right rude), and it was hard to penetrate the clique. No one laughed at the new guy's jokes on the rides, and I found myself sitting alone in the hotel room while my teammates went out to dinner. I was accustomed to being close with my team, so the exclusion was hard to deal with. Since then, I've always made it a point to watch out for the new guys. If anyone should get his ass kissed, it's the guy who's getting no salary, whose job is to bring bottles to his teammates.

DON'T LISTEN TO DOCTORS

Jonny Clarke was also new to the team. Son of an Olympian and younger brother of top sprinter Hilton Clarke, Jonny had been groomed to be a pro cyclist by the Australian Institute of Sport and was already a seasoned pro at age 25. Jonny helped with a lot of the little things I didn't know yet, like not to be afraid to ask for the keys to the team car if I had to run an errand, because that's what it's there for.

He scored points for being a nice guy, but it was a conversation I overheard at camp that made me really respect Jonny. The team doctor had made an appointment with each rider for a physical, which included an asthma test. I went first, blowing several times into a tube, which measured the power and volume of the output.

According to the doctor's chart, the needle didn't move far enough, and she concluded that I had asthma.

"But I've never had an attack," I protested.

"Do you find yourself out of breath at the top of the stairs?" she countered.

"Well, yeah," I admitted. I should have asked, *But who doesn't?*

"I think you'd benefit from an inhaler." She wrote me a prescription for Albuterol.

I was skeptical of the diagnosis, but she was a doctor after all, and the idea that I could go faster with something as simple as a legal inhaler was appealing. I filled the prescription.

Jonny Clarke had his physical after mine, while I sat in the next room. He went through the same routine and result with the tube and the needle, but handled it differently.

"I don't have asthma," came the response in Jonny's Australian accent. My ears perked up.

"Well, if you look at the results here, it shows that you do have—"

"No, I don't."

"Do you ever find yourself out of breath at the top of stairs?"

"Nope. Not once," he lied, daring her to challenge him.

"Well, according to this test, you could benefit from—"

"No, I wouldn't."

I didn't realize what was going on at the time, and the doctor wasn't doing anything illegal, technically. She was just taking advantage of the fact that Albuterol was legal in competition. Science says that inhalers don't help you perform if you don't have asthma, but it was rumored that over half of the European pro peloton carried inhalers prescribed by their team doctors, and I was unwittingly being asked to join their ranks, taking a legal shortcut against my better judgment, while Jonny pushed it away. He wasn't interested in shortcuts, and he'd made his decision long ago.

HUG THE INSIDE

Camp wasn't all bad. We raced up Mount Palomar, and I went to the front and dropped everyone who'd been pissing me off all week. With my legs, I finally made a statement I'd been holding in, and the guys had to respect me a little after that. Most important, I was on a pro team now. Gone were the days of finishing a ride and checking my tires, washing the frame and chain, and adjusting the cables. Before the ride, the mechanics asked what wheels and gearing I'd like, and the soigneurs would find out if I wanted Gatorade or water in my bottles. When we got back, I'd leave the bike on the rack, and it would be cleaned and tuned for the next day. Having all those details sorted out for me really added up.

Although my pay was pathetic, the sponsors treated us well, with piles of clothing, sunglasses, luggage, tires, tubes, and a whole lot of candy. With every meal taken care of, I hardly opened my wallet on the trip, which made the light paycheck easier to handle. Easier, but still not easy. When your salary is $166.66 a month, you don't forget it.

We ended training camp with a local criterium. It wasn't a big race, but it was a good chance to work together, racing for our sprinter, Brad Huff, and I had a rare view (for me, anyway) of the front of a crit. The guys showed me to ride on the far inside of the straightaways, swinging out at the last second to take the turns at full speed. Holding the inside made it nearly impossible for anyone to attack into a corner, and easy for the team to control the race. I'd been a victim of this tactic countless times and never knew it. I was going to learn a lot if I kept my eyes open. We had 11 guys in the race, so it was pretty funny when Rahsaan Bahati (riding for Rock Racing, with no teammates) dive-bombed the last turn and won.

TAKE AS MUCH CANDY AS YOU CAN

I went back to Florida and spent hundreds of dollars on lab testing to see whether I really did have asthma. The results: of course I didn't. My VO$_2$max was 88, and my lungs were in perfect shape.

I threw out the inhaler. Albuterol was the closest I ever came to any performance-enhancing substance, and I was angry at myself.

Riders were always doing dumb things with legal substances. The year before, at the high-altitude Tour of Qinghai Lakes in China, a few of the guys bought some knock-off Chinese Viagra at a pharmacy as a joke. In addition to providing a long-lasting erection for those who need help with that (at the Chinese massage parlors, for example, which some riders were known to frequent), Viagra dilates the blood vessels, which helps performance at high elevation. In China, you can walk into a pharmacy and buy pretty much whatever you want with no prescription, but it's hard to say what you're getting (the "Viagra" I saw there included "bull semen" on the ingredients list). One of the riders ultimately tested positive for strychnine (a chemical used in rat poison, and banned as a dangerous performance-enhancer), presumably from tainted pills. He was starting a new job as a construction worker when I joined the team. Nobody wanted to talk about it.

When I did the medical history with the asthma specialist, he saw "Pro Cyclist" under "occupation" on my form. He closed the door, sat down, and looked me in the eye. "All right, so what are you on?" He asked. "EPO, 'roids, what else?" I winced. I was on nothing, of course, and it was sad to learn what the general public thought about pro cycling from reading the news. Then he noticed that my skin was peeling where I'd missed a spot with the SPF 45, and asked how many times I'd been sunburned. "I don't know. A thousand?"

I was only home for a few days before I hopped right back on the plane for the Tour of California. The trip started with a long drive to Fairfield, to tour the Jelly Belly factory. Walking around all day and sampling candy wasn't ideal preparation for the biggest race of the year, but we got to raid the gift shop on our way out.

We arrived at the start in Sacramento the next day, and my first race as a pro started ominously: a 5 a.m. knock on the hotel room door for mandatory blood testing. We lined up in the basement of the hotel, rubbing our eyes and squinting at the light. Welcome to pro cycling.

Lance Armstrong had come out of retirement, and the ToC was his U.S. comeback debut. Autograph-seeking fans were everywhere. Lance must have been hard to get to, so lots of fans asked for autographs from me and my teammates, just for souvenirs. It was fun to push through crowds filled with people thrusting pens, posters, and T-shirts at us. Sometimes, I forged Lance's signature, just to be nice. If you sold that on eBay to some sucker, you owe me a cut.

My parents flew in from Atlanta to watch the prologue. My mom and dad were never huge cycling fans, so I was glad they got a chance to see a real race. They knew I wasn't making a living, and they probably thought that racing was some sort of phase I was going through, but when they saw the crowds and watched me sign

Me with my mom at the Tour of California. I grew a sleazy mustache so my friends could pick me out on TV. That's my story, and I'm sticking to it.

autographs, it was clear that their son was at least getting somewhere, even if he finished 91st out of 120 that day. We were all hoping the bad results were just a phase, too.

My mom saw a few Garmin riders pass by after the stage, and briefly thought their jerseys said "Gaimon."

"Phillip!" she said. "That team is your destiny."

I rolled my eyes, because she had no idea how good they were. "Yeah, keep dreaming," I told her.

EURO PROS ARE GOOD AT WHAT THEY DO

From the very first kilometer, cold rain dulled the excitement and fanfare of the Tour of California, making for a crash-heavy, generally miserable week, which would have been hard enough in perfect conditions. Jonny Clarke summed it up, looking out the RV window as we pulled up to the start. "Cunt of a sport," he observed dryly.

Near the end of the first stage, a hard climb forced a selection with all the GC riders. I'd started near the back but shot through the field when the road kicked up. As they put the pressure on near the summit, Fränk Schleck—who had worn the yellow jersey at the Tour de France the year before and was considered one of the best climbers in the world—opened a gap in front of me, and we both came off over the top, just by a few seconds. We chased with two other riders for a few kilometers, but only lost time to the leaders, and were eventually absorbed into the field. The selection stayed away, and the GC was between a group of 18.

At the meeting that night, Danny looked at the results. I thought he'd be angry that we'd missed the crucial selection, but he listed the names of the guys in the front group, and said, "Yeah, this group is all of the biggest names in the world. It's okay we missed that." Phew.

The rest of the stage race was a constant humbling at the hands (or legs) of the ProTour riders. Once we were out of the GC, we went for stage results, but that proved impossible every time we hit the "10 km to go" sign, as the Euro teams would ramp it up to a speed that we could barely hold onto. In stage 4 I'd worked my way up to the middle of the group with 15 km remaining. As we climbed a short hill into a crosswind, I looked over my left shoulder to see Tom Boonen—Belgium's dominant rider in all the big one-day races—sprinting up the side, his whole QuickStep team behind him. By the time we reached the top, they'd shredded the field into five groups of 20 riders, and Tom was driving the front group. I finished well behind the leaders.

By the midpoint of the Tour, I'd already gone twice the distance of any race I'd ever done, and I'd picked up a nasty cold that was spreading throughout the peloton thanks to weak immune systems and mediocre dinner buffets. The team gave up on GC the first day, and now it threw in the towel on stage results, so the goal became to make the early break and get Jelly Belly on TV. My goal was to finish.

IF YOU HAVEN'T PEED THERE, YOU HAVEN'T BEEN THERE

For stage 5, the organizers closed the Golden Gate Bridge for us to cross, and I relieved my bladder right over the side, checking an item off my bucket list. My moment soon ended, as we turned into a crosswind/tailwind and attacks started flying to establish the early break. I soon found myself at the back of the group, spinning my biggest gear as fast as I could. The race radio crackled in my ear: "KRRRK. Three riders at 10 seconds. It's Tyler Hamilton, Mancebo, and Jens Voigt. Need somebody up there. KRRRK."

There wasn't anything I could do about that right now. Besides, at this speed, I knew the break would come right back. They were stronger than me, sure, but the guys attacking had the same gears I did, and it was physically impossible to maintain that pace in a 53x11. I put my head down and gave it all I could, just to stay in the group. The race radio crackled again. "KRRRK. Three riders, now at 30 seconds. KRRRK. Need somebody up there NOW. That's going to be the break and we're—." I took my earpiece out before I heard the second KRRRK. It wasn't helping.

With the break gone, the smart move would have been to recognize that the plan had failed and sit in the group until I felt better, or at least take an easy day without digging myself into a hole, but I lacked the experience for that, and I still thought I needed to prove myself. The field slowed as we approached the first climb of the day, and the break still was only 45 seconds up the road, so I attacked. Astana was riding tempo, and that was the first time I actually saw Lance in person that week. Lance always rides at the front, and I hadn't made it up there a whole lot.

I managed a 10-second lead before I came back. A failed attempt, but I was doing my job. That is, I was trying to do my job, but I was physically unable. Either way, Astana was offended and indignant at the perceived disrespect of attacking after the break was established. I was on the far right side of the road, and as each rider passed me (Lance and Levi included), he'd flick his rear wheel just enough to force me into the dirt, a gesture that says, "Fuck you for attacking without our permission."

The snow-covered ground at the top of the climb was crowded with spectators, including one wearing a bee suit (for the Livestrong colors), wielding a bazooka-sized needle, with "EPO" written on the side, like "NASA" on a space shuttle. As he ran next to the field hollering at Lance, I watched the seven-time Tour de France winner shove him, sending the poor bee stumbling into the snow, antennae-first. I was mostly impressed at Lance's bike-handling.

The group stopped to pee in the next valley, allowing the gap to go out to the three leaders. I stopped beside Floyd Landis on the edge of the road. Shivering in our black Gore-Tex jackets, which we hadn't taken off all week, we urinated into a cold puddle. He laughed. "This is the best part of the whole day. You've gotta enjoy the little things."

"I hope you're not talking about your dick," I said. He'd walked into it.

I sat in the group for the rest of the day and finally had my revenge on Astana for riding me into the dirt. They had four guys riding at the front, and we were nowhere near the finish, so the pace was relaxed. One of my teammates rode up to me and said he wanted to show me something. We slotted in at the front of the group, where he took a full water bottle and threw it as hard he could at a metal speed limit sign.

"DOOOONNNGGG," the sign rang out, vibrating from the impact. The Kazakh riders flinched from the sound and looked around to see if there was a crash. My first bottle missed, but the second one nailed a stop sign. The leaders jumped again, but they'd seen the bottle this time, and fired back at us with Bond Villain-esque Eastern European scowls, which weren't quite intimidating enough for us to stop. Other teams soon got into it, and Boonen sent one of his teammates back for more ammo (I mean bottles). Floyd was right about the little things.

The next morning I lined up at the front. If I couldn't get a result and couldn't be in the break, I would have to stand in front of the cameras to get on TV. Lance stood beside me, probably recognizing me from the day before. "What kind of brake pads are those?" he asked. I couldn't figure out why he was talking to me.

"Uhh. SwissStops," I replied, looking down to read the logo.

"Do they work all right in the rain? We've been going through these cork pads like crazy."

I was sore from fatigue, with my nose running from the cold, and tired from coughing all night. Brake pads weren't in my top 50 concerns. "They're fine," I choked, as the start counted down.

I'd like to apologize to my readers and cycling fans everywhere. This was my opportunity to punch Lance right in the testicle, and I regret letting it slip by.

Once again, our goal was to make the early breakaway, and attacks flew early and often. Finally, three guys went up the road with a small gap, and I was about to go across when Levi cruised up to the front.

"Who has to pee?" he asked.

Knowing that the pee stop was the traditional nail in the coffin for anyone hoping to make the early break, I asked Levi if it was okay for me to go across while he took a nature break. "We've missed it every day," I explained. "Somebody's going to get fired if we do it again."

As he pulled over, Levi laughed and told me to go for it. At least he recognized that we also had a job to do.

Five minutes later, some of the riders had managed to pee, the field had shattered, Levi was back in the group after a hard effort, and the breakaway had been absorbed. I'd tried to go across solo, but Tom Danielson hadn't overheard my conversation with Levi, so he went to the front and chased me down out of principle.

"Didn't you see Levi pull over? Do you know how disrespectful that is?" he asked. It was funny how all the rules for respect favored the big teams. I didn't feel like taking a lashing from Danielson.

"Levi said I could bridge. You're the one that made the field go hard with the yellow jersey stopped, instead of just letting me go. Now fuck off, Christian." I called him the wrong name on purpose, pretending I thought he was Christian Vande Velde. My teammates and I had been doing that all week. I wish I could have raced in a sandwich-board sign that said "I make $166.66/month, so everyone give me a break."

Thanks to Tom, the breakaway reshuffled, this time with Jelly Belly's Matt Crane in the mix, so I'll say we actually accomplished something that day. Crane had a pre-race ritual. On the way to the stage, he would go back to the bathroom in the RV and masturbate, and he wasn't shy about it. Matt's motto: "When in doubt, rub one out."

Levi rode up to me around the halfway point of the stage. I'm not sure if he felt bad for flicking me into the dirt the day before. Maybe he found out I was writing a blog for *Bicycling* magazine and wanted to suck up to me. Whatever the reason, we had a friendly conversation while his team rotated at the front. Levi asked if any of the Euro sponsors had been around longer than Jelly Belly.

"This is Jelly Belly's 10th year," I informed him. I'd paid attention during the factory tour. I also could have listed the steps in the all-natural flavoring process, or told him that Ronald Reagan kept a jar of red, white, and blue Jelly Bellies on his desk.

Levi hit the button and talked into his radio. "Hey Johan, what year was it with Rabobank that you rode off a cliff?" He looked back at me. "That was 12 years ago." So maybe we were the second longest-running team. And people say race radios are unnecessary.

Since Levi was in yellow, riding next to him meant that I was on TV for close to an hour. It was much easier that way than trying to get in the break.

Later that day, with nothing else to think about, I had to pee again, but with the slippery, pothole-filled roads, I didn't feel safe trying to pee off the bike as usual. I went to the back of the group and let it go in my shorts. I was ashamed of myself, until I looked to my right, where Thor Hushovd was doing the same thing. He smiled at me. "Much warmer now, eh?" he said, in his thick Norwegian accent.

The next day was the time trial, and I was glad just to have a rest to try to get over my cold. The kitchen table at the back of the RV was set up with a set of plastic drawers, each one filled with a rider's favorite flavor of jelly beans, and labeled with his face. I scarfed the last handful of peanut butter from the "Phil" drawer. On the way back to the hotel, I fell asleep while we drove, spread out on the floor like a liquid.

When I stepped out of the elevator onto the fifth floor at the Hilton that afternoon, I noticed a room service tray in the hallway. Too hungry to resist the untouched chicken finger on the plate, I ate it. Yes, that's gross, but what are the odds that the original diner licked it?

By the penultimate stage, my legs were empty. Sick with mucous and fever, I was dropped from the field the moment the hostilities started. Thanks to the strategic pessimism I'd brought into the week, I was pleasantly surprised to make it that far, and I don't think the team had expected much more from me. That night I was quarantined to my own hotel room, so I got to sleep in, and woke up just as the racers were lining up at the start. Desperately wanting to contribute, I asked Danny if there was anything I could do to help out. He handed me a scrub brush and a bucket. While the guys raced, I washed the RV.

Only 84 out of 130-something riders finished the race, so that was actually a decent performance for my first race as a professional. Starting the Tour of California as my first pro race was a lot like driving the Batmobile in a driver's license exam, but I learned both how close and how far I was to the top of the sport, and there's nothing like a swift kick in the butt to get motivated.

I took a few days off when I got home, and did some easy riding by the end of the week. That Sunday I finally felt recovered enough to ride three hours. Meanwhile, Thor Hushovd had finished the ToC, and he won Het Volk that day.

EVERYONE IS LAZY, AND IT CAN COST YOU

A few weeks after that rough start to the season, the regular domestic racing schedule began with the San Dimas Stage Race. San Dimas isn't on the National Racing Calendar, but since it's only a short drive and a few days before Redlands, all of the big teams show up.

I finished sixth in the opening uphill time trial, two spots behind teammate Will Routley, but the race always comes down to the second stage: an 84-mile, hilly road race, on a twisty, white-knuckle course. Fly V Australia controlled the pace, with the yellow jersey on the shoulders of its climber, Ben Day. The race split often on the climbs and narrow roads but came back together into a select group with one 7-mile lap to go. With his team suffering, I watched Ben bring back a dangerous break by himself, and I counterattacked alone up the right side of the road.

My lead went up to 30 seconds, but the field was gaining on me when I crested the final KOM, with only a 1-km descent and an 800-meter flat drag to the finish. I bombed the corners and looked back twice on the finishing stretch as the chasers breathed down my neck. Team cars aren't allowed on the course at San Dimas, so Danny and all the other directors were leaning on the fence by the finish, making

Winning the stage in San Dimas. See the field way back in the distance? No time gap, huh? But I'm not bitter.

bets on who would win. "Well, we know it won't be a Jelly Belly," Ouch's director joked. Everyone laughed until I came by with my arms up. I was still celebrating after I crossed the line, as the sprinting field shot by me on both sides.

"Later, suckers," Danny laughed. He must have felt like a genius. A lot of pros in the United States were making $50,000 or more, and most wouldn't win a single race. Danny had found a guy that could win one for $2,000.

I took the Points jersey and the Best Young Rider jersey, but the officials didn't give me a time gap in the results. The 20-second bonus for the stage win put me into second overall, and if I'd finished just a second ahead of the field, I'd have been in yellow. I wondered whether we should file a protest with the officials, pretty standard practice in the circumstances, but I didn't want to cause any trouble that might ruin the day. I'd never experienced a greater thrill, and I doubt if I'll ever match it. Years later, I can still feel every pedal stroke of that last lap, and it gives me goose bumps every time.

I'd been sort of an outcast on the team up to that point. No one wanted to talk to me, and there were a few guys who'd been hazing me mercilessly, which was getting hard to deal with. Suddenly I'd won a race, and it was like I'd flipped a switch. On the drive home, everyone was my friend, and they laughed at all my jokes, blatantly sucking up now that I was a winner. I enjoyed it for a minute and then shut up when I noticed the change. Fuck those guys.

When I saw photos from the finish line, they clearly showed a gap of three to four seconds. I probably would have worn yellow if we had protested.

That evening, we discussed the plan for the crit the next day. There was one sprint lap in the middle of the race, with green jersey points and a five-second time bonus up for grabs. I wanted to go for it.

My teammates knew that if I won the bonus and took yellow halfway through the race, they'd have to ride on the front to defend it for the second half, and they didn't want that responsibility. Instead, it was decided that I should go for the time bonus at the finish.

My team forgot a number of key factors in this scenario:

1. To win the intermediate sprint, I'd only be sprinting against Ben Day, a climber, whereas to win the final sprint, I'd be going up against all of the best sprinters in the country.
2. I'd never contested a field sprint in my life, or been anywhere near the front with three laps to go in a big crit.
3. If Ben placed in the top three in the intermediate sprint—which we'd decided not to even contest—I'd be out of contention altogether, no matter what happened at the end.

I should have spoken up, but that wasn't my place on the team. They promised I'd get a great lead-out for the finale. I'd never had a lead-out, and for all I knew, I'd sprint fine with enough help.

The crit went about as I would have guessed. I had trouble staying at the front and needed constant help from the guys to hold position in the top 20. Fly V put Ben in second place in the intermediate sprint, clinching the GC, but none of my teammates did that math, so they still tried to position me for the field sprint as I floundered 30 to 40 guys back in the group. At the end, we weren't even close. I was 23 years old, I'd finished second overall and won a stage in my second race as a pro, and I was honestly disappointed in myself for letting everyone down.

However you look at it, I'd shown great form at San Dimas, clearly setting myself apart as one of the best in the country (at least in March), but I still didn't make the Redlands roster a few days later. I'm not sure if the team didn't want to waste the plane tickets they'd already booked for other guys, or maybe they thought my win was just luck and I wouldn't be useful at Redlands. Brad Huff sent me a handful of encouraging text messages. I didn't know him very well, but Brad recognized that I'd been gypped, and it was nice of him to say so.

I went straight from the biggest win of my life to sleeping on JC's sofa, staying nearby in case someone got sick and the team needed a backup. But I never got the call. Instead, I showed up for the Redlands Pro-Am criterium, where a strong field raced the same course the pros had used for the NRC race. I lapped the field twice that day, with all the directors watching. Luck, huh?

ATHENS TWILIGHT IS NOT A BIKE RACE

Since I was enjoying the crits so much, my next race was the Athens Twilight Criterium, infamous for its crashes. I knew I shouldn't do it, but did I listen to my intuition? No. I'm a bike racer, which means I like to ignore that voice in my head, because racing is fun.

I finished 13th in the prologue time trial, which put me on the front row at the start, where I hoped I'd be safe. It also earned me the ominous number 13 on my jersey.

The spectacle of Athens Twilight did not disappoint. Intoxicated college students were out in full force, and a manhunt was under way for a professor who committed a triple homicide that afternoon and was at large downtown (you can't make this stuff up). I had to fight through crowds and climb over a barricade to get to the course for the 9:30 p.m. start.

Per superstitious tradition, I pinned the 13 upside down, but it didn't help. On the first lap, I only made it through one turn before that 13 caused me to crash. Or maybe the crash was caused by Alejandro Borrajo, who took the far inside line of the turn, in an attempt to go from 30th place to first in 10 feet.

It's funny what happens to your mind and your body during a crash. What you thought you were doing and what you expected to happen next are suddenly tossed aside. A second ago, you were racing and having a good time. Now you're on the guardrail, or against a curb, or sliding on the pavement, and you have to deal with that. As my senses were heightened and my brain hit the "record" button, instincts kicked in.

What did I do?

I sat on my knees, head facing forward, hands protecting my head.

Where did I learn this position?

Ms. Cumbie demonstrated it during a tornado drill in kindergarten.

Did it work?

Yes. One rider plowed into my side and flipped over, but other than a tire burn, his impact did no harm.

What did I hear?

Pained groans and expletives from crashed riders, mixed with the roar of the crowd, excited to see a wreck up close.

What did I observe when the noise died down, and it seemed safe to open my eyes?

A pile of colorful spandex to my immediate left, and an overweight frat guy on the other side of the barrier, wearing a red UGA polo shirt and a John Deere hat, reflexively pulling his beer-filled, red Solo cup back to protect it from the racers piling into the ground in front of him. His blood alcohol level was likely approaching 0.15 percent, which meant that his reflexes, motor control, and reaction time were all impaired, so much of the beer spilled as it sloshed toward him. He jumped back, keeping the cup stable in his hand, but it was too late; the shirt was soaked, and the rest of his beer spilled into the street and trickled into a sewer, whereupon it eventually entered the Atlantic Ocean via the Upper Oconee watershed network.

To my right, Olympic track racer Bobby Lea was similarly crouched in a tornado-drill pose. I wonder where he met Ms. Cumbie.

What did I suddenly appreciate?

Balance, low centers of gravity, and traction, any of which could have prevented this fiasco.

What was the effect?

A series of scrapes along my right side, and a wide area of skin removed from my upper thigh, due to a combination of the road surface acting as a cheese grater, and burns from friction between flesh and pavement. My wheel was broken into a taco shape, the rear derailleur hanger was snapped in half, and a shifter was crushed. Spectators had stolen my sunglasses and helmet.

How did I feel?

Angry that I'd crashed yet again, and irritated that I'd bothered to pin the number upside-down yet still failed to avoid this misfortune. Then again, perhaps I was fated to decapitate myself in that crash, and the minor road rash was in fact good luck.

The next morning I called Danny to ask him to send a new helmet, and he wasn't surprised about what happened. "Yeah, that race is always a bloodbath. I don't know why I sent you there." Danny always knew how to make me feel better.

The race had ended close to midnight, and I had to get up early to make it to another crit the next morning. If someone had hit me with a tranquilizer dart the second I crossed the finish line, I might have managed six hours of sleep. Lacking tranquilizers in any form but full of pain, endorphins, and adrenaline, I went home and stared at the ceiling all night. I decided to get some sleeping pills for the next twilight crit.

I'd planned to race the whole Speedweek series after Twilight but thought better of it after a very quick DNF the next morning. I had no hope of limping into any prize money that week, but I did have a pretty good chance of crashing again, with five more crits on the schedule. It was better to heal up from my road rash and bruises and focus on a race that might suit me better.

YOU'RE VULNERABLE

I moved back to Pennsylvania for the summer, this time to a house rented out by the Mountain Khakis team. It was infested with stink bugs but the price was right. There was no soap in the shower, and I forgot to steal some from a hotel (buying soap was out of the question), so I used a pinch of Tide detergent powder each day.

My win at San Dimas was overshadowed by my DNFs (you're only as good as your last race), and I was left off the team roster for most of the summer. The next team event was the Tour of Qinghai Lakes, an eight-day stage race on the Tibetan plateau in China, starting at 10,000 feet, but I had over two months with nothing on the calendar. Danny offered to pay for a flight to Boulder, where I could acclimate to altitude and train with Kiel Reijnen. Instead, I suggested that I sleep in my altitude tent and use that money to fly to Oregon, so I could race Mount Hood. I wouldn't have a follow car or teammates there, but at least it was a race.

I hoped that if I got some decent results, the team would take me off the bench. Aside from a sixth-place finish on the first mountaintop stage, though, Mount Hood was another disaster. On stage 2 I was caught behind a crash, shredding my tire as it skidded toward fallen bodies. I stayed upright, but it took several minutes to get a neutral wheel, and I never made it back to the group.

When I told Danny about Mount Hood, he said, "Well, that's bike racing." Most jobs aren't like that. Imagine if an architect focused weeks of work and research designing a skyscraper and somehow lost all of his plans right before construction started. He wouldn't brush it off with a laugh and say, "Well, that's architecture!" He would completely reevaluate how he worked to ensure that such a catastrophe could never repeat itself. You don't have that luxury in pro cycling. You have to accept your vulnerability, even at the highest levels, and you can't make it if you're not willing to put in the same time, energy, and effort that I did at Mount Hood, knowing that something out of your control could go wrong and make it all for nothing.

PRIZE SPLITS ARE NICE

Just as things that you can't control may break your spirit, they can also brighten it. My teammates raced a three-day crit series in

Tulsa, where Brad Huff won two stages and the overall. Our policy was set up so that riders at the race got most of the cash, but I still got a check for $1,100, without setting foot in Oklahoma. I suppose I owe Huff a beer.

JUST SIT IN THE GROUP AND DON'T DO ANYTHING STUPID

I had three weeks of training in Pennsylvania to shake off my Mount Hood experience and mentally prepare for Fitchburg, another stage race I was doing without team support. I started off well, placing 18th in a 9-mile time trial, so I decided to ride conservatively to maintain my GC. After all the DNFs, finishing in the top 20 would be fine, so I sat in the field and stayed out of trouble. Some of the pros had to sacrifice for their team leaders or sprinters, so they lost time, and I finished 14th overall. Prize money was only $280, but least I didn't have to split it.

BRING A SENSE OF HUMOR TO CHINA

I was excited about the trip to China at the end of the summer. I'd never raced outside of the United States before, nor even been to Asia. My legs were good, and I had another chance to contribute to the team and give them some reason to bring me back the next year.

The Tour of Qinghai Lakes was a UCI.HC-level race, meaning it carried the same level of competition and prestige as the Tour of California. One of the guys who'd raced there before gave me good advice. He said to expect a lot of mystery meat and nothing I'm used to, and to bring some snack food, a sense of humor, and a picture of home. I packed nine cans of honey-roasted peanuts, a pound of milk chocolate chopped into small chunks, and some protein powder.

Powers at the Olympic training center in Duoba, China. Note the racewalker on the right.

We flew into Xining, an enormous industrial city the size of Los Angeles but just out of the top 10 biggest cities in China (don't worry—I'd never heard of it, either). Twenty hours in a plane was the closest I'd ever come to prison, and we all arrived hungry, sore, and disoriented. Jeremy Powers was in a bad mood. On his flight, an obese man in the next seat kept coughing. When he tried to raise the armrest to overflow into Jeremy's seat, Jeremy smashed it down, looked him in the eye, and said, "No! That's an 'us decision!'" Inspirational.

I was so disoriented that night, I used the skin lotion instead of shampoo in my hair. When I told the guys at dinner, Matty Rice said, "Just don't jerk off with the shampoo, eh, Phil?"

Each team had a brand new car to use for the race (the odometer was straight zeroes), and we each got a pile of ill-fitting clothing with race logos and brands we hadn't heard of, ironically endorsed by African American NBA stars. Our lodging was the Duoba High Altitude Olympic Training Facility. The racers were housed in a block of dorms there, along with Chinese gymnasts, swimmers, and other

Olympic athletes. I was passed and dropped by a racewalker on my way to dinner that night.

The race assigned us a translator, and we all got off to a bad start. His English wasn't very good, and Danny complained about it to one of the organizers. "Fuck shit!" I heard our translator mumble, under his breath. It reminded me of a Vietnamese classmate in elementary school. We never heard him speak a word of English, but our teachers always passed him on to the next class. Someone picked on him in the bathroom in fifth grade, and he finally had enough. After staying mute for six years, he yelled "Mother fuck fuck shit bitch!"

Most of the team had sleeping pills, but we were all awake by sunrise, so we headed to the equipment area to put the bikes together. The space was divided into open cubicles with metal fencing; I shared one with Jeremy and Kiel Reijnen. Jeremy had just spoken to Danny and confirmed that the only wheels we brought were SRAM-branded deep carbon clinchers. The team was sponsored by the wheel maker Zipp, and we had (literally) a truckload of Zipp 202s, 303s, all the way up to 1080s—high-end racing wheels made for tubular tires. SRAM had recently acquired Zipp and had provided the clinchers specifically for training. But gluing tubulars would have required a second mechanic, which wasn't in the budget. The team would not be sponsored by Zipp the following year. Funny how that works.

Jeremy, ever the equipment geek from cyclocross (he could squeeze a tire and tell you within 5 psi what pressure was in it), was livid. He wasn't looking forward to high-altitude climbs on heavy wheels, with tires more likely to flat on all the poorly paved, pothole-filled roads. It was infuriating that we flew all the way to the other side of the world only to have our potential undercut with second-tier equipment (mother fuck fuck shit bitch!).

Jeremy looked around to make sure no one could hear him, and then started whispering to me and Kiel.

"Listen guys, it's too late for me," he said. "I've been on this team for six years, and I've got a good thing set up with my 'cross schedule. But you guys need to get the hell off this team. It's a fucking joke. You guys actually have potential, and you're wasting it if you spend more than a year or two here."

Kiel and I looked at each other, and then nodded at Jeremy, not sure what to say.

After building the bikes we went for a short ride into Xining. We passed a meat market, where butchers hacked up yaks in the street, but we managed to keep our tires out of the bloody gutters.

PACK PLENTY OF UNDERWEAR

The next morning the riders climbed into a chartered bus and headed to the course. After a 30-minute drive, we stopped in front of a brand-new hotel in the middle of nowhere. We weren't spending the night there, but we could use the rooms to change for the prologue and shower afterward. A row of women in ceremonial costumes bowed as we entered, and a bellman took our bags and showed us to our rooms. He explained that the hotel was built specifically for the race, and completed just a week prior. It was hard to imagine, but based on the plastic screen covers still on the TVs and the strong scents of paint and carpet glue, we believed him.

Huge crowds must have been bused in for the prologue, all clad in matching T-shirts. *Chi-Oh,* they chanted, which translates to "Step on the gas." Buddhist prayer flags were draped above the roads and down the buildings every few feet, forming a sea of color as we blasted around the corners to the roar of the spectators.

TAXIS ARE CHEAP IN BEIJING

My gratitude for our first-class treatment turned to horror after the prologue, as we spun away from the course to cool down from the effort. Riding along a ridge parallel to the highway, we could see that the valley below was a giant tent city: thousands of people living under blue tarps, wading in the polluted, shit-scented river. Children played in the water, using big blocks of Styrofoam as kickboards, some of which probably came from the brand new TVs in our hotel rooms. The race had spent all that money to impress us with new hotels and caviar, with incredible poverty just down the road.

In the places we visited, I noticed that all of the construction was just a little bit off. The doors didn't close right, and water pooled in the corners of shower floors. The worst example was the plumbing at the Duoba Training Center. The commode jammed up before a team meeting in Danny's room, so he called the front desk. Minutes later, in walked a 14-year-old girl with a plunger. Danny felt so bad that he gave her a Jelly Belly jersey before she left. When I walked by his room a couple hours later, the toilet had clogged again, and the girl, now wearing our team jersey, was ramming the plunger into the commode, sweating profusely. Danny took one look at me, read my mind as I reached into my pocket, and yelled, "Don't you dare take a picture, Phil!"

Faced with all the poverty and hardship, there wasn't anything to do but joke about it. If somebody left food on his plate, we'd unleash a powerful guilt trip. "Kiel, finish your food. There are people starving in . . . wait, they're right over there!"

The crowds of spectators and fans were heavy in the cities. After stages, everyone wanted pictures with the tall Americans. To avoid a throng of cameras, I went the back way to dinner one day, sneaking through the kitchen, but it was a bad idea to see where our food was coming from. Chickens ran amok, with shit and feathers on the floor, where a young boy was also washing a bucket of lettuce for the salad buffet. I stuck to rice and pasta.

The course took us up to 14,000 feet, and almost back in time. We passed through remote villages where the only spectators were nomadic herders, often dressed in animal skins, living as their ancestors had for centuries, seemingly ignorant of electricity, currency, or government. Not only were the herders not fans of cycling, but they stared like they were wondering what type of animal we were, and whether to attack us.

The race was the easy part. There was no getting used to the altitude, but everyone was affected equally. I made it through a few hard, rainy stages and was climbing well, usually making the front groups with Kiel. The rest of my teammates were racing conservatively, as usual. Some had made careers that way, consistently finishing hard stage races like Georgia and California but never going for the win. It made them solid riders, so they were more reliable teammates than I could have been that year, but they never left their comfort zone. I was always more the "race for the win or die trying" type. A healthy medium might have been ideal, but finishing in the third group didn't sound bad when I crashed into a giant pothole on the opening circuits of the fourth stage. I was able to chase back into the peloton, but my knee was hit hard, and I couldn't hang on over the climbs. I finally jumped into the broom wagon for yet another DNF. The race doctors sprayed my wound with something to kill the bacteria but refused to wash it. They said the tap water in Duoba wasn't clean enough.

I stayed behind the next morning while the racers left for four days of point-to-point stages around Bird Lake. No one spoke

English at the training center, and I had no means of transportation to leave other than my bike, which didn't bode well with my swollen knee. It was hard to think about five more days without speaking to anyone, and the pain was bad enough that I wanted to go home and see a doctor, so I pressed the travel agent who arranged our flights to move up my return a few days. He said he would try, but he wasn't optimistic. In the meantime, I learned that one-way tickets out the following day cost $1,100. I did what any mature adult would do in that situation: I asked my mom for money. She said I could put a ticket on her credit card if I needed to. Safety net.

The travel agent came through at the last minute and saved my mom's wallet, booking me on a flight the next day, with a nine-hour layover in Beijing. For $40 I took a cab from the Beijing airport, saw the Great Wall and Tiananmen Square, and grabbed takeout for dinner. If nothing else, bike racing had gotten me a free trip to China, and I was damn sure going to take advantage of it.

TO GET BETTER, YOU MUST TRAIN MORE, OR REST MORE

A week later my knee was fine, and I was racing with the team again, this time at the Tour of Elk Grove in Chicago. Brad Huff had won a stage there the previous year, but with only a few days at home between Qinghai and Elk Grove, most of the guys were tired at the start, and no one was enthusiastic about the race.

Danny followed me in the team car during the prologue time trial (TT), honking if I went too slow. I was so distracted that I rode straight through a turn and off the course (boy, did he honk then). Another dumb rookie mistake was all I needed, but Danny laughed it off since he didn't think I'd do well anyway. He did say that I needed to work on cornering on the TT bike because I was taking the turns like "a complete pussy." I hadn't been permitted to bring my time trial bike home to train on, so that was my first ride on it since the Tour of California six months before.

Danny was angry at the meeting that night, but only at our time trial specialists, who didn't do as well as expected. "Bryce! Bernard! Why did I give you guys a TT bike to ride at home if you can't do better than this?" he yelled. "All of you guys. I don't know if you need to train more, or rest more, or what, but you need to be better." With that rousing speech, Danny slammed the door. We all looked at each other, dumbfounded.

The real reason that we weren't that good: We were one of the lowest-paid pro teams in the United States that year. If Danny wanted guys who could win, he knew who he could have hired, but he didn't have the money. Whose fault was it that we couldn't compete? Hell if I know.

Low pay or not, I was still desperately trying to prove myself, attacking solo with 80 miles left in the Elk Grove road race. I got a 90-second gap and didn't have much trouble holding it for a few laps—not that the field was panicking about a climber up the road on a technical, pancake-flat circuit. Rain started to pour, so I took the corners even slower, fighting the urge to bomb through them after my poor cornering on the TT bike the day before. In my head, I had to risk life and limb to stay away for another lap before the field inevitably chased me down for a field sprint, or the team would damn well find someone else to take my place next year, and that guy would be glad for the opportunity.

I approached a corner that was filled with standing water, so I grabbed a handful of brake to scrub my speed. Better safe than sorry, but I thought I was kind of taking it like a pussy this time, and maybe Danny had a point. And then I found myself on the pavement. So I was right to take it easy in the corners after all, at least when they were wet. Being right doesn't always feel so good.

I never had any hope of staying away to begin with, so the wreck just made their chase easier. I was caught with 10 km to go and cruised in to the finish. I don't think anyone even realized I'd hit the deck.

Our team was powerless against the bigger squads in the field sprint on the first stage, so my teammates decided that we would take the front for a full lead-out the next day, just as the Ouch team had the day before. In their view, we were just as strong as Ouch, so of course we could go to the front with 15 one-mile-long laps to go. The idea of taking the front is to hold it to the end so your sprinter is in perfect position, and the only way to do that is to keep increasing the pace so the other teams can't overtake you. Fifteen miles would have been a long way to go, even for a strong team like Ouch. Five laps might have been reasonable, since we could each put in half a lap, or maybe a full lap all-out, and then be done. Three laps each was laughable.

I tried to make eye contact with Jonny Clarke. I knew that he would feel the same about the plan, but his look told me to keep my mouth shut, and Jeremy proved him right. "Wait. You know what? Fifteen is kind of a round number. I bet someone else is planning to take the front with 15 to go right now." I could say with certainty that no other team was that dumb. I love Jeremy, but he chugged the Kool-Aid straight from the bottle and with it came dumb race tactics. "So let's take the front with *sixteen* to go, when no one's going to be prepared for—"

"Shut the fuck up, Powers!" Jonny interrupted. He had a way with words.

STOP AND SMELL THE HAM SANDWICH

From Chicago, I met up with my family in Bethany Beach, Delaware. I rode west every day, surprised to find a ton of nice, flat, low-traffic farm roads. I rode with my jersey open and my sleeves rolled up, to combat the heat and the five years of tan lines I'd built up. The result was a slightly improved gradient between the two ends of the Caucasian skin spectrum on my body, and a large U-shaped shadow on my chest from my bib shorts. I've seen bike racers at the beach wearing leg and arm warmers so only their whitest parts are exposed to the sun.

The vacation was a good break before a trip north to defend my Mount Washington title. I liked my chances, since all of the best climbers in the country were at the Tour of Utah, which Jelly Belly didn't attend.

On the way up to New Hampshire I picked up my girlfriend at the airport in Boston. She'd spent the summer in Florida, and agreed to fly in to watch the race and then keep me company on the drive back down. We took a quick detour to have lunch with my old teammate Steve Weller and his fiancée Darcy at the Lady Killigrew, a quiet café on the Connecticut River in an old mill building in Montague, Massachusetts. While I enjoyed the conversation (and a grilled sandwich with ham, mustard, cheddar, and sliced apple), I wondered if I'd be visiting any of my teammates from Jelly Belly in the following years. With pro teams, you fly in, you race, and you fly out. I'd become friends with some of my teammates, but I couldn't tell if it would be like Fiordifrutta, where we lived together, traveled together, and really bonded. I sacrificed for my pro teammates because it was my job, but I wasn't sure if I could ever turn myself inside-out for them like I could for Steve or David Guttenplan.

The way my season had been going, I half expected a poorly timed flat tire or some other disaster to keep me from a good result on Mount Washington, and two impressively strong old men from Colorado beating me would have qualified. I didn't get rid of them until the final kilometers, but I won the race. I took a minute off of my time from the previous year, but it was still nowhere near Tom Danielson's best time, and still a few seconds slower than the women's record, set by Geneviève Jeanson in 2002. On the other hand, I heard she was so doped up that she had a beard on her penis.

YOU CAN'T ARGUE WITH CRAZY

After Mount Washington, my girlfriend and I drove two days straight back to Florida, where I had time for one more training block before the next races. I managed 20 hours on the bike in four days, but the training only tired me out for USPro National Championships in Greenville, South Carolina, the following week.

Somehow, despite the fact that the team had only won two races all year, everyone was optimistic about our chances at nationals, and since Jonny Clarke wasn't there (U.S. citizens only for nationals), I was all on my own in a room full of crazy at the meeting. The plan was to outclimb all the world-class pros the last time up Paris Mountain. It wasn't clear if the whole team was expected to drop Levi Leipheimer, or just one of us. Maybe they thought I could do it? Danny wasn't specific, focusing instead on what to do after our hypothetical star climber made the small selection over the climb.

"And listen," Danny advised. "If it's just you and George together on the finishing circuits, you don't have to pull through, not once. You just tell him to fuck off, sit on his wheel, and beat him at the line." This anger at George Hincapie was in response to Andy Bajadali's ride on that course a few years ago when he was on the Jelly Belly team. Bajadali had made it over the climb with George and Levi, who, in the version I heard, then offered him third place. Baj probably wasn't going to do better than third anyway. But he wanted to win, and you have to respect that. He refused their offer, they attacked him mercilessly, and Baj fell back to finish fifth.

So the plan was to win, and the rest of the meeting was devoted to a more important topic: the design of the stars-and-stripes jersey after we'd won the national championship. Red, white, and blue jelly beans, obviously. Don't count your jelly beans before they hatch.

UNTIL YOU HAVE A CONTRACT IN HAND, ASSUME YOU'RE FIRED

With the upcoming championship race signaling the tail end of the season, I needed to talk with Danny about next year. They say that money doesn't matter when you get to do what you love, but at some point, you sort of need it, and if I wasn't getting a nice offer I'd have to talk with other teams. Sure, my season hadn't been stellar overall, but my win in San Dimas was arguably the team's best result that year, and that had to be worth something. I knew that the more established guys on the roster were making around $30,000. I wasn't expecting that much, but I'd spent a year on the road and gotten a whole lot of bottles for those guys. I just needed somewhere between $12,000 and $18,000, which was enough to live on as long as I could maintain my coaching business on the side. No matter how many DNFs I had, you can't say that's greedy.

Danny assured me that my spot was safe and I'd get a reasonable raise. "I don't have our budget worked out, so I can't get into numbers yet, but don't worry, we want you to stay."

"So I don't need to talk to other teams?" I asked.

"No, no. We'll take care of you." Isn't it cute that I believed him?

I felt 50 pounds lighter from that conversation, but it wasn't enough to get over Paris Mountain with George Hincapie and Levi Leipheimer. I came off the climb in the third group and took a shortcut to where the team van was parked. Kiel had made the second group and would finish in the top 20, but the rest of the team was already seated on folding chairs in the parking lot, listening to the race announcer in the distance. It was peaceful until the team car came squealing into the parking lot and skidded to a stop next to us. Danny opened the trunk and flung the toolbox as hard as he could, scattering wrenches in all directions. John Sessa had to clean it up. He left the team after that year for some reason. Maybe Powers had a talk with him in China about his wrenching talent.

BACON IS YOUR FRIEND

After Greenville, we headed out to the Tour of Missouri, another high-level international race, but with Lance's absence the crowds in Missouri were more relaxed, and no one pretended to want my autograph. We went for a short ride to get our legs moving, and ran into a few European teams. I overheard a conversation between two Garmin riders who were both purchasing vacation homes, debating the pros and cons of different locations. I could totally relate to their problems. My trailer really needed to be hosed out.

Mark Cavendish and his team, Columbia, had dominated every field sprint in the world that year, so with the roster they brought, it was pretty clear how each stage would play out:

1. Columbia lets a small break get away.
2. Columbia rides the front.
3. Columbia brings the break back.
4. Mark Cavendish wins the field sprint.
5. The rest of us die a little inside.

THERE'S NOTHING WRONG WITH A GREASY BREAKFAST

After a few early stages, we finally had an afternoon start. I was sore and exhausted from an autograph signing for Jelly Belly at a candy shop the night before, glad for a morning to relax. Matt Crane and I trudged toward the dining room like we were headed to the gallows, for yet another dreaded meal of race-provided oatmeal and pasta, when we noticed "Ryan's All U Can Eat Breakfast Buffet" across the street. We veered left at a brisk jog, gave the cashier $4.99 each, and loaded our trays with pancakes, eggs, sausage, buttery Texas toast, and bacon. When we packed up our hotel room and headed to the bus a couple hours later, I caught myself taking the stairs two at a time. My legs were feeling good.

This was the last road race stage, and with only a circuit race the following day, BMC and Garmin were pushing the pace in the headwinds and crosswinds, pressuring Leipheimer's Astana teammates to work hard leading up to the final climb. The high speeds kept any early breaks from getting away, so when I attacked with a QuickStep rider with 40 miles remaining, we were the only sustained break of the day. I won the points sprint into the next town, and it looked like we might actually have a chance of staying clear to the finish. But we hit the final climb with a 30-second lead and tired legs, and were soon caught and dropped by Yaroslav Popovych of Astana, followed by the entire Garmin train going bananas to catch him over the top. I was relieved that I at least had the legs to contribute in a top-tier race like that, and I made a mental note to have a big, greasy meal whenever I was starting to fade during a stage race. All I'd needed was more energy.

I'd dug deep trying to stay away on that stage, though, and no breakfast buffet the next morning would get me out of that hole. A text message informed me the team meeting before the final stage would be in the RV at 9 a.m. I went early and fell asleep on the sofa. When I woke up it was 10 a.m., and I'd missed the message that the meeting had moved to Danny's hotel room. He assured me that all they'd said was, "Good job on yesterday's stage, Phil." After eight months on the team I'd finally earned some kudos, and I slept through it.

I only made it a few laps in the circuit race before coming off the back with a small group, racking up another DNF for the season. That night, I drank a few beers out of the big brass trophy I'd won for the sprint the day before.

LEARN TO NEGOTIATE

With a beer or two in him, Danny had mentioned that his budget was finalized, and I was looking forward to getting my contract all sorted out when I got home. He had promised to take care of me, and the time had come to get those numbers in the form of an official offer for my second year as a pro. I'd finally be rewarded for five years of hard labor, for all those cold, rainy training rides, the cross-country drives, the skin I'd left on pavement in nine states and two continents, the bottles I'd delivered to teammates, and the time away from friends and family. You see where this is going.

"We can do $6,000," Danny said.

"Six thousand? That's the offer I turned down from Time to ride for you last year. I've paid my dues, Danny. You can do better than that." I don't think I sounded convincing.

"Well, you'll have to pay them again." I could tell he felt bad about that one, but not enough to raise the offer. "Look, I know it's a shitty number, so you can take a few days to think about it." Wasn't he supposed to at least try to convince me it was a good offer?

I had until Friday to decide. It was Monday morning, and I was deflated. Yes, it was triple my salary from the previous year, but the whole point of taking Jelly Belly's offer over Time's was to get my foot in the door to a living wage, and they had just smashed my toes rather than letting me in. There wasn't much difference between $6,000, $2,000, or $0, because at those sums bike racing wouldn't pay the bills. To make matters worse, I hadn't even talked to other teams, and now it was almost too late to get another offer. I'd been betrayed, and I'd let it happen.

I didn't have much leverage to negotiate. Yes, I'd won San Dimas, but that race was early enough in the year that other teams had forgotten about it or chalked it up as a fluke after all the DNFs. There were hundreds of guys who were 95 percent as good as I was, who would happily race for free. Besides, I didn't have any other offers on the table, and wasn't this a supply-and-demand situation? Pro cycling is a business, after all. It wasn't personal. I just hadn't made the cut, plain and simple.

BE REALISTIC

I had to weigh some tough questions. If my best offer after five years of work was $6,000, maybe it was time to quit. I'd overcome 1,000 to 1 odds to get this far, and the returns should be better for that kind of gamble, but would quitting be giving up on a dream after all the work I'd put in? Maybe this shitty offer meant that I'd failed the dream already. What's it worth to follow a dream, anyway? Is that just garbage they tell you when you're a kid, or is there something inherently noble about putting all your energy into a lofty ambition, even if that ambition doesn't bring home the bacon (or even the bacon bits, in this case)? Is it more courageous to keep fighting a pointless fight, or to recognize when you can't win and start another battle from scratch? What's the meaning of life? Why do men have nipples?

When I started racing, I'd stared in awe at the Jittery Joe's riders, and I wanted to be like them. I suddenly realized that I'd made it to their level and it wasn't what I'd expected at all. But young riders were now looking at me with admiration. Who would I be without bike racing? Would my friends still like me if I quit? If I moved on, what could I do? Successful men said that they were living vicariously through me. They thought that success as a bike racer meant success in life. They'd almost convinced me, but the magic trick always means more to the audience than it does to the rabbit crammed in the hat.

The hardest part about quitting was that deep down, I knew I could make a living doing something I loved, and I wasn't going to be happy with anything less. It didn't seem like it was my decision, though, so maybe it wasn't my right to be happy. It was time to accept the fact that I was living a lie, not a dream. I enjoyed being a pro athlete, but it was a façade, just like it probably had been for the pros I'd looked up to when I started, and it was time to move on. I resolved to start a new chapter in my life and work to be my best at that. I opened up practice books for the GRE and the LSAT and printed out graduate school applications.

I stopped riding, even though there was one more race left for the season, the Tour of Hainan, a nine-day stage race in China that didn't start for several months. I'd use Hainan as an opportunity to take my revenge on bike racing. My plan was to stop training, grow out my leg hair, and put on some weight. Maybe I'd lie on my back underneath a soft-serve machine and have it spew ice cream into my mouth for a day. I would show up in China completely unfit, looking like the guy who ate Phil Gaimon, just to see what they would do with me. The team wouldn't want to buy a plane ticket to send me home, and the race was pretty flat, so I could probably hang on for a few stages and get in the way. At least I would have the last laugh and say I retired in style, on my own terms.

I'd only gained a pound when I got a phone call from Frankie Andreu on behalf of Kenda Pro Cycling. Frankie and his wife, Betsy, had given testimony in 2006 that Lance Armstrong had used EPO, and when the court documents were later leaked their honesty ruined Frankie's career. He'd been accused of lying, was attacked in the media, and then was fired from his previous director job. The Andreus went through a rough time, trying to raise three kids when telling the truth wasn't paying the bills. Everyone who understood the sport knew that the Andreus were right all along, and you had to admire them for standing up against Goliath. With guys like Floyd and Lance dropping like flies, Frankie was a safe hero to have.

Kenda was Frankie's ticket back to the sport. And he wanted to talk to little old me on the phone.

Kenda had been the lowest-ranked pro team that year, so it was the only one I hadn't already begged for a last-minute offer. But having Frankie call on their behalf made them legitimate enough. He assured me that their budget was going up, and he was already signed on to direct. The boss, Chad Thompson, called next, asking how much I needed to stay in the sport. I told him $18,000. He said that would be no problem, and I'd be the team's designated GC rider. The offer was barely above the poverty line, but I felt like I'd hit the jackpot.

Despite Frankie's celebrity, I didn't really want to ride for Kenda. I wanted to race the Tour of California again, and Kenda would never get that invitation. I called Danny as soon as Frankie hung up. Based on my understanding of how market value worked, I was pretty sure he'd match Kenda's offer.

"Phil. Have you made your decision?" Danny was always terse on the phone. It was almost like he didn't care.

"Well, no. Kenda just offered me $18,000."

"Oh. So you're leaving Jelly Belly then?"

"Well, I was hoping you could match it."

"Oh! No! We can't do that. We don't have any more money." He seemed distracted, like he was getting another call.

"Well, can you do $12,000 then?" I'd be eating a lot of ramen, but I thought I could make $12,000 work.

"No! No. Six. That's your offer. That's all we can afford. Are you leaving?" He sounded almost excited about it.

"I guess I'm riding for Kenda next year then."

"Okay. Good luck—WAIT! You're still coming to China, right?"

"Uhh, yeah."

"Good!" And he hung up. Five minutes later, I got a text from my friend Jon Chodroff, an amateur on a team from New York. Danny had just offered him $12,000 for 2010.

I'd been thinking about the meaning of life and the joys of racing so long that I knew more pondering wouldn't help, so I called Frankie right back and told him I was in. A "letter of intent" arrived from Kenda, promising a salary of $15,000–20,000, depending on final budget. I should have asked why it wasn't for the $18,000 I was offered, but I figured that Thompson just wrote it that way so he could use the same document for a handful of riders within a certain salary range, and I didn't want to rock the boat before I even started with my new team. When I got the actual contract the following week, the salary was $15,000. Pro cycling was like grasping at a beach ball floating in the water: Every time I walked closer to it, the wave from my body pushed it further away.

I should have seen that one coming. The lesson I learned—for the bargain price of $3,000—was that the new boss was the same as the old boss. But there's a Catch-22 in domestic pro cycling: Anyone who thinks he can assemble and manage a team has to be at least slightly crazy to start with.

Most teams aren't run by the sponsor, even though the jerseys may make it look that way. Teams are started by individuals to be a marketing vehicle, and then the sponsorship is sold. For example, Jelly Belly didn't create the team that Danny Van Haute ran. Danny assembled the riders and staff, and then he convinced Jelly Belly, and then the clothing sponsor, and then the bike sponsor, and so on to be a part of it. It's a crazy gamble to start a team and try to earn a living managing it. The sponsor value, risk-reward ratio, and pay potential are all ridiculous. And the riders, inhabiting the lowest rung on the ladder, are in the most ridiculous position of all.

NO ONE CAN HELP YOU

As I was sorting out my contract, getting screwed over, and figuring out how to scrape by, I was bombarded by friends, acquaintances, and strangers, all seeking my help to join a pro team. Every Cat. II who'd ever beaten me on a group ride wanted me to recommend them to Jelly Belly or Kenda or Fiordifrutta. Jeremy Powers might have put in a word to get me onto Jelly Belly, but I hadn't asked him—

or anyone else—for favors when I was coming up. I lived out of my car and passed out a lot of bottles to get where I was, so I resented everyone coming out of the woodwork, trying to skip those steps.

Besides, the real truth is that no one can get you on a team but yourself. The contract comes when you have results at big races and you've shown that you're good enough to contribute to a pro team. If you're ready, you don't need my help finding a team. And if you're not, I wouldn't want to help you anyway.

The requests would usually come from guys who had no chance of ever making it. I was barely afloat, they were nowhere near as good as I was, and they'd been at it much longer. Not wanting to shatter any dreams, I tried to give friendly advice about how to write a race résumé and who to send it to. If I had really wanted to do them a favor, though, I would have told them to give up.

ONE OUT OF FIVE IN THE BREAK IS PLENTY

With a new lease on pro cycling with Kenda, I couldn't follow through on my revenge plot against cycling, so I resumed training. When it was time to leave for Hainan, my form was good, and I was excited to improve on my previous experience in China.

When I landed in Hainan the team's second mechanic was being his usual difficult self, refusing to lend me a 5-mm Allen wrench to tighten my seatpost, treating his tools like Chuck Heston clutched his Winchester at an NRA rally ("FROM MY COLD, DEAD HANDS").

To be fair, although he couldn't spare a wrench, our mechanic did put wheels on the bikes and pump the tires before each stage. Most professionals check their bikes before the start, or at least the skewers to make sure the wheels aren't going to slip out, but he was insulted by that, so Danny told us that we needed to trust the mechanic and let him do his job, meaning no more skewer-checking, at least not in sight of the boss or staff.

Once again, the team race plan was impossible. We started five riders while most teams had eight, so we were already at a disadvantage to the handful of Tour de France and Giro d'Italia stage winners in attendance. Then the guys decided that Jelly Belly should either make up half of the break, or, if it got away without us, chase it down. Lance's U.S. Postal Service team in its prime wouldn't have tried a plan that lofty.

For the first five days, if we had two riders in a break of six, they would both sit on the back while the rest of the team chased at the front of the field. On the rare occasion that we did get two out of four or three out of six, of course the riders from other teams refused to work, because they were outnumbered. Our efforts were a comical waste of energy.

Thanks to intermediate time bonuses I won on a long breakaway during the first stage, I was sitting sixth overall. At the start each day, the announcer introduced the top 10, but with his accent, he couldn't pronounce the "L" sound. It was hard to keep a straight face when the crowd roared to the sound of "PHIIIRRRRRRRR, from JERRY BERRY."

WHEN IN ASIA, GET A HAIRCUT

Hainan is a small island in the South China Sea, known for its spas, golf, beach resorts, and a tropical climate that most of us weren't prepared for. Kiel had been riding in the snow in Boulder, so he'd let his hair grow out for the winter (it doesn't occur to bike racers to cut our hair unless it sticks through the helmet vents, which never happens if you wear a hat in the cold). Sick of the heat in China, he took a pair of scissors to himself in a dark hotel bathroom, and showed

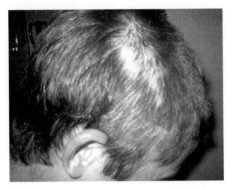

Kiel Reijnen's head.

up for the meeting looking like a mangy animal. Some areas were still long, but others were down to the bare scalp. Kiel was my age, a great bike racer, and an interesting character when you got to know him. He's the rare type who sincerely couldn't care less what people think of him (most people only pretend not to care), and it was fun to observe. The stares he got in public didn't seem to bother him, but the next day I dragged Kiel to the hotel salon, insisting that we would both get haircuts.

A crowd gathered around the high swivel chairs as we tried to express that we wanted Kiel to look like a human being and I just wanted a trim. To break down the language barrier, I tried to find the number-four clipper attachment, but after digging through all the drawers, all I came up with were clay curlers, rusty scissors, and the edging attachment from a vacuum cleaner. I couldn't stop laughing.

We gave up and told them to just start cutting (universal code for that is the scissor motion with the index and middle fingers). The two hairdressers were young and nervous, especially now that a crowd had gathered at the window, pointing at the mangy American. They seemed to be cutting one hair at a time, and it took them over an hour to finish, but Kiel looked much better, and I thought mine came out quite well. When I worked out the exchange rate, the price was $4 each. Tips aren't customary in China, but I insisted. We tipped like Sinatra, if you calculate by percentage.

CHECK EVERYTHING ON YOUR BIKE

Going into stage 5 of 9, I was looking forward to holding onto my top 10 overall when my bike suddenly ground to a halt. My cassette lock ring had come loose, several cogs had slipped off entirely, and the chain was wedged in between. When the mechanic changed into easier cassettes for hilly days, his policy was to thumb-tighten them all first, and then go around with the tool to tighten them all down, but he often forgot the second step. This was the fifth instance of loose cassettes that season.

I got a wheel from neutral support, but with the team car following a teammate in the early break, I was off the back alone for over an hour before Danny came to rescue me (none of my teammates waited for their GC guy). By then, I was a couple minutes behind, on pace to miss the time cut, so there was no choice but to hold onto the car window for a free ride back to the peloton. I wasn't proud of it, but there's a difference between using a car to get back on because you didn't make it over a climb versus using it after a mishap. It's technically against the rules, but in the case of a bike malfunction or a flat tire, most riders don't consider it cheating, and officials look the other way. The road was long, smooth, and straight, and I gripped the inside of the window with white knuckles, life flashing before my eyes as Danny pushed the speedometer to 75 mph. The officials caught us and decided to make an example of me. I was disqualified. From hanging on the car all that time, my right arm felt like it was an inch longer.

THE TRUTH GETS YOU YELLED AT

With nothing to do for the next few days, I wrote a blog about the race, explaining what happened with my mechanical issues. The mechanic had been rude to me personally, and my mishap was his responsibility, which deprived me of a good result, wasted weeks of training, and thousands of dollars in team expenses. Given all of that, I was pretty merciful. My message was that sometimes you can do everything right but it can all fall apart anyway, and "that's bike racing." It didn't make the team look great, but the editors thought it was an interesting story, and they paid me more than Jelly Belly did, so at that point I owed more loyalty to my readers than my team.

My honesty earned me a tongue-lashing from Danny and a series of angry e-mails from an executive at Jelly Belly, but what could they do to me? Give me a shitty offer for next year? That already happened. I apologized, but looking back, it's pretty amazing how quickly everyone turned on me. I'd been working my ass off for the team all season for almost no pay. How much loyalty did they expect from a 23-year-old rookie?

Everyone has a temper when the team isn't racing well, myself included. At the time, I had a lot of malice toward the team, but I realize now that this is how the business works. Jelly Belly is a great sponsor and Danny does a fine job with the team, but the way the sport is set up, the low man on the totem pole is expendable, and he's treated accordingly. It wasn't fair, exactly, but I wouldn't have experienced much better elsewhere, and it certainly could have been worse. Danny buys me a beer every chance he gets, and that's close enough to an apology. I'm pretty tipsy from one beer.

THERE'S ALWAYS A BIGGER LOSER

At the end of the week, still trying to get three out of six in every breakaway, the guys finally got tired and missed a split in a cross-wind, the whole team falling out of the top 30.

I felt better about my fate when I saw how the GC competition ended. With three laps to go in the last stage, the race leader, Boris "the Blade" Shiplevsky (Russian National Team), suffered a flat tire. There was a lot of prize money at stake, and Team Sparkasse from Germany had apparently made a deal with the Russians, because they'd been pulling together all week. (Why didn't we think of that? Oh wait, it's against the rules.) Sparkasse had one of its riders give Boris a wheel to chase back on—a pointless move since the other teams would have slowed the race for the yellow jersey. The illegal wheel change cost Boris a two-minute time penalty, knocking him out of the race lead. That was $22,000 in prize money down the drain, and suddenly my week didn't seem so bad. Everything is relative.

The highlight of Hainan was the market in Sanya, the host city for the start and finish of the race. Immune to trademark issues, local manufacturers made impressive knockoffs of products from Nike, Rolex, and even Apple. Some of the copies were so good that only a very discerning consumer could tell the difference. But not all.

"Look! I got iPhone!" boasted Boris the Blade, shaking his new device, his arm jingling, weighed down by "Tag Heuer" watches. Then he pulled out the phone's antenna.

"That's great, Boris!" We tried to stifle our laughter.

Just as Hainan was coming to an end, I heard an inspirational story about another rider who was also sick of being taken advantage of and who had also been insulted with a lowball offer. Unlike me, who planned my revenge but gave up on it like a sucker, this guy left his team in style. He made his exit at the Sun Tour, a stage race in Australia. He'd flown into Sydney for the race, done all his pre-race duties with the team, and started with everyone else. Then he pulled out on the first stage. Right after that, he met a woman who'd showed up to watch, and the two of them took off. No one knows where they went, and the rest of the team barely saw him until the day they all flew home. He'd taken a vacation, showing his team exactly the loyalty it deserved. While everyone else was racing, he posted pictures of himself on the Internet with roadkill kangaroos. He'd burned a bridge on purpose, and he wasn't afraid, because to him it was a bridge worth burning. I'd tried my best to suck it up, and look where it got me.

SET GOALS OUTSIDE OF CYCLING

With racing over in mid-November, I was in for a short off-season. My first year as a pro hadn't quite gone as I'd expected. I'd joined Jelly Belly hoping to develop, but it was hard to tell if it worked. Now that I knew what it meant to be a pro, it was scary to think I might be doing it for another 10 or 15 years. I thought about Jonny Clarke, who'd focused on racing since high school and joked that he'd barely learned to read. Bernard Van Ulden had a degree in chemistry but set it aside for years while he raced, which would make it harder to work in the field when he hung up his wheels. I could hear him contacting a prospective employer. "Please read my résumé, and then eight seconds later, when you're finished . . ."

To keep my head on straight, I started a small business that fall selling cycling jerseys online. The idea was huge text on the back for motorists to read, with messages like DON'T RUN ME OVER and DON'T HONK

AT ME with a reflected THANKS! on the front, to be visible in rearview mirrors after they'd passed. I invested $9,000 that I'd saved from coaching, and spent several weeks learning how to build a web site to accept credit cards. My friends thought I was crazy, but I started selling a few jerseys every week to cyclists across the country. I packed and shipped everything myself, writing the addresses by hand with a marker.

I still wanted to make some use of my English degree, so I made a reading list of 200 books and started reading 50 pages a day, with the goal of starting a book of my own when the list was done. I started carrying a voice recorder, and I wrote notes every evening in a journal. I sent my pitch of a column called "Ask a Pro" to all the major cycling magazines, got a monthly page in *Velo* magazine, and moved my blog to its site.

With a contract signed, I'd be racing for at least another year, but I didn't assume it would be forever. It made me feel better to think that I was still improving myself, learning, and building a résumé. A big goal like starting a business or writing a book can be daunting at first, but all you have to do is break it up into little pieces and keep working at it. You could eat a school bus if you ground it up and sprinkled some on your oatmeal every morning. Juggling it all was stressful at first, but it was also satisfying to get things done. Everyone is always searching for happiness, but satisfaction is almost as good—and much easier to achieve.

EVERY LITTLE BIT COUNTS

Jelly Belly stopped sending me jelly beans by the end of the year. When I finally ran out, I trained with a plastic honey bear bottle for a few weeks. I even won the state road race championships with it. I'd recommend honey bears over race gels, but it was pretty messy.

My contract for 2009 was $2,000, so each month from January through November I got a check for $166.66. But if I got the same amount all twelve months, my total earnings would only add up to $1999.92. I was concerned. How would I pay my bills? To my great relief, on December 1 my last paycheck arrived, for $166.74.

5

KEEP RACING AS LONG AS YOU CAN

At the start of 2010 my inbox began filling with questions from Kenda's Chad Thompson, the new boss. What airport are you flying out of? Which saddle do you want on your TT bike? Multiply that by a new e-mail for every logistical detail, every part on the bike, and every article of clothing imaginable. No one understood why he couldn't have just sent us each a single spreadsheet. Thompson marked all his e-mails urgent, and if a rider didn't respond within 24 hours he'd send a passive-aggressive note to the entire team. It was great to see that things were so organized.

Training camp was in Macon, Georgia. The Kenda team had stepped up financially from previous years, but it was still a low-budget affair compared to Jelly Belly, and the little differences were hard to get used to. Our lodging was a cheap motel by the interstate, between a Hooters and a Kmart, with an algae-filled swimming pool. Thompson had found the cheapest hotel in town, negotiated a group discount for all the rooms, and another discount for telling them we didn't need cleaning or linen service, but the team still didn't pay for a single meal for the riders all year. Day-to-day, it was a far cry from what Jelly Belly provided, but at least I was getting a monthly paycheck with four figures on it.

What we lacked in perks, we made up for in atmosphere. No one had dinner alone. After the cliques and attitudes I'd dealt with at Jelly Belly, enjoying my team's company was by far the most important thing, and I had a blast with the new teammates. Chad Hartley and Jonny Sundt tried on the new shorts, each pulled out one testicle, and went around asking, "Do you think this fits right?" or "Did I sit in some gum?"

He kept his testicles concealed, but I quickly made friends with my teammate Jim Stemper, a college graduate and nice guy from Wisconsin. I asked why he walked around wearing scrubs all week. He explained that he was hit by a car a few months back, and the ER technicians told him his X-rays indicated a broken hip. "So I just started bawling. I was never going to ride again, I'd never get to be a pro, and I totally lost it and cried like crazy. Then the nurse came back in and said they looked at the X-rays again, and it wasn't broken after all."

Guilt ridden, the nurse asked Jim if there was anything she could do. "I couldn't think of anything, so I said I'd take some scrubs. They're really comfortable!" The best part was that he was man enough to admit that he cried.

FIND MONEY

Everyone got along, but I noticed a few guys on the team who didn't quite fit in. For pro teams at the "continental" level, the UCI, cycling's governing body, requires that half the roster be under age 28, so it's rare for someone to get his first contract above that age if he hasn't been winning races. I learned that some of these guys brought sponsors with them in one way or another, so the "pay-to-play" guys made up a significant portion of the roster. It didn't seem like a very sustainable team model.

DON'T LISTEN TO BIKE FITTERS

One of the team sponsors was a bike-fitting company. With laser technology and computer software, the fitters took measurements of the riders and then adjusted all of the seat heights, handlebar positions, and so on for maximum comfort, power, and efficiency. At the end of an hour-long process, it felt like I was riding a pile of dog shit. I told the fitter that the saddle was low, hoping he would recheck the measurements or calibration of the machine, but he ranted about his PhDs and his vast knowledge of physiology, insisting that I needed to get used to it before I took out the wrench and ruined everything.

When I still felt uncomfortable a week later, I raised the saddle to where I wanted it (about a mile higher), and that's been my position ever since. We have fitters at camp every year, and now I say, "No, thanks," and set everything up myself. I don't care how many doctorates you have; I sit on a bike all day and I know what feels right better than you do.

DO LISTEN TO FRANKIE

The Tour of Taiwan was the first race for the team that year, and it was a big target. Kenda Tires is based in Taiwan, and the company was sponsoring the event and paying "off budget" for the trip. When we got to customs in Taipei, the agent looked at Jake Rytlewski, an average-height, average-build, blond American; Jonny Sundt, with his sprinter's build and a blond mullet; and me, a taller, scrawny American with shaggy brown hair. "You all look same!" he said, laughing. Fair enough.

With Frankie Andreu as a director, I was relieved to follow the advice of a competent tactician. A good director can't make bad riders win a race, but a bad director can definitely make good riders lose one, and it was refreshing that Frankie didn't make the same mistakes that had baffled me the year before. He was appropriately conservative at first, telling us to be attentive, follow breaks, to assess who was strongest, and decide which teams and riders to watch out for. After the meeting, we watched Oscar Friere win the Milan–San Remo one-day classic on TV.

"Huh. They must have changed the last 2 km," Frankie observed.

"How many times did you do that race?" asked Jonny.

"Oh, 10 or 11," was his reply. Frankie probably knew what he was talking about.

The opening stage was brutally hot, but coming from Florida, I had a leg up on my teammates, who were from Milwaukee, Indianapolis, and north Texas and weren't even accustomed to riding outdoors. The racing in Taiwan was aggressive. Within an hour or so, I followed wheels into a huge break, but lacking teammates, I didn't pull through. The gap went up to over two minutes, until the Polish team decided to bring it back. They nearly tore the field apart in the effort, and our noncooperative break came back like we'd opened a parachute. I attacked solo as soon as we were caught, and five riders came up to me out of the field. The Poles were completely destroyed, missing the front split. Insert your own lightbulb joke here.

I worked in the smaller break, with no idea who was with me. I expected us to get caught as soon as the group was organized, but big time gaps formed in the heat, and a British rider attacked the break with 5 km to go (all slightly uphill). Realizing that my companions were hurting, I followed soon after and spent the rest of the stage about 10 seconds behind the solo rider. He turned out to be Dave McCann, billion-time Irish national champion and 11th at the world championship time trial the year before. McCann had served a six-month suspension in 2002 after a positive urine test for nandrolone.

On my wheel (but unwilling to help) was Will Clarke, an Australian. In the long drag to the finish, we all died gradual deaths, going slower and slower, but time gaps stayed the same, and Clarke went around me at the line. He was hoping I would drag him up to the Irishman for an easy stage win, but it was poor tactics on Clarke's part because we lost time on the GC that day that we never got back. If he had the gas to sprint, he should have used it to limit our time losses. I explained that to him after the finish, remaining calm and polite. No yelling or cussing from me. No, sir.

My efforts did earn me the green jersey and the protection of my teammates. I wasn't expecting to be in the GC, and the pressure was mentally and physically exhausting. I didn't have much appetite and barely slept at night. I counted down the kilometers until it would be over.

The island of Taiwan is a narrow strip about 90 miles wide by a few hundred miles long, with one interstate connecting the north to the south. The area around the main highway is dense with industry, but the rest is mostly farmland. Somehow, despite the small size of the island, we had two to four hours of bus rides before and after every stage, which didn't make for great recovery. Nor did the race buffet, with little to eat other than rice and mystery meat, and only orange Tang to drink. Yes, Tang.

Fortunately, there was almost always a McDonald's or KFC nearby. In the United States I wouldn't enter a KFC without a gun to my head, but in Asia, thanks to American health standards, those were the only places with clean floors and employees who were guaranteed to wash their hands, which eased the guilt of fast food. I ate like I was on death row and rode just fine fueled by Big Macs and fries.

Despite the difficulty of being so far from home (or perhaps because of it) the team was a family. We weren't winning the stage race, but I can safely say that we had more fun than anyone else. Our table at the buffet was always roaring with laughter, making it easier to stare into our dreary bowls of congee every night. It was a big contrast to some of the races with Jelly Belly, when half of the guys weren't speaking to each other. On most pro teams the staff usually does their own thing, but even our soigneur was part of the gang. Halfway through a massage, I asked to use the restroom, where I smeared Nutella all over my ass. When I returned and lay face-down on the table, she jumped in disgust.

A few minutes into stage 3, I flatted in a pothole. The team car with spare wheels was ahead of us following a teammate in the breakaway, so Hartley gave me his wheel. Neutral support blew right past him, so Hartley chased alone for three hours, finishing 25 minutes behind. With 2 km to go, officials told him to get in the broom wagon because he'd missed the time cut. He used some words that they didn't understand and stayed on his bike to the finish. Frankie had to argue with the officials so he could continue to race the next day. For several years, every time Hartley needed a favor he mentioned the wheel he gave me in Taiwan.

The field was weak for a UCI race, with just a handful of good riders. When the roads pointed uphill, I was consistently the strongest, so we waited until the fourth stage, which had the biggest climbs of the race. I put almost two minutes on the leaders over the second climb, but with a 40-km-long open descent to the finish, it was impossible to stay away, and I was caught by the field with 3 km to go. I did take a three-second time bonus, which moved me up to second overall.

Kenda seemed pleased with my finish. The company hosted a banquet that night and took us for a tour of the tire factory the following day, which is about as glamorous as you'd expect, only hotter. Strangely, I didn't see any Kenda tires in the whole place. The majority of its business was in making tires for other companies, and the walls were covered with Michelin Pro 3s and Specialized Armadillos. Everyone always jokes that all the bikes in the world are made in the same factory in Taiwan. Tires too, apparently.

It was my first time inside a factory. The night before, I drank champagne at the banquet, and now I was watching an old man cut hot rubber in an assembly line, with an industrial fan blowing the sweat off of his face.

The race was a great start to the season, but rather than feeling pride in my result, I was more relieved that I hadn't let my teammates down. I'd led a team for the first time, but I knew I wasn't really a leader. Frankie and my teammates were guiding me along, telling me what to do.

While we were on the other side of the world, Jelly Belly was racing the Redlands Classic. Will Routley won a stage, and Kiel finished second overall. I was surprised to find that I was happy for them.

GO TO EUROPE

After a short rest we headed to upstate New York for the Tour of the Battenkill, a one-day UCI race known for its dirt roads. I made an early break, but it was doomed by the tactics of bigger teams, and I watched from the sidelines as Caleb Fairly came in for a solo win. Caleb was known as a climber, but I'd been about at his level when we were racing as Under 23s together. Caleb had started racing younger, though, and managed to get onto Garmin's development team, so he'd spent a few years doing hard races in Europe, getting his teeth kicked in. That made him stronger, and now he was winning big races. I wondered if I could ever make up that difference.

MAKE FRIENDS WITH *BICYCLING* MAGAZINE

I got home from Battenkill on April Fool's Day, so I was suspicious when I saw that my e-mail inbox was filled with sales notifications from my online store. Orders had been trickling in for months, but I sold 40 jerseys that morning, which didn't make sense until I learned that *Bicycling* magazine had featured my DON'T RUN ME OVER design as Jersey of the Month. *Bicycling* readers obey those selections.

It was great to have some success, but the business that I'd started as something between a joke, an educational process, and a labor of love suddenly became real work. I immediately sold out of half the designs and found myself flooded with backorders and operations issues. For example, now that I had enough volume, I could order directly from a manufacturer, cutting my inventory costs in half. I also needed to set up a credit card gateway on my web site to accept cards directly (rather than through a third-party source that charged a 4 percent fee), register as a limited liability company (LLC), and open a bank account. I also had to leave town in a couple days for the Tour of the Gila. My English degree just sat there, not helping at all.

Still feverishly handwriting addresses of customers onto boxes and taking them to the post office myself, I knew I needed help, but the sales still didn't justify hiring anyone. I was concerned that the

Jon (*right*) and I hard at work with Frank, the company mannequin.

stress and time would affect my sleep and training, so I turned to Jon Ciaccio, a business major on the school cycling team who'd been helping with the web site. I made a deal that Jon could have half the company in exchange for handling inventory, shipping, and any other work that required someone with a more stable schedule. Jon agreed, and I had fewer balls to juggle. When you register an LLC in Florida, the form has a blank space for the title of each partner. Jon wanted to be CEO, so I filled in "King and Tyrant."

I also quit my role as UF's cycling coach, unable to reconcile the time commitment with everything else I had going on. After Gila, I'd be moving with my girlfriend to Baltimore, where she was starting graduate school. Maryland isn't a huge cycling destination, but I knew it was time to leave Florida.

PLAYING H-O-R-S-E IS NOT IDEAL RECOVERY

Business stress didn't turn out to be a limiting factor in my race at the Tour of Gila. That job was easily done by guys named Armstrong, Leipheimer, McCartney, and Zabriskie. A loophole in the rules allowed top-level riders to compete as long as they weren't registered under their official team name, so riders from BMC, RadioShack, and Garmin showed up as prep for the Tour of California, and they worked together against the domestic teams. We had no chance.

Leading up to the race, I found myself comparing my own activities to Lance's. When I stayed up late mailing jerseys to customers, I wondered if Lance was similarly boxing Livestrong bracelets, or loading a Michelob Ultra truck. I thought of several differences:

1. Lance wouldn't have eaten nearly as many chocolate chip cookies as I did.
2. Lance probably didn't put cheese in his oatmeal.
3. Lance didn't spend half the week playing phone tag with landlords from Craigslist, trying to determine if their cheap apartments in Baltimore were a good deal or were in neighborhoods likely to get him murdered.
4. Lance most certainly did not fly coach.

The biggest difference was that Lance's team didn't put him up in a gym, while my team was hosted by a Baptist church on a dirt road just outside of Silver City, where we slept on cots lined up against a wall, like you might see in news footage of disaster-relief housing. It was no hurricane or tornado, but nine dudes in one room did qualify as a disaster. At least we could cook our own meals and pass the downtime playing H-O-R-S-E. Jim Stemper's bed and belongings were under the basket, and they took a serious pounding.

The kitchen was set up to feed an army, with redundant appliances, enormous skillets, and a cabinet filled with nonperishable goods. I found a novelty sized chocolate Easter bunny and hid it in my suitcase, finishing it over the course of the week. With 10 guys sharing one echoing room, it became a symphony of burps, farts, coughs, loogies, crunching, slurping, and snoring. An anthropologist could have observed us for the week and published an article: "A Study of Male Habits in an All-Male Environment."

Unaccustomed to the altitude, we floundered in the race. I lost enough time in the first road stage that I treated the next few days as recovery, hoping to snag a stage result later in the week.

Our bike sponsor didn't make a TT bike at the time, so it bought frames from a Taiwanese manufacturer and had them painted to match our road rigs. They were some sort of low-grade carbon fiber at least, but these prototype bikes were barely safe to ride. The seatpost slipped down, the rear wheel slipped forward because it didn't fit right in the horizontal dropouts, and the chain slipped off because the braze-on for the front derailleur was in the wrong place. Our mechanic was supposed to build the bikes at training camp, but a pro team with 18 riders should have two mechanics, and he never got around to it with everything else going on. At Gila, with eight bikes to put together in one evening, he threw his hands up and came into the gym where we were playing Jenga, bored out of our minds.

"You'll just have to ride your road bikes, I guess," he informed us. Given the competition, we already had little hope of results. Putting us on road bikes in a flat time trial against Lance and Levi would place much of the team dangerously into time cut territory.

"What did Frankie say?" I asked.

Frankie was in the trailer gluing tubulars while the mechanic complained to us about how hard he was working. I hadn't been a pro cyclist for very long, but I knew that Frankie Andreu had earned the right to never glue tires again.

Stefano got up without saying a word, spent 15 minutes in the trailer, and got everything working perfectly on his bike, mostly thanks to a Dremel tool. He'd taught himself to work on cars, and this was much simpler than building an engine. The mechanic watched, and then reluctantly finished the bikes for our other GC riders.

I made the early break on the last stage, but a flat tire took me out of it. When I tried to hang on to the car like I'd learned on Jelly Belly, poor communication with Frankie sent me to the pavement. As the front group came by, I looked over and made eye contact with Lance. He glanced at my shorts, ripped and bloody, with half my butt coming out. "Ouch," he winced. Ouch indeed, Lance.

I stopped in the feed zone at the top of the climb, planning to take the van back with the staff. Frankie pulled over in the team car and told me to get back on the bike. "Everyone else DNFed already. We have to finish someone," he explained.

"Fuck. How far is it?" I asked.

"It's like 20 miles, all downhill," Frankie lied. I suppose he had to.

I rode cautiously on the descent and started climbing up to the finish. After 20 miles, I saw a race sign that said "25 km to go," and I could tell there'd be plenty of climbing. I pressed on, with no other means to get home, cursing Frankie with every breath. Then it started snowing.

That night, instead of braving the snow on the way to a crappy restaurant or cooking another box of pasta, we ordered Papa John's pizza, enjoying our last night in the gym and our first chance to hear some of Frankie's stories.

Somehow, politics came up. This was around the time that the media was accusing Barack Obama of Kenyan birth and lying about his U.S. citizenship. "Yeah, I could totally believe that Barack isn't a citizen," Frankie said. If he could fall for that, I thought maybe my new director might have been mistaken about some of the doping scandals on U.S. Postal. Perhaps Lance was telling the truth all along.

Nah.

Our mechanic didn't join us for dinner. He became the scapegoat at Gila for the time trial bike debacle but was immediately picked up by BMC for the Tour of California. He fell up.

WAIT UNTIL THE CONTRACT IS SIGNED

I had no chance to rest after Gila, packing a U-Haul and driving up with my girlfriend to our new apartment in Ellicott City, Maryland, just west of Baltimore. I was getting over a cold and still healing from road rash, so adding moving to the mix made for a less-than-perfect prep for the 150-mile UCI road race in Philadelphia the next weekend.

Chad Thompson showed up for the race, the first time we'd seen him since training camp. He'd had a meeting with Mercedes-Benz about sponsoring the team next year. In his head, it was a done deal, and it was all Thompson talked about. He hinted about the new sponsor on the team's Twitter page and walked around wearing a Mercedes baseball cap. Shortly after that he must have gotten word that the sponsorship was not going to happen because we never heard about Mercedes-Benz again. I'd bet my house that he bought that hat at the gift shop, no discount.

BRING YOUR OWN DRINK MIX

Only one of our guys made the front group at Philly, and he barely had the energy to sprint. I realized that the biggest difference between our team and the Europeans wasn't necessarily talent, or even budget, but that racing the Tour of California and the Giro d'Italia makes you stronger than you can possibly be from the events we were doing. Even if we had the same talent and potential as our competition, we lacked the miles and speed in our legs to compete. For my personal development, I needed to ride some bigger races, and I felt the clock ticking on my career if I didn't.

BEWARE OF TORNADOS WHEN YOU'RE GOING FOR THE EARLY BREAK

At the Nature Valley Grand Prix, no one in the team cracked the top 20 in the prologue. That earned us a nasty e-mail from Thompson, not because we raced poorly but because Jelly Belly beat us. Van Haute had "stolen" a potential bike sponsor from Kenda, starting a one-sided Kenda vs. Jelly Belly feud. I began a habit of skimming and deleting Thompson's e-mails, which were almost always unmotivating and frustrating. After how hard I worked for so little at Jelly Belly, I'd learned to establish boundaries. I was up to $15,000 for the year, so I was happy to devote more training and publicity effort to the team, but I'd need a zero added to my salary to get yelled at for not placing well in a time trial.

I hung on the crit stages, anxious for the first road race, where I attacked solo with 55 miles remaining. Soon, my gap was just over a minute, and it was clear that I was going to be the break of the day. I had little hope of winning the stage, but with the first two climbs of the race coming up, it would take an act of God to keep me from nabbing the KOM jersey. Then the lead motorcycle official rode up next to me and instructed me to stop, due to a tornado warning nearby.

"What?" I yelled.

"Stop! You see that up ahead?" He gestured to dark clouds in the distance. "They're canceling the race."

When I looked back, the field had turned around, headed back to the cars. My polka-dot jersey hopes were dashed, and now that they'd left without me, I went from off the front to off the back, and I had to ride hard to catch up.

Only a road race remained in the whole six-day "stage race"—a 120-mile rolling course with a few decent hills. Gunning again for the early break, I attacked often, but I was out of place when the break finally went, so I tried to get across to them, riding all-out across the flats. I knew there were six strong riders in the breakaway pushing hard to establish a gap; if I didn't get there fast, I'd be stuck in no-man's-land.

After a few minutes I looked back to check my gap on the field and noticed that I had a passenger: a big, goofy-looking Texas Roadhouse rider had been on my wheel all along. He must have been six foot four and 220 pounds, and he was having a rough time staying with me. I demanded he take a pull, and he shook his head. If he wouldn't pull, he wasn't getting a free ride from me, so I surged on a short kicker, but the kid held on, still begging me to slow down.

"Hi. My name is Pat Lemieux," he huffed. "I ride here all the time [huff]. If we just go steady over this next hill [huff], there's a valley, and we can catch them there."

The balls on this guy! Telling me to slow down! We were bridging to a breakaway at an NRC race. There's no slowing down! And if he had the energy to speak, he should have been using it to take a turn in the wind. I decided to get rid of him. "Shut the fuck up and take a pull, you piece of shit," I demanded politely.

He came around and took his pull, going much slower than I had been. I attacked as soon as he swung off, sure I'd never see that sucker again.

I joined the break on the next climb. John Sessa, the good mechanic on Jelly Belly, cheered from the window when I passed them. Danny gave him a dirty look. The KOMs were too short, and Brad Huff beat me on both of them, which means that I accomplished nothing that week.

BETTER TO HAVE NO TEAM THAN EIGHT GUYS WHO DON'T WORK TOGETHER

Frankie's leadership was the duct tape, rubber band, and chewing gum holding our team together, so when he went to France to announce the play-by-play for the Tour, I knew that racing without him would be a disaster. Lacking funds to hire someone else, the full team showed up in Fitchburg without a director.

The trip started with horrible flashbacks that kicked in when we found ourselves crammed into a dorm suite at Fitchburg College. When I left the dorms after my freshman year at UF in 2005, the pizza boxes were stacked to the ceiling and my roommate's towel smelled of spilled bong water. I couldn't get out of there fast enough. Years later, having made it as a pro cyclist, I returned to dorm life, dining hall meals and everything. I was sad to learn that the toga party was canceled.

With a team to help me, I was hoping to improve on my GC finish from the year before, maybe slotting into the top five or 10. The

GC would most likely come down to the time trial, so Stefano walked me through more modifications he'd made to his bike to make sure we didn't repeat the issues we had at Gila.

Together, we modified the braze-on so that the front derailleur would mount five millimeters higher (enough to not grind the chainring). Next we welded a small nut into the horizontal drop-out, so the wheel could go forward just to the point where the tire wouldn't rub the frame. I shimmed the slipping seatpost with an entire can of Arizona iced tea (don't worry, fellow Southerners, I'd never drink that crap, but Arizona was a higher-volume can, with thicker material to cover the massive gap between the seatpost and the frame). I then sprayed several thick layers of 3M spray adhesive into the frame, onto the shims and all over the seatpost. I measured the saddle height twice, because I knew there'd be no adjusting it after that. The time trial bike was team property, and at the end of the year, when Thompson asked me to send it back so he could sell it, I told him he'd better find a buyer with legs the same length as mine, because that thing wasn't budging. I think the frame is still in my attic.

The first stage was a long road race. When we discussed the plan, I thought it would be understood that I was the designated GC rider, so the guys would cover the early moves and I could start following attacks near the end. That's what I was hired for, and I'd been the strongest on the team in time trials and road races. Some of the guys were on the same page, but most of them chose to ride for their own results. Kenda was a low-budget team, so most of the guys were paid less than a living wage, and most wouldn't ever be the strongest guy on the roster. If they raced selflessly every weekend, they'd never get a result to earn themselves a raise. Just like Danny Van Haute had done to me, they'd work for the team and get nothing to show for it. When you're not paid a living wage, racing for your teammates is doing yourself a disservice.

I didn't want to argue or look selfish, so I kept my mouth shut. We all missed the deciding break, cruising in with the field 10 minutes behind the leaders.

CHOOSE YOUR CRASHES CAREFULLY

With nothing to show for yet another stage race, I was angry going into the criterium the final day and decided to take my emotions out on the tight circuit in downtown Fitchburg. I was active in some early breaks and was feeling good until I overcooked a turn and took my emotions right into the pavement. Luckily, Gila had taught me to pack a first aid kit and road rash gear in my bag. After the volunteers scraped out my wounds, I jumped in the car and headed to my aunt and uncle's house in the Hamptons, meeting up with my family for a summer vacation.

Being among the mansions of the wealthiest New Yorkers— away from the world of crappy hotel rooms, stink bugs, and bike racers—gave me some much-needed perspective. Bleeding all over the nice sheets, I realized that I'd become too careless about crashing. I'd somehow accepted that I'd crashed before, I'd crash again, and I'd be covered in scars. It wasn't worth it. I'd never broken a bone or dealt with anything worse than road rash, but limping around with bruises was getting old. My crashing was caused less by being bad at bike riding and more by my willingness to take risks, even when there wasn't much potential reward. Fitchburg was a great example. With my weak sprint, I could have been first into the last turn and still wouldn't have finished in the top 10, but it would have taken a podium finish to earn a raise. I was lucky to keep my bones intact so far, but if I was going to be a pro cyclist for the next few years I needed to choose my crashes better, or I'd be killing my chances at races that did suit me, with a lot of miserable nights and ruined bed linens in the process.

THE BEST FISH TACOS EVER ARE AT LA PARILLA GRILL IN BEND, OREGON

It was only July, but the team was officially out of funds for the season. One of the "pay to play" riders wasn't happy with his race schedule, and the sponsor he brought never wrote the team another check. At least, that's the story we got from Thompson, which I'd take with a grain of salt (or maybe a salt factory). Our salaries still came, but the team didn't send us to any races after Fitchburg. I found out that Frankie forfeited several months of his own pay to make sure the riders were all taken care of.

I knew I'd never move to a better team or earn a raise from Kenda if I stayed at home, so Jonny and Stefano agreed to race the Cascade Classic with me on our own dime. Jonny borrowed a car from a friend and picked us up at the airport in Portland.

The race took place in Bend, Oregon, and I quickly fell in love with the town. After my stay in the Hamptons, where everyone was wealthy and spent money on fancy cars and empty tennis courts, Bend was more my style. Bend people put their money into mountain bikes and kayaks. A river flowed through the small downtown area, always filled with locals floating on colorful inner tubes.

Jonny and Stefano had raced in Bend before. Stefano knew a good spot to put our legs in the water after hot stages, and we took our dinners at La Parilla Grill, Jonny's favorite fish taco stand. Our host house was huge, with bedrooms for each of us, a 20-seat movie theater, and a woman who baked nonstop. I wanted to eat healthily, so I limited myself to 30 to 40 cookies before bed, just to be polite.

The race was a media circus thanks to Floyd Landis's participation, simultaneous press conferences with French media, and accusations about U.S. Postal's doping timed to shake up Lance's return to the Tour de France. Floyd had started the season racing for Bahati Foundation, a new pro team out of California. He wanted to race, but he also wanted to tear pro cycling up from its roots, a weird contradiction that drove sponsors away from his new team, which folded early in the summer. Floyd raced stages at Cascade in T-shirts and various jerseys covered in beer logos. I think he was wrestling a combination of feelings: a need to prove his abilities as a clean rider, bitterness that so many had gotten away with doping while he was crucified for it, and an urge to get his name back into the headlines for attention's sake. Whatever it was, Floyd was making himself an unwelcome distraction in the U.S. peloton, and the riders mostly resented his presence. Hartley told me that if Floyd missed the break, I should tell him, "It's okay, Floyd. You can make up eight minutes tomorrow. I saw you do it that one time."

Our three-man hit squad had a fun week, but we didn't accomplish much in the race. I finished in the front group on the climbs and quit halfway through the final stage, worried I'd miss my flight home out of Portland. When I dropped out, Stefano and Jonny were relaxing in the feed zone. A young boy stood nearby with a yo-yo, making it sleep and then pulling it back up. I'd mentioned to the guys that I was second at the Georgia State Yo-yo Championships in fifth grade, and they didn't believe me. (I was also spelling bee champion. It was a big year.)

I asked the boy if I could borrow his yo-yo and did the "brain twister," the most impressive trick I could remember. When it was done whirling through the air at high speed, I gave the toy back to its owner. Seeing someone much better than you can have two effects: It might motivate you to work hard and improve, or it could intimidate you into giving up. The boy looked at the yo-yo, looked at me, and put it in his pocket. He didn't have what it takes to be a champion.

BOULDER IS MECCA

The next race was the Tour of Utah. After my dismal performance at Gila, I knew I needed some time at altitude first, so I flew to Boulder and spent two weeks on Stefano's sofa. Stefano and I would go climb for a few hours, grab lunch in town, and soak our legs in a cold creek on the way home.

We had a good time, but Stefano was going through a rough patch. He'd been racing since he was a kid in Brazil, and he went pro right out of high school. He eventually landed on the Toyota-United team, where he got great results (and a nice paycheck), but he'd been unable to find a good gig when Toyota didn't keep him. Stefano was offered a spot on Kenda, but he wasn't having a great season thanks to a knee injury over the winter, and it didn't look like they'd be hiring him back for 2011. Bike racing had been Stefano's main focus for so long that he didn't know what else he could do. I didn't worry about him too much, though, because Stefano's a smart guy. Besides, his family owns a successful business, which gave him a good safety net. You know how rich people own a yacht? Stefano's uncle has a yacht factory.

With a mixed field of domestic and ProTour teams, Utah was my last chance to earn a better contract and Stefano's last chance to get an offer, but lacking team support, just getting into the race was no easy task. We scrambled to afford the entry fee and find enough guest riders to fill the minimum roster.

DIRECTING A TEAM ISN'T EASY

I'd done my best in preparation, but the race was a nightmare before it even started. Stefano and I had to attend the manager's meeting (usually Frankie's job), pick up all the guys at the airport, make sure they had groceries and all the basics they'd need for the week, and find a ride back home from the finish the following day, which was 80 miles from the start. As we were getting everything together, I got a frantic call from one of our guest riders.

"Phil. I have an emergency."

"Shit. What?"

"We went to the Whole Foods by the host house and they didn't have Peanut Butter Puffin cereal. I saw there was another Whole Foods that you'll pass on the way back from Salt Lake City. Can you swing by and get a couple boxes?"

He'd used the word "emergency" about Peanut Butter Puffins, and he was dead serious. Team leader also meant that I was a babysitter. I had a glimpse into Frankie Andreu's job and I didn't like it one bit. I will not be a director when I retire from racing.

The neutral feeds we were promised in the race guide never materialized, so I did the whole 104-mile opening stage in the dry Utah heat with only two bottles. I bridged to the winning break, and three of us stayed clear over the final climb. With a solid gap on the field entering the short descent, and Livestrong's Alex Dowsett doing the majority of the work, I was pretty much guaranteed a second-place finish behind Fly V's David Tanner, a sprinter who'd managed to stay with us on the climb. By the top, though, my dehydration had caught up with me, and I was cramping and covered in salt. Dowsett sprinted out of the hairpins on the descent, and my quads locked up every time I tried to accelerate. Unable to straighten my legs, I watched Dowsett and Tanner ride away. The front group caught me with 2 km to go.

I couldn't even complain about my fate when I returned to the house because no one else on my team had finished. They'd all missed the front group on an early climb and finished outside of the time cut. One of our guest riders took a 6 a.m. flight home the next day and didn't even take his bike, promising to pay me back when I shipped it for him. Stefano was already in his car, halfway back to Boulder by the time I got out of the shower. I didn't blame him.

The upside was that Kenda was sufficiently panicked at my near miss on stage 1. Frankie told Thompson to get me a contract before I won something and demanded more money, so he offered me another year at $15,000. I bluffed, telling him that I thought I could get better offers from several other teams. Thompson didn't fall for it, insisting that he couldn't afford more. He did agree to a compromise, though: a two-year deal, the first for $15,000, and the second for $20,000 with a guaranteed $5,000 raise if the team budget went over $400,000 from the new sponsors he was talking to. Looking around at all the strong amateurs in the race and the guys from the defunct Bahati team looking for contracts, I felt fortunate to have anything.

I agreed to the offer over the phone, but when the paper contract arrived a key point was missing: It had no mention of the promised raise if the budget increased. That $5,000 was a big difference for me. I could live off of $20,000, but anything less meant I was still working side jobs. I'd felt gypped out of $3,000 with the letter of intent the previous year, and I wasn't going to let it happen again. I told Thompson that I needed the agreement in writing, because if the budget increased after he already had me on the team, he'd naturally want to do more with it—like sign another rider or add a race to the schedule—rather than give more compensation to guys he already had. He was hurt and insulted that I could accuse him of hypothetical dishonesty. "My word should be enough. I'll put it in writing, but you should trust me after everything I've done for you," he said. It was nice to know that he considered it a favor to allow me to work for $15,000 a year.

Later that day I caught up with Nick Reistad, my former teammate from Jelly Belly. Nick had moved away from his training base in Athens, Georgia, starting a job at a marketing firm in Wisconsin. After complaining about my team, I asked how he was enjoying it.

"Let's just say, you should keep racing as long as you can. I know it's rough, but it still beats this boring life," he replied. That's what I figured. Cycling isn't easy, and the uncertainty can be downright menacing, but there's also menace in the mundane.

I didn't have a lot of results, but every year, there was a day—or even just a moment, like that near miss in Utah—that my mind could grab onto, and that was all I needed to feel that I was still getting better, that I shouldn't quit yet. All I needed was another contract, another year of getting to races, and everything would be fine.

SOMEONE IS ALWAYS LUCKIER THAN YOU

Around the time I signed back on for another year at $15,000, I read an article about the new Leopard-Trek ProTour team. Its roster included Will Clarke, the guy who'd finished a spot behind me in Taiwan by virtue of hanging on to my wheel for dear life as I raced for the win. He was friends with Stuart O'Grady and had apparently found a good agent, putting him on one of the best teams in the world with a salary I estimated at 10 times what I'd be getting. The press release listed his Taiwan result as his biggest accomplishment. I didn't know how to contact the big teams, or how to find an agent.

Other confusing signings were coming from my own team. Stefano was gone, but Thompson told me they'd picked up a young guy from Texas Roadhouse who'd ridden well at the Tour of America's Dairyland. I knew immediately it would be Pat Lemieux, the big kid I'd yelled at and dropped during the road race at the Nature Valley Grand Prix.

NICE GUYS DOPE

That summer Jon Chodroff's name showed up on a list from an EPO distributor, and my good friend announced that he was leaving Jelly Belly and professional cycling. Strangers instantly turned on him, and Jon was blasted in vicious online forums. Anyone who knew him was blown away by the revelation because Jon wasn't the kind of guy you would think of as a cheater, and we couldn't imagine hating him in the way that you'd want to hate a doper.

It's easy to say "dopers suck" and dismiss them all by definition, but I'd seen Chodroff hold doors for old ladies, and I couldn't hate him. You have to judge morality by someone's entire body of work, and one mistake shouldn't condemn an otherwise moral life. I knew that he was a good guy, even though he did this bad thing. I'd always suspected that if I was around cycling long enough, it was only a matter of time before I'd be faced with a friend who let everyone down, and I pondered how I'd feel. The news made me sad, but I still considered Jon a friend and wished him the best.

I'd always wondered what might happen to make a rider dope for the first time. I'm sure every situation is different, whether it comes from a doctor, outside pressure from staff or teammates, or a just a dark moment of personal desperation. I thought about what I would do if, by some miracle, I was signed to a top team and someone handed me a needle at training camp, explaining that I'd be on the next flight home if I didn't take it. After all I'd been through to get there, would I have the courage to say no? It was a scary thought.

I wanted to raise the stakes on myself, to help remove any temptation I might encounter, so I decided to get a tattoo. The design would be a bar of soap with the word "CLEAN" on it. If I was ever tempted to take something, a tattoo would be another incentive to avoid it, and maybe enough of a statement that my next doctor wouldn't close the door to ask what drugs I was on. I'd place it on the inside of my lower bicep, to make it plainly visible in a victory salute.

I'd never gotten a tattoo, so in the spring I mentioned my plan to my friend and former employer, Adam Myerson. Adam was covered in piercings and tattoos and had always been outspoken about racing clean. He must have liked the idea, because he got the tattoo himself later that day.

DON'T GET A TATTOO IN SPARTANBURG, SOUTH CAROLINA

Jon's EPO admission convinced me to pull the trigger on my own tattoo. I talked with my teammate Nick Waite about it at national championships in Greenville, and we decided to get it that night, peer pressuring each other into action. Our options on a Sunday night in rural South Carolina, however, were limited. I made some phone calls and convinced one shop to stay open. It was such a simple design, Nick and I didn't think we needed to go somewhere good. What could go wrong?

We hesitated when we arrived at the small building behind a gas station in nearby Spartanburg, South Carolina. A tall African American man was walking out. He'd just gotten his son's name on his chest, and was showing it to a friend, who wondered why he hadn't gone with his wife's name. "See, my son's gonna be my son forever," he explained. "But my wife? That bitch could leave me any day."

Nick and I held strong. We explained our idea to a heavily pierced female tattoo artist with a shaved head. Pale and overweight, she wore a leather jacket filled with shiny silver buckles and spikes, and her teeth looked like a box of crayons. I went first. Nick looked at my tattoo, which ran the full width of my puny arm, and got the same design 25 percent smaller.

Her work was shaky; maybe she had never dealt with an arm as scrawny as mine. Nick and I both had to get our tattoos touched up a few weeks later, but we'd joined a club with Adam Myerson, and the three of us made a pact. We'd do our best to spread the word and convince more athletes to get CLEAN tattoos. And if anyone doped, the rest of the club would come and scrape it off with a cheese grater.

NEVER TRUST A HARLEY ON A DESCENT

Late in the year Kenda was invited to a low-level UCI race in Korea. It was hard to train for a race that started in mid-October, but I showed up in pretty good shape.

The race was called the Tour of the DMZ, set along the Demilitarized Zone on the North Korea–South Korea border, and the course went along the DMZ line, full of barbed wire, armed soldiers, land mine warnings, and walls rigged with explosives to quickly topple in case of invasion. It made for a strange setting, but we're bike racers. Give us a start line, point us in a direction, and we'll pedal.

The race was three days: two long road races and one short one, for a total of about 300 miles. That created a dismal travel-miles-to-

Jonny Sundt and Chad Hartley on the penis cannon.

race-miles ratio of about 100 to 1, but since the race organization had offered to pay our travel and expenses, Thompson didn't see any reason to say no.

We drove north from Seoul to the start of the race in a bus full of other teams. When the driver stopped for gas, we wandered out into the only building in the vicinity, a museum and gift shop devoted to the penis. Jonny Sundt, Chad Hartley, and I wondered if we might be dreaming. We posed joyfully with eight-foot-tall penis statues, climbed the penis cannon, and bought penis trinkets at the gift shop, laughing uncontrollably. Other teams stared.

We raced the first stage with dust kicking up around us from low-flying military helicopters. With two huge climbs, my job was pretty simple: Stay with the leaders, and try to beat them at the end. The race exploded into groups of 10 on the first climb (land mines didn't play a factor, thankfully), and I made the front split, but my job proved difficult when we rounded a fast, blind corner on the descent where the lead motorcycle had crashed and was lying unavoidably sideways in front of us.

I once read a physician's advice in a magazine on the best way to crash a bicycle. He recommended tucking your chin down and holding your arms behind your head. Using arms to brace a fall is the natural reflex, but it makes you much more likely to break a collarbone or wrist, and any way of avoiding or minimizing impact to the head or spine is a good idea.

Intellectually, that makes sense. However, in my many experiences of flipping over handlebars, washing out in corners, and being innocently knocked over by incompetents, I'd never had time to think about a course of action or take any conscious steps to protect myself. My stages of crash reaction are as follows:

Stage 1: Denial
Stage 2: Screaming profanities

If I die in a bike race, my last words will almost certainly be four letters at high decibels.

I don't remember much about the crash in Korea. We all flipped over the motorcycle at over 40 mph. My chin hit first, and judging by the scrapes and scratches, I slid down the road on my chest like a penguin. The moral of the story is that the lead race moto should probably be something sportier than a Harley-Davidson cruiser, and the moto pilot should maybe familiarize himself with the course ahead of time. But what do I know?

I crawled to the guardrail in a daze, looking around for the team car and watching as the first riders from every group crashed the same

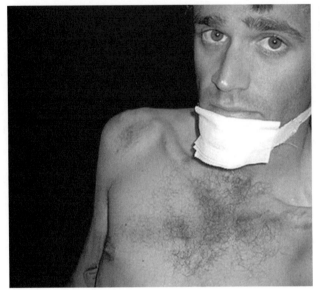

Post–Korea
face-plant.

way I had. I never saw Frankie pull over, but the car was stopped directly in front of me when the mechanic woke me up (I didn't try to finish the race). The race doctor said my split chin would be okay without stitches, which didn't seem right, but I wasn't interested in seeing the inside of a Korean hospital, so I took his word for it.

The accommodations that night were interesting. In Korea, the custom is for the husband to move in with the wife's family when they get married, so the countryside is filled with cheap hourly rate motels, where a shy couple can have discreet sex away from their families. The tiny rooms consist of a bed, toilet, and sink. Fine with me—I was glad to have a room to myself. I knew I'd lost consciousness in the crash, so I looked up how to treat a concussion. Various web sites said that it was best for the patient to stay awake so that he could seek medical attention if any dangerous symptoms arose. I figured I could knock on the soigneur's door and wake her up, but

I didn't want to bother my teammates or staff since they still had racing to do, so I bought a six-pack of Coke at a 7-Eleven and walked laps around the neighborhood all night. It occurred to me that this probably wasn't a safe place for a foreigner to be alone, but then again, who was going to mess with the tall white guy with bandages all over his face? I wouldn't.

For the next few days I hung out in the feed zones, and I also got away from the race to experience South Korea. I explored dozens of tiny villages in the country, and ate delicious foods I was never brave enough to try in the United States, including a traditional Korean barbecue (with all the intimidating side items) and many forms of kimchi, a pickled cabbage dish that tastes much better than it sounds.

The rest of the team stayed upright, but the Tour of the DMZ was horribly run and dangerous throughout. My teammates and I agreed that even if a race was willing to pay for us to participate, it might be worth a little more research to determine if it was worth the trip. "In fact," I pointed out, "if a girl offered to write me a check to take her on a date, I'd be less likely to go out with her." We hoped that Thompson wouldn't put us in that position again. My biggest regret was that I couldn't find a metal plate while I was there. It had been a lifelong dream to put a plain dinner plate from Vietnam or Korea on my mantelpiece, so that when someone asked me about it, I could say, "I got that metal plate in Korea," and then gaze off into the distance.

STOP AND SMELL THE PISTACHIOS

I finished the 2010 season with 67 race days under my belt and took a few weeks off at home in Maryland, working on my business and taking long naps. When I started riding again, I'd almost forgotten how. It's amazing how alien riding can be after even a short break. It felt like I was riding someone else's bike, or that I'd put it back together from the trip with all the spacers and measurements off. After a few minutes, though, sensations were back to normal, the bike was once again an extension of myself, and I could feel that I was recovered from the long season.

My first ride took me over two swinging rope bridges crossing the Patapsco River and through the horse farms just west of Baltimore. I saw a racehorse urinating in a grassy field. He pissed like a . . . he pissed a lot. The ride ended with a pistachio muffin at my favorite coffee shop. With a two-year contract signed and sealed, I watched trout jumping in the river and enjoyed the crunch of colorful leaves under my wheels.

6

HOLD IT DOWN

═══

At the end of the season, coach Colby and I would look over the files from my power meter to review my training as a whole and set goals for the next year. All I remember from that conversation was that according to the computer, I had coasted for over 30 hours in 2010.

That winter, Colby had me add plyometrics to my training, alternating core and yoga exercises with lunges, squats (with no weight), and various jumps. He recommended that I do these in a park, on grass. Public displays of yoga might be okay in Boulder where he lived, but in Baltimore, I found myself looking over my shoulder during the "boat position," to make sure no one was coming up to shoot me. I survived, though, going through the routine of lunges, jumps, and sit-ups in various snow-covered parks. I wore a baggy hoodie, thinking no one would mess with me if I looked like Rocky.

The workout finished with picnic table jumps. The first time I looked at a picnic table in this context, I wasn't sure whether I could make it to the top, but I planted my feet, took a deep breath, and barely got there.

I did 10 picnic table jumps that day and added two more in each workout, with no issues until the final week, when I'd built up to 30. I'd grown cocky in my jumping, and I was going faster now (up-down-up-down-up-down), not taking the time to set my feet, breathe, and prepare for each jump like I should have. On number 28, my toes slipped off, and my shins scraped down the edge of the cement table. I dragged myself back to the car, leaving a trail of blood in the snow.

Despite the gash on my shins, I liked having new workouts where I could see fast and consistent improvement. On the bike, I'm lucky to improve 3 percent on my power output in a year. In the gym, I might struggle with 180 pounds on the leg press at first, but I'll throw around 1,000 pounds 10 weeks later. When the steroid-fueled body-builders stood up, this skinny guy told them to leave all the plates on, and then added a few of his own.

My company had built a respectable line of clothing, including some funny jerseys for recreational riders. We designed a LIVECLEAN jersey, a spoof of Lance Armstrong's cancer foundation that played off its colors and fonts, but after a few "cease and desist" letters from Livestrong's lawyers we took the jersey off the web site so they wouldn't sue us for "brand dilution." In case you were wondering where that yellow bracelet money went.

I'd worked my way back into the UCI's drug testing pool, so my girlfriend and I often awoke to the sound of USADA pounding at the door. I didn't like the 6 a.m. part, but it was good to learn the process. The test kits arrived wrapped and sealed in foam and plastic. I opened them myself while under supervision, to confirm that there hadn't been any tampering or contamination. Then I signed some forms, inspected the bottles, and matched codes on the bottles to codes on the sheet and packaging, to prevent a mix-up. Next, I'd go to the bathroom and let a stranger watch me pee into a cup, and it's not like I could put my back to him: He had to watch it come out, and he stared. Once the cup was full I'd pour the contents into the two sample bottles with locking lids, seal up the packaging, and be glad that my girlfriend had a sense of humor about my ridiculous job. It's not easy paying the penalty for the crimes of others.

The samples were probably then shipped to France or Switzerland, where they were thrown around at random and all the labels mixed up. At least that's what I hear. When the results came back, I joked that I'd tested positive for pluck, moxie, and grit.

It was strange settling into domestic life after all that time on the road, but my girlfriend and I always got along. She told me about a coworker named Drew she didn't like, and I was on her side immediately. "I hate anyone whose name is a past-tense verb!"

"What other past-tense verb names do you know?" she asked.

Caught off guard, I couldn't think of one until days later when she was at work, so I sent her a message. "Claude. Total asshole." You know what just occurred to me? Doug.

STAY IN THE SOUTH

Winter in Baltimore was the first time I had to wear real gloves and a jacket, and I wasn't enjoying it. I couldn't find a way to keep my toes from going numb during a four-hour ride in 20 degrees, or my bottles from freezing shut, and it was hard to stay motivated when snow was falling. With no one to train with nearby, my best friend was a pig at a farm on a dirt road, a few miles west of the apartment. If I had any energy bars left at the end of a ride, I'd stop to see him.

All of his friends fled to the far side of the pen, but Snowball came up to the fence and ate from my hand. A photo of Snowball still sits on my mantle. It was hilarious how bad he smelled.

The first snow arrived on Thanksgiving, and it never quite melted as the air cooled down. With my Colorado-native coach's help, I came up with a routine: I'd get dressed for the cold, including outer layers, shoe covers, and jacket, and warm up for 15 minutes on the rollers inside, so I'd be hot when I went out. If the weather was particularly nasty, I would stop at a coffee shop or gas station to thaw, and when I got home, I'd do another 15 minutes on the rollers, riding no-handed as I threw off all the layers. Every day ended with me sweating in the living room, with a pile of jackets, warmers, and gloves forming a puddle of sweat and melted snow.

Some days were so miserable outside that I would have to do my entire ride on the rollers, but nothing could be more mentally taxing than a long ride literally going nowhere, just watching television. All I could do was count down the minutes until I'd be finished. Two minutes into a four-hour ride, I would think "I'm 1/120th done with this ride. Just have to do this 119 more times." I got pretty good at fractions that winter.

Riding a bike as a job is supposed to be awesome. If someone offered you a contract that required you to ride a Jet Ski every day, you'd be ecstatic at first, but eventually you'd have a day where you went out, saw it floating there, rolled your eyes, and wished you could go back inside.

After Christmas, I'd made it through a month of days in the 20s or colder, and many hours inside on the rollers. When the weather wasn't impossible, I rode around alone between the dirty snowbanks while my girlfriend was at school. Meanwhile, my father's test results hinted that his cancer might be coming back. It was all I could think about on the bike. On January 2, I did my usual warm-up inside, then headed out to the street hoping to get in a few hours of training before the forecasted blizzard arrived. I was already worrying about my dad, and I could tell it was going to be a difficult day. My motivation ran out before I made it to the end of the parking lot, and I turned around to go back in. Two hours later, I'd packed up the car and was heading south on I-95. My girlfriend was disappointed to see me go, but after watching me sweat on the rollers for weeks, she understood that I couldn't chase my dream and live in Baltimore. I thought I was just leaving temporarily, but she had a few years left on her graduate school program; over the next few months we realized that we weren't going to work out, and said our good-byes.

HOLD IT DOWN

The blizzard came sooner than forecasted, so it wasn't safe to drive over 30 miles an hour, even on the interstate. Slush from my skidding rear wheels sprayed onto the side of my bike rack, forming 2-foot-long icicles. I made it out of the storm and into Florence, South Carolina, that night to hunker down at another cheap motel. After I checked in, I walked across the street to a busy gas station for a snack.

The man in front of me in the line was wearing baggy jeans, work boots, and a do-rag. He looked at me and whispered conspiratorially.

"Hey man. You know, you can run a car, just like normal, on cooking oil instead of gasoline?"

I don't know much about cars, but this didn't sound right. "Really?"

"Yeah! I was watching this thing on Discovery last night, called, 'What if there was no more oil?' And they said you could put it right in the gas tank, and it runs the same."

"What does cooking oil cost?"

"Less than gasoline!" He laughed. "Damn. They shouldn't have told me that."

I liked this guy. It was nice to interact with someone new. People don't talk to strangers outside of the South, and I'd missed it, so I kept him going with a conspiracy of my own. "I heard that after World War II, General Motors got together with tire and oil companies, bought up train systems all over the country, and then closed them down so they wouldn't have the competition." That's true. They were accused of conspiracy to monopolize interstate commerce in 1949.

"Shit, I believe that, man. I believe that!" said my new friend, his voice jumping several octaves as he approached the cashier. "And Obama a puppet!" he yelled. Everyone stared at him, and then at me.

As he paid for his pack of Newports a few feet away, my mind started buzzing. I knew he'd want to say good-bye, but I wanted to sound cool, and I didn't know how cool people said good-bye these days. I didn't want to say "Later," because of course I wouldn't ever see him again.

I was starting to panic when he turned around and came to my rescue. "Hey, man, hold it down," he said. "Hold it down."

I told him I would, and I meant it. I needed that advice.

The hotel that night was a new low (definitely not a good start on "holding it down"). I learned that there's a type of prostitute called a "lot lizard." They roam motels and gas stations to do business with lonely truckers, and they're scary as hell. I paid $60/night for a queen bed in room 116 with a mattress wrapped in plastic. Police cruised the parking lot, checking between all the 18-wheelers to keep an eye out for unsavory characters, but it was the paper-thin walls that ruined my night. First, I heard sex noises in room 117, which was entertaining until I realized that both voices were male.

Later, I could hear the guy in 115 snoring, and the noise was keeping me awake. I finally called his room to wake him up with the ring, then quickly slammed the phone and fell asleep before the snores resumed. I awoke at 6 a.m. when the trucks started firing up, and joined them on the road for an early start.

Back in my collegiate racing days we would book the cheapest room within 20 miles of the race, cramming it full of people and bikes so we could split the $40 cost seven ways, and no one ever complained. I'd gotten too old for that.

A WIN IS A WIN

When I arrived in Florida, the housing situation was only slightly improved. I settled in at the home of my friend Ryan, who was staying with his girlfriend nearby because her house had central heating. It was cold (even in Florida) that week, with lows in the 20s and highs in the 40s, and Ryan's house was on a raised foundation, with gaps between the floorboards big enough to see the ground beneath, so the temperature inside was the same as the temperature outside. I carried a space heater when I was there, hugging it tightly to my chest. Ryan was so cheap that he even set the refrigerator on the warmest setting to save electricity. It took me a few days (and one spoiled gallon of milk) to realize that the temperature outside the fridge was colder than it was inside. I called Ryan and told him to stop being such a cheap asshole.

Still, with no snow and plenty of friends to train with, life was better in Florida, and my dad turned out to be cancer-free after all. Worries about my fitness from all that miserable time in the cold were squashed when I won the first local races, with the help of David Guttenplan.

The Gutt and I
on the podium.

We hugged after another one-two finish, but then he ruined it.

"It's sort of pathetic how great it feels to win another podunk race for the fifth year in a row," David said. He was right. Whatever chemicals the brain produces for a victory couldn't tell the Swamp Classic from the Tour of California. When someone posted a picture of one of my wins on the Internet, one of my teammates pointed out that the only spectators were garbage cans on the curb.

GET EVERYTHING IN WRITING

When I arrived at training camp in February, pro cycling was abuzz with the demise of the much-anticipated Pegasus team. Kenda picked up Ben Day in the aftermath. It seemed like every year there was another story like this. Rock Racing was the most glorious example in the United States. It signed big names, got tons of press, and then blew sky-high with financial woes and a doping scandal. The team folded after 18 months. Some of its riders were never taken to races, others didn't get clothing or bikes, and paychecks were lost in the mail. Pegasus was a similar situation on a larger scale, leaving some of the best riders in the world to scramble for teams at the last minute.

When you're talking contracts with a new team, it's hard to know if you can trust the manager. You're afraid to offend a potential employer, but the sponsorship situation had gotten so bad that a rider at any level had to ask those questions: "Hey guy who just offered me a lot of money to ride a bike, do you actually have that money? Are your sponsors just promises, or are contracts signed? Is there real money? Is it in a real bank? Are you a crazy person?"

I wasn't happy with Ben's signing at first. He was a top climber and a GC rider at Fly V, and having him on our team meant that I'd probably find myself in a support role just when I finally thought I might have been ready to lead. I wanted to hate him for stealing my thunder, but Ben was my roommate at camp and he never complained about the crappy hotel room, the disorganized rides, or the teammates who didn't take their training and recovery as seriously as they could have. He showed me some stretches, talked about training, and seemed enthusiastic about growing our team and working with what he had. We were Ben's best option, and even though his pay was probably a fraction of what Pegasus had promised him, he was prepared to make the best of it. It was obvious that I could probably learn a lot from him.

I got along well with Ben. I'd always enjoyed the Australian sense of humor (Australians are a beautifully vulgar breed). Every time I handed him something, I'd say, "Here's your knife" and he'd oblige with a Crocodile Dundee reenactment. "That's not a noif!" Priceless.

Ben's arrival had a big influence on the team's schedule. Since he'd won San Dimas, Redlands, and Beauce in the past, I was thankful that we wouldn't be skipping those again for the Tour of Taiwan or Nature Valley Grand Prix. I probably wouldn't be the team leader, but at least I'd be at the right events.

The biggest improvement from adding Ben to the roster was the snowballing effect it had on the team's budget. Now that we had a top-shelf GC rider, we were assured an entry for the Tour of California. All the sponsors kicked in a little extra since they were going to be on TV, and 5-Hour Energy came on board as a cosponsor. Our name became a mouthful—Kenda–5-Hour Energy Presented by Geargrinder—but our team was getting attention.

The new sponsor and team name were announced at a morning meeting, after which the guys went off for a ride while I stayed behind for a fit on my time trial bike. Because the fitting company was a team sponsor I was required to do it, but not required to actually listen. If the fitter had changed anything, I'd have argued and moved it back when he wasn't looking. We spent 15 minutes measuring my angles and watching me pedal on a monitor, and the results said I was perfect. I was proud to learn that while most guys took three sessions to get it right, I was the only rider that the fitting company's software didn't change at all. Or maybe the fitters had heard I was a stubborn bastard and decided not to waste their time on me.

After the fit, with the rest of the team still out training, I expected to go for a short ride by myself when Thompson came around the corner and invited me to join him for a spin. We talked about Ben, the other new riders, and the California invite, but I steered conversation to the budget, hoping to hear that it was now enough for my $5,000 raise, per our agreement when I'd signed in August. Pro cycling is a hard job, and I was getting sick of doing it for 15K.

"So is the budget over $400,000 now?"

"Oh yeah. Way over that. Way over," Thompson bragged. Our agreement on this was so plain and simple that I just assumed there was an automatic raise in my future. But you know what happens when you assume. First, people use the obnoxious cliché about making an "ass" out of "u" and "me." Then, you're disappointed.

"Great! So I get that raise. That's a huge relief."

"Well, no. See, we have Ben on the team now, and we'll need the extra money to do the Tour of Utah and Colorado."

I didn't know if I should laugh or cry. When he promised me the raise, I'd told Thompson that if the budget increased he'd want to do more races rather than compensate guys he already had, and he'd been insulted that I could accuse him of such disloyalty. Now, he was doing exactly as I predicted. How did I know my boss better than he did? Had he simply forgotten that conversation? Most important, how could I possibly stop being a pessimistic asshole if I was never wrong?

When we got back to the hotel, I sent a carefully worded e-mail to Thompson and his father, Bruce, the team lawyer, reminding them of our agreement, and attaching a copy of it. Thompson saw my note, canceled the team meeting, and demanded to meet me in his hotel room.

The meeting didn't go well. I'd put my foot down, and it sank right into the ground. I sat on the bed as Thompson paced by the television. "You can't take something I said in innocent conversation and then use it against me to get a raise!" he explained. "Our ride today was not a contract negotiation!" Apparently I should have recognized that he was only informally bragging about ripping me off for $5,000, and it was wrong of me to absorb that information. He really seemed sad at first. How could I be so inconsiderate?

I didn't say much, nervously defending each point as best I could. I'd never dealt with Bruce, and I assumed they'd be teaming up against me, but he mostly tried to calm his son down. "Now hang on. Phil didn't say that in the e-mail," Bruce interjected several times, much to my relief. I don't know what I could have done without him. Still, despite Bruce's best efforts, sadness turned to anger, and Thompson stood over me where I sat, yelling into my face like I was a little boy. His main point was that I wasn't worth $20,000, and I was an ungrateful ass to expect such a lofty sum. What kind of spoiled princess needs that kind of cash, after all?

With all the yelling, I feared that I was about to get fired, and I was prepared to cave on the raise. Thanks to low self-esteem, I agreed that I wasn't worth $20,000, or I would have had that offer from someone else. Besides, $15,000 was more than I had contributed to sponsors, or society in general. Heck, if we based it that way, I should pay him money. I recognized that the budget was finite, and I wanted to do Utah more than anyone (I'd paid my own money to race there the previous year, after all). Still, an agreement is an agreement, so I wanted something. I would have happily settled for $2,500, or $5,000 added to my contract for the following year, or even a race bike to take home at the end of the season. If Thompson had offered any small bonus or gesture to make me feel better, I'd have shaken his hand and accepted, just to make the screaming stop. But then he threw me a curveball.

"So you'll get your $5,000 raise, and it'll be reflected in your next paycheck!" Thompson screamed. "And if you tell anyone on the team about this, you're done!" He slammed the door and stormed into the hallway. I sat on the bed for a while. My heart was pounding, my shirt soaked with a mixture of sweat and Thompson's spit.

I walked out to the hotel parking lot as guys were piling into the van to get dinner. They wanted me to join them, but I took a walk through the orange groves to clear my head. I thought about how well that conversation could have gone. He could have just said, "Yes, here's your raise. You're worth it, and we're happy to have you." Thompson would have won my undying loyalty if he'd given me the end result without the verbal onslaught, but he beat me down until I was willing to compromise or even forfeit, and then gave me 100 percent of what I'd asked for. It might have been one of the most pathetic negotiations in the history of mankind.

I eventually learned that a lot of other riders on the team had been promised the same raise, but as far as I know I was the only one who got it. I didn't feel great about that. Every team contract I've heard of states that riders can't tell anyone what they make, and somehow that conspiracy always holds. We're afraid of being punished, but also ashamed of how little we work for. If everyone gets 25 percent less than they think they're worth, it's not hard to keep quiet about it, but long-term, the secrecy only hurts everyone because no one knows what he can ask for. I've always made it a point to talk about contracts during the season with a few riders I trust on each team; it gives me somewhere to start in negotiations, as well as an idea of whether a handshake from the boss will be good enough for little things, like keeping a bike at the end of the year, or if everything needs to be chiseled into granite and handed down from Mount Sinai.

Best team photo ever. *From left*: Chris Monteleone (who was shy, apparently), Bobby Sweeting, Spencer Gaddy, Ben Day, Pat Lemieux, Gregg Brandt, Chad Hartley, me, and Luca Damiani.

SAVOR YOUR MALE BONDING AND PROTECT YOUR TESTICLES

Thompson and I avoided each other for most of the year, which made it easier to enjoy my time with the guys at camp. After a few months cooped up at home with wives or girlfriends, we were all itching for dick jokes and male bonding. The team took photos for the web site on an abandoned construction site (camp was in central Florida at the beginning of the mortgage crisis, so the area was filled with ruins, not unlike ancient Rome). The next day, we rode back to the same spot and took our own pictures, this time with our genitals out, and slipped it into the photographer's slideshow. Someday, I'll frame that photo and put it on the wall.

JUST BECAUSE YOU WON IT ONCE DOESN'T MEAN YOU CAN DO IT AGAIN

Kenda brought a strong team to California for San Dimas and Red-lands. I knew my only hope to lead was to beat Ben in the uphill prologues, and I thought I had a decent chance. It was two years since I'd finished sixth in the time trial and second overall at San Dimas, and my legs had felt better than ever in Florida.

It's a funny thing when you're used to improving year to year. You assume that you'll finish a few spots higher just by virtue of being older, but it doesn't work out that way at every race. I was just coming off the Tour of California the last time I'd raced San Dimas. No amount of training or racing in Florida could compete with the fit-ness I got from that. This time around I finished ninth in the San Dimas prologue, five seconds slower than the last time, and Ben won.

We defended Ben's lead without any issues that weekend. With five laps to go in the crit, the Jamis team took over the front of the race to lead out their sprinter, and we started to fade back, job done. I coasted out of the top 10, where all the sprinters were fighting in the closing laps. Someone got pushed into the barriers in front of me, and I had to skid and put a foot down to avoid the resulting pileup, safely coming to a stop between fallen riders. The rest of the field buzzed past, and the victims stood up, dusted themselves off, and watched the race ride away. It was too late for free laps, so we all knew we were done. Everyone looked around, trying to decide if there was someone to blame.

"It's alright, guys! I'm okay!" I yelled, sarcastically. "Everyone can relax. I'm not hurt at all." The goal was to break the tension, and even the guys with road rash laughed as they exited the course, but one of the sprinters was not amused.

"Shut the fuck up, Phil!" he yelled, veins throbbing. A lot of guys had been waiting the whole weekend for that field sprint. This sprinter wasn't hurt, but he was understandably angry finding himself on the ground instead of the podium.

"Sorry, dude. Just trying to lighten the mood, you know?"

"Well this is no time to try to lighten the mood, when people are crashed and pissed off."

When people are mad, I think that's exactly the time to try to lighten the mood.

That night, the team celebrated our first-ever GC victory at a Japanese restaurant. The team paid for the food (the first time I'd ever had a meal on the team), but champagne wasn't in the budget. Ben paid for that out of his pocket.

ALWAYS CARRY A SHOVEL

With San Dimas behind us, I was excited for my first crack at Redlands with a team, and I didn't want to mess up another opportunity at a stage race that suited my abilities so well. The opening time trial was always the most critical stage; it mixed steep and gradual climbing with short downhills and corners. Choosing the right equipment and getting my pacing correct during the race was always complicated. How hard do you go on the first kicker? How much do you save on the climb up to the highway? Do you bother trying to recover on the short flat stretch to save energy for the steep finale? Do you want a disc wheel or regular race wheels?

Ben had won the stage twice, so I asked him for advice. Opening a handwritten notebook, he looked up what gearing was on his rear wheel in previous years, where he'd used his little ring, and where he'd stood up to get to speed, walking me through it, meter by meter.

Apart from e-mails providing my coach with race reports, I had no such records of previous races. This was what it took to be a winner. My training log got a lot more detailed after seeing Ben's, and it sure was nice of him to give me all that advice. I repaid his generosity by riding really slowly and finishing 19th. Imagine what would have happened if I didn't have that insider info.

The highlight of my Redlands experience was sharing a room with Luca Damiani. He usually rode criteriums, so I'd never spent much time with my Italian teammate, and it was good to finally get to know him. Luca was a funny guy to begin with, but his accent and the occasional misused word made it even better. When I arrived, I put my bag down by the bed and then headed to the bathroom. Luca stopped me in my tracks with a stern warning: "Listen. When you roommate with me, you flush, everything!" Luca must have roomed with someone who didn't flush the toilet after they peed. I made sure to leave a good shit in there for him every day.

Luca was from a rural part of Italy, up north in the mountains. Jim Stemper, Roman Kilun, and I gathered around the breakfast table to hear a story from his youth.

"In Italy, we would raise lots of animals. We had one, how you say," Luca paused, looking at the ceiling as he grasped for the word.

Jim tried to help him out. "A cow?"

Luca shook his head.

"Sheep?" offered Roman.

"No, no, no. It has the horns."

"A goat!" I was sure I had it, but Luca's head was still shaking.

"No! The horns go like this," Luca twirled his fingers around his ears.

"Ohhh. A ram!" Teamwork.

"Yes! A ram!" Luca pointed at me, raising his eyebrows, like a schoolteacher commending a student. "We had a ram. And all he want to do is run at you."

"WHOA. He would try to ram you? What did you do?" Jim asked, flabbergasted.

"At last moment, you step aside, and you hit him as hard as you can, with a —." Luca gestured a hard swinging motion to help us guess the weapon, and so began a macabre form of charades.

"Holy shit! A baseball bat?"

"No, no, no," Luca was staring at the ceiling again, repeating a swinging motion, now lower to the ground. The rest of us looked at each other, wondering if we wanted to know more.

"A golf club?"

"A sledgehammer?"

"An ax?"

"No! You use it to dig," Luca gestured again.

"A SHOVEL?" We all guessed at the same time, horrified, preparing to call PETA. "You hit him with a shovel?"

"Yes! Shovel!"

"Well, what did he do after that? Did it kill him?"

"No, no! He love it! He come back to do again! Is a game for ram," Luca explained, laughing.

So it wasn't cruel after all, and now we'd learned something. I've always appreciated bike racing for putting different kinds of people together. I'd never have met anyone like Luca otherwise.

YOU MIGHT AS WELL TOSS UP BOTH MIDDLE FINGERS

I was on early break duty the next day in the 120-mile Beaumont road race, and had no trouble getting a move established with four other riders. I won the KOMs and the field gave us a long leash, so we never had to work too hard. Getting caught was inevitable, and we didn't want to kill ourselves in the heat.

With 30 miles to go, our break still had nearly three minutes, but the gap was coming down, and the officials informed us that one rider from another team was bridging, two and a half minutes behind. I didn't recognize the name, but none of us wanted another rider in the break, so we ramped up the pace. When officials came up to give another update, we expected him to be back in the field, but instead he'd gotten a full minute closer.

No matter how hard we pushed, the gap kept coming down. The rider joined us with 15 miles left in the stage, and then he went immediately to the front for a long pull. My computer said it was 109 degrees, and this guy was wearing arm warmers. We started going 5 mph faster, and two of my break mates were soon dropped.

Matt Koschara had once told me that arm warmers are good not just for warming arms but also for covering needle marks. I thought that I might be witnessing an enhanced performance, so when he flicked his elbow and looked back, asking me to pull, I was riding no-handed, with both middle fingers in the air. I gave him a big smile and said, "Fuck you!" He went harder and dropped me on the next hill. After the stage, I heard that someone found an empty medical blood bag in one of the port-a-potties, but that rumor was never confirmed. I suppose it's not fair to think someone's doping purely because he's better than you. You want to trust your instincts, but the truth is that you just don't know.

The team was out of the GC after the Beaumont stage. My KOM jersey gave Kenda a consolation prize to work for, but I lost it by one point on the last climb on the Sunset stage, so the team went home empty-handed.

Francisco Mancebo won the overall. He'd been top five in the Tour de France, national champion of Spain, and had a very strong career, but he hadn't gotten any good jobs in Europe after he was pulled before the start of the 2006 Tour de France just as the Operación Puerto doping scandal exploded. The reports at the time said that he had suddenly decided to retire from racing, but after a couple years off, he crossed the Atlantic to beat up on the NRC. Mancebo claimed he had neither retired nor unretired from racing. It was a puzzling story: A guy named in the Operación Puerto report suddenly leaves the sport and then two years later shows up in America. But how he got here wasn't the issue anymore. I just had to figure out how to beat him.

REFLECT

I replayed the whole stage race in my head on the flight home. I'd worn the KOM jersey for three days, finally on the verge of achieving something at an NRC race. Redlands had beaten me down every time, but I knew what I needed to work on, and I couldn't wait for another shot at it. I was Luca's ram.

ULTIMATELY, YOU'RE RESPONSIBLE FOR YOUR OWN RESULTS

At Gila, the team put us back at the gym disaster relief housing. Ben and Shawn Milne had heard enough to get their own hotel room down the street. Ben also showed up with his own time trial bike, a Scott Plasma. It looked a lot faster than our knockoff Taiwanese rigs.

Some of the guys were a little turned-off that Ben was staying in a hotel instead of with us at the gym, and I'm sure our sponsors and management weren't too happy about that new bike. I'd always done my best with what I was given, but on this team that often meant going down with the ship. Ben knew that if he wanted a better contract next year, he couldn't do it with what Kenda was providing him, so he had to make it happen on his own—even if that meant a little headache and spending his own money. His was a winner's attitude, and I needed to learn it.

Ben worked his way into second overall thanks to a strong TT on that new bike, but he couldn't stay with the climbers on the last day, leaving the team once again with no result overall. Adding insult to injury (or vice versa), after the race ended we stayed at the gym for three more days. The idea was to give us an extended training block as final prep for the Tour of California, but the effect was to completely kill our motivation and morale, especially since everyone else had fled toward lower altitudes and less humidity. After five days of racing at our limits, we didn't have much energy to train, but we did our best, riding five to six hours that Monday and Tuesday, with lots of climbing and motorpacing drills behind Frankie in the car. On the final day, we couldn't take it anymore, so we convinced Frankie to ride with us. We dropped him on the first climb and rode back across the continental divide into town, where we sat at the only coffee shop in Silver City all afternoon. My teammates and I hid our bikes around the side, and sure enough, we had to duck when the team van cruised by, with a soigneur peering through the windows to make sure we were still out riding.

Before we left Silver City we did get the wireless Internet to work for long enough to see Luca and our team's crit squad win the Athens Twilight Criterium. Seated on camp chairs, we gathered around the screen in the gym kitchen, getting goose bumps while Luca, Chad Hartley, Pat, and Isaac Howe were mobbed by the crowd of drunk spectators in downtown Athens. We stage racers weren't quite holding up our end of the bargain, but their success made it easier to swallow.

GRASP YOUR MILK TIGHTLY

The Tour of California a week later was my first time in Tahoe, and my first thought was that it was just as beautiful as Qinghai Lakes. If you live in California, there's no need to ever get on a plane for a vacation. You've got it all.

We took a ride around the lake enjoying the scenery until Chris Horner came by us doing intervals to open his legs up for the first stage. He passed me so fast, I was sure he must have been holding onto a car. No amount of motorpacing we did in New Mexico was going to prepare us for this.

That night was the team presentation, where we dressed in track suits like a boy band (or in team Jelly Belly's case, like extras from *Willy Wonka and the Chocolate Factory*) to be introduced to a room of VIPs. Backstage, we got to chat with other riders, and Luca was doing this great joke, where he plays up his Italian accent and asks for translation help. I got him to try it on Jeremy Powers.

"Jeremy. I need ask you somefing."

Jeremy knew Luca from cyclocross. "Sure, Luca. What's up?"

"What is . . . blowjob?"

Jeremy looked around, uncomfortable, not sure how to answer. "Luca, I uhh, you uhh, you don't know what a blowjob is?"

"Last night, Chad Hartley say, 'Luca, I want you . . . come on my face.' What is he mean by this? I don't understand why he tell that to me."

I watched from the other side of the room, in tears.

Heavy snow came down that night in Tahoe. The stage was canceled at the last moment (they let us all get carb-loaded at breakfast and stand in the snow at the start for half an hour). We went for a short ride just to get our legs moving, and then hopped into the cars and turned the heat on. Some of the other teams had similar ideas but better execution. RadioShack went a little farther up the same road, and must have had lunch ready for them when they stopped. As we rattled along in the right lane toward the next hotel in our rented, weekend-getaway-sized RV, the "Shack" team passed on our left. Our cramped seating area darkened from the shadow they cast, and all we could see out of the windows was a solid, glossy black, like a massive space ship in *Star Wars*.

The new lodgings were at the other side of Lake Tahoe, where the stage would have finished. We showered and changed, then ransacked the buffet (it had been seven hours since we'd eaten). Before we left, I ordered some skim milk in a to-go cup to complement the cookie I'd brought in my bag. Luca thought it was coffee, and since we had coffee in the room, he slapped it out of my hand in the street, like he was forcing me to fumble a football. Luca felt horrible when he saw the white liquid in the street and realized his mistake. My day was ruined. Cookies are worthless without milk.

PUT ON A GOOD SHOW

Ben Day started with GC aspirations, but Frankie had reasonable expectations for the rest of us, emphasizing opportunism for the team and putting on a good show to prove we deserved the invite. My previous Tour of California was the first time I'd ever found it difficult to hold a wheel in front of me, just sitting in the pack on a flat road. Two years later I was fine in the group most of the day, and I didn't have any trouble until the speed ramped up with 5 km to go. Ouch, but progress!

Jim Stemper was rooming with Chad Hartley that week. Hartley is lactose intolerant, but he's still tempted to eat cheese from time to time. Jim and Hartley had been traveling to races together in vans for a long time, and Jim was well familiar with the smells that resulted from Hartley's cheese consumption. Our vile sprinter would smile as he sprinkled parmesan on his pasta, and it took all of Jim's self-control to keep from diving across the table and tackling the plate to the floor.

One thing I liked about the Tour of California was getting to be an underdog. It's much easier than trying to win, and it's more fun. Since our goal was to animate the race, no one had a problem with me attacking from the gun in stage 3. As soon as the red "neutral" flag came down, I was off. Five guys followed me, and that was the break of the day.

It was my first time in a long breakaway at a race of that caliber, and I was in over my head from the beginning. Four hours into the stage, I'd burned over 5,000 calories, equivalent to the hard six-hour training rides I'd been doing at home, and I hadn't eaten nearly enough to maintain it. I drank a Coke and ate an energy bar, but it was too little, too late. Out of gas, I went back to the field, the first of the breakaway to get swallowed up.

The team was low-budget as always, but we did our best to fake it for the biggest event of the year. When the race was over, food and drink were waiting for us in the RV. At the hotel, we were handed our room keys and the bags were already waiting by our beds, along with a room list and massage schedule. The hotels were provided by the race, so instead of the usual host housing or La Quinta with the leaf-filled swimming pool, we stayed in Doubletrees, with long, uniform hallways just begging for a Scooby-Doo chase scene.

Every night, Jim would unpack his suitcase into the hotel drawers, only to pack it all into his bag again each morning.

"Why do you do that?" I asked. "Isn't that a waste of time?"

"Hotels are the only place I have drawers," he admitted. Jim had been staying in unfurnished apartments and crashing on friends' sofas for a long time.

The morning after the breakaway, I woke up feeling like I'd been sadistically beaten. The rain hadn't let up since we left Tahoe, but the sun finally came out 20 km into the stage to cheers from the peloton, which then resumed beating the crap out of each other. Making the early break on the first stage would have meant the end of my stage race two years before, but now I was able to recover and finish in the group without a problem.

We coasted back down the hill to where the RV was parked. Bruce Thompson was helping out for the week, not in his legal role but as a bus driver. As we ate our sandwiches, he steered us toward the hotel and hit an old Datsun hatchback on the way through the parking lot. It was a low-speed collision, so he didn't damage anything, but we all watched, eyes wide but unable to protest with our mouths full of sandwich, as the car moved three or four feet into another parking spot. Bruce looked straight ahead, oblivious, listening to something on his headphones (we guessed the Rat Pack). Bruce had been driving the RV alone all week, and we wondered how many babies he might have run over. With his bald head and thick, black-rimmed glasses, he looked like Mr. Magoo.

WHEN A TEAMMATE ASKS FOR WATER, BE PROMPT AND POLITE

One of the longer, more boring stages of the ToC wound through strawberry fields for hours. Just when I thought I hated my life, we passed a crowd of laborers taking their lunch break on the tailgate of a pickup truck. "That's what I'd be doing if I couldn't sprint," said Luca.

With 60 km remaining that day, Roman asked me to go to the car for more water. Drifting to the back of the field, I noticed that I had a flat tire, which was perfect timing since I was going back anyway. When the team car pulled over, I was surprised to see Thompson step out instead of Frankie. He'd been following in the second car in the caravan all week, with Frankie in the first one tending to the riders. Thompson and "car two" were more of a backup if we got a guy into the breakaway (and that was a big "if"). "Where's Frankie?" I asked, as the mechanic changed my rear wheel. I probably displayed a little more concern than I should have.

"He's at the back of the caravan today. You guys took all of Frankie's bottles, so we swapped," Thompson said, nonchalantly.

My boss wasn't very experienced at motorpacing or driving in a caravan, and trying to stay with his car as we chased back sapped my energy on the hills and had me braking on the descents. Normally, it would only take a minute or two to get back to the field with a new wheel, but after 15 km on Thompson's bumper, Bobby Julich, who was driving a car for Saxo Bank, felt bad and came back to help. I jumped in behind him and was back in the field in no time.

I still hadn't grabbed the water that Roman had asked for. It was hot, and everyone probably needed more to drink by then. The course had taken us to the Pacific Coast Highway north of Santa Barbara, with the ocean to our right and a salty smell in the wind. I asked the officials to call Kenda's team car up to the front for feeds.

Thompson was insulted that I'd abandoned him and followed another car. "What?" he asked.

"I'm sure everybody needs water. Might as well get bottles while I'm back here."

He nervously reached into the cooler, eyes on the road as he handed me the first bottle he grabbed. It was filled with endurance mix, not water, and after 200 km our stomachs wouldn't have handled it very well. I put it in my pocket anyway, thinking maybe one of the guys wouldn't be picky. "Let me have water now."

Still scared to take his eyes off the road, he handed me another mix.

"Do you have any water?" A can of Coke came next.

"Water," I pleaded.

Thompson continued to hand me bottles of mix and Coke, until my jersey was filled with drinks that no one would want.

"Water!" I said as I put my hand out for the fifth time, starting to lose patience.

When I looked down, my hand was filled with sample bottles of 5-Hour Energy, our new sponsor. I took one look, transferred them to my left hand, and hurled them over the car and into the Pacific.

"FUCKING WATER!" I yelled.

The mechanic had been watching in silence. He leaned forward from the back seat, dug through the cooler, and passed up some water. I pushed off of the driver's side mirror and back into the field.

As I worked my way up to Roman, I saw the "30 km to go" sign. I'd been in the cars for 45 minutes.

"Where have you been?" demanded a thirsty Roman, as I handed him a bottle.

"FUCK YOU, DUDE!" I screamed at the top of my lungs. Everyone heard it. Peter Sagan looked over and smirked at us. I apologized later. He had no idea what I'd been through.

On the way to the hotel, Hartley pointed out a new Volkswagen hatchback that had passed our poor little RV, and the guys were debating its pros and cons. "It has great gas mileage," Shawn said.

Roman didn't like Volkswagen's new offering. "No, it doesn't. That thing gets crap mileage."

Shawn took out an iPhone to make his case. "Look! It gets 31 miles per gallon."

It looked like Shawn had him cornered, but Roman didn't miss a beat. "Thirty-one isn't good mileage for a car that size." Before he started racing professionally, Roman went to law school at Berkeley and passed the bar exam in California. He couldn't help toying with us. Shawn was raised in Massachusetts by a lobster fisherman.

The debate started to turn to car size and reasonable fuel efficiencies. I had no dog in the fight, but we all had to gang up on Roman in these cases, or we'd never stand a chance. "He's reframing the argument, Shawn!" I pointed out, proud I'd caught one of his fancy lawyer tricks. "Don't let him get away with it!"

Roman was in no rush to actually practice law, but he kept his skills sharp with his teammates. There was no talking to him without arguing, and no arguing without losing, but it was a fun game to play. If someone said "Roman, your cock is so long and wide," he'd have said something like, "Well, wide is a relative term."

My teammates weren't making the breaks or even cracking the top 20, but there was no one I'd rather be stuck with in traffic on the 405.

IF THE RAPTURE COMES, MOUNT BALDY IS THE WRONG PLACE TO BE

The next day was the dreaded Mount Baldy stage, starting with the Glendora time trial course that we were all so familiar with from the San Dimas Stage Race. Appropriately, the date was May 21, predicted to be Judgment Day by various crackpot religious groups. The dinner-plate-sized granny gears on our wheels at the start seemed to agree, though.

I didn't impress anyone with power-to-weight ratios that day, but I made the select group over Glendora, and with 15 km to go I came out of the dwindling field a couple minutes after Johan van Summeren did. I'd just watched him win Paris-Roubaix a few weeks prior, so I figured that ought to be good enough.

TACO TRUCKS ARE GREAT FOR POST-RACE RECOVERY

My teammates arrived about 20 minutes later in a large group that was dropped on the first climb. They reported that Lars Boom, former cyclocross world champion, was with them all the way up the climb only to quit with 1 km to go, when he passed his parked team bus. Lars handed his sunglasses to a fan and took his DNF with only one short and flat stage left in the race.

The consensus was that for what Lars probably got paid, he could have at least finished the stage race, but to me, Lars's move was one of a true champion. Moreover, it put things in perspective. This was our biggest race of the year, so finishing the Tour of California was important to us, but for some of these guys it wasn't even worth one more kilometer.

When we got to the hotel by the Staples Center in downtown Los Angeles, we couldn't wait for the buffet to open, so Shawn and I went across the street and each bought a bag of chicken tacos from a truck. I was starving, and the average taco truck in Los Angeles beats the best Mexican restaurants in Georgia. Frankie caught us with the fast food, and I asked if Lance ever ate out of trucks when they were teammates on Motorola. He said no. I guess Lance just ate out of needles.

After a shower and massage, we sat down for second dinner at the buffet, and I finally noticed signs of fatigue among the European teams. More and more riders were lost in the hallways, trying to find their soigneurs' rooms or the race buffet. Each day, they came back from the salad bar with less lettuce on their plates, and more croutons, cheese, and dressing. So it wasn't just me who was hurting.

DON'T LET THE BASTARDS GET YOU DOWN

Our meeting for the last stage went about as you'd expect: Thompson telling us how horrible we'd been racing, that we needed to try harder, because obviously that was the problem, and vague threats about what would happen if we missed the early break again. I guess some guys are motivated by that sort of talk, but I never responded well to it. If I didn't get motivation from within, I wouldn't have been there in the first place. I think most of my teammates probably felt the same. We certainly weren't doing it for the money.

We missed the break. HTC set up a blockade to keep more riders from going across. I pushed and elbowed my way through, and then I started to attack, riding just 10 feet ahead of the group. A chorus of teasing and discouragement came from the riders at the front, reminding me that to go now would be an impolite breach of protocol. For a second, I gave in. I looked at the guys and waved, assuring them that it just looked like I was attacking but that I was only giving myself some room to pee. Then I changed my mind again and shifted down a few gears. When they rounded the next bend, I was gone. Fuck those guys.

I'd escaped the field, but the break was too far ahead by then. As they caught me after my failed bridge attempt, each HTC rider had something rude to say about my disrespectful breakaway, as though they hadn't already said it with their legs.

The domestic guys all appreciated my gesture. "Good for you, dude," Michael Creed applauded. Creed was known as one of the few Americans to go to Europe to ride for a big team, refuse the drugs, and get sent back to race domestically, which made him a personal hero. His approval was enough validation for me.

We started the last 8-mile finishing circuit in Thousand Oaks, and I found myself in the cars, unable to hold the speed of the lead-outs. I had my head down, struggling to fight back to the group when Frankie passed me.

"Relax, Phil," he said. "Just cruise in to the finish. Good job this week."

Frankie made a good point. Sometimes you just have to accept that your race is over, and you might as well look good for the crowds. I felt better for taking a breather, but I still went looking for the HTC guys to tell them all they were assholes, and possibly fight somebody. It was a blessing that I couldn't find their RV.

TEAMS CAN FALL INTO BAD PATTERNS

We had five days between leaving the Tour of California and starting national championships in Greenville (if you're not good with geography, that's the other side of the country entirely). With our failures out West, all the talk at the pre-race meeting for nationals was about making the break. I was told to save energy, to see if I could stay with the front group the last time over the climb. I wasn't optimistic.

The break went, and my teammates were all at the front, so I stuck my neck up like a giraffe. I was watching for someone to jump across before the gap stretched, but it never happened. Apparently everyone was either tired or racing for themselves again, so I had to do it myself.

I worked my way to the front and attacked, hoping to bridge the 15 seconds to Timmy Duggan (Garmin), Jason McCartney (RadioShack),

Jesse Anthony (Optum), and Brent Bookwalter (BMC). That 15-second gap took me 10 minutes to cross, and I was destroyed when I got there. We still had over 100 miles to go.

I struggled the next time up Paris Mountain, so I stopped working in the break. Jason McCartney didn't like having a passenger; he insisted that I take my pulls. There's an unspoken rivalry between the European and domestic teams, even among riders of the same nationality. We all feel a natural jealousy and bitterness anytime someone is better, more famous, or making more money, and it goes both ways. Just as a student from Harvard might look down on community college, riders on BMC or RadioShack would walk right by me in the hallway at a hotel: no eye contact, no smile. We considered them a bunch of stuck-up, rich, doping bullies; they'd probably call us bitter, no-talent, whiny losers. Anyway, I was in no mood to take shit from Jason McCartney.

"Sorry, dude. If I pull any more, I'm going to get dropped," I said. "I barely made it over that last climb. It's not like I'm saving it to attack you."

"What kind of a pro are you? Pros work in the break."

"Oh wait? What do pros do? Please explain how bike racing works." I started pedaling backward and swerving. "Wait! How do I do this? I push the left foot down first, and then the right foot?" And what do I do with this bent handle thing in the front?" Jesse Anthony was laughing.

Jason rolled his eyes. "Fuck you," he said.

I had a great comeback for that.

"Fuck *you*!" I said, emphasizing the "you" part, but then I kept going. "If you were any good, you'd be at the Giro right now."

From the look in his eyes, I knew I'd won the verbal battle, but then Jason won the war, dropping me on the next hill.

None of my teammates cracked the top 30. I was quiet at dinner that night, trying to keep from yelling at a few of them. As I boarded my plane for the flight back to Baltimore the next morning, I got a call from Frankie. "Thanks for being the only guy who always tries," he said. "I know the early break isn't what you wanted yesterday, but we're glad you did it." I needed that.

IT'S OKAY TO SKIP A WEEKEND

Most of the team—already cooked from California and nationals—went straight up to Philadelphia to race the Liberty Classic. I opted out and went home for a weekend off. Any time I feel like I'm not at my best, there are two instincts that I have to fight. First, I want to lose a couple pounds. Everyone remembers the least they've weighed in the past five years and obsessively tries to get back to that number. When your legs are good, though, the extra weight doesn't matter, and it's never worth all the stress. The second instinct is that I need to train more, but all that does is dig you into a deeper hole. I forced myself to stay on the couch while the guys tried to "race themselves into shape" in Philly. They mostly DNFed.

LEADERSHIP COMES TO THOSE WHO DESERVE IT (JUST BE READY)

The weekend off meant that my legs were fresh going into the Tour de Beauce. Beauce is a region of Quebec just north of the U.S. border. The team flew us to Vermont and drove the six hours up in the van instead of paying extra for international flights. A customs agent stopped us to ask a few questions at the border.

"Are you carrying cash over 10 grand?" he asked.

"I have a dollar," Jim told him. "But I left my credit card at the Olive Garden by the airport."

They let us go after that.

The start countdown at the Tour de Beauce was in French. I can count up to 10, but hearing it backward threw me off.

Halfway through, I looked over at Bobby Sweeting. "I lost count," I confessed.

"I'm just waiting for *trois*," he replied.

The first day, Ben and I made our way into a large breakaway, gaining 22 minutes on the group. Ben had won the last two editions of the stage race, so he was the undisputed team leader. With 10 km to go, he told me I should attack, to put pressure on Francisco Mancebo. I went for it, but when Mancebo caught me, Ben was barely hanging on. He lost 10 seconds that day, and I was down almost a minute.

Stage 3 was the decisive mountaintop stage. We all watched Mancebo, knowing he was going to drop us at some point, and then he dropped us, and we watched him (from a slight distance) win the stage and take yellow. It was only a 10-minute climb, but Ben lost several minutes. He said he was sick, but my guess was that he realized he didn't have the legs to win the stage race again, and it was mentally easier to pass leadership to me than it would have been to try to defend his position in the top five. I'm probably overanalyzing it, but I'd call it a generous move on Ben's part to give me that opportunity. Whatever it was, I became the team's only GC hope, down a minute thanks to the time I lost attacking on the first stage.

EQUIPMENT MATTERS

Stage 4 was a rolling out-and-back time trial. I hadn't had a good TT in years, and I'd always secretly blamed our crappy bikes, but ever since Ben boycotted our team frames at Gila, the floodgates had opened on nonsponsored gear. Bobby was working for Cannondale as an engineer, and he got Roman a deal, so they each showed up with brand new Slice time trial bikes. I faced a dilemma: I could borrow Roman's bike, which I'd never ridden before, or I could ride my team-provided machine, which I knew from experience had no chance of helping me get a good result.

I warmed up on my team bike, feeling awful and prepared for another placing in the 30s, which might have kept me in the top 15 overall. When Roman finished, I borrowed his bike and raised his saddle to match the height on my road bike, and went straight to the start line. I felt amazing from the first pedal stroke, and it never wore off. My cadence was high, and I gave it a little extra juice over the top of each hill. Frankie followed in the team car, with Roman shouting encouragement and time splits from the passenger's side.

I finished fourth, behind three Euro guys who weren't in the GC, and 10 seconds ahead of Mancebo (who'd won almost every time trial in the United States that year). I'd moved up to fifth overall. I wasn't sure how I did that on a bike I'd never touched before that day, but I told Bobby to order one for me. Lance says it's not about the bike, but I have a sneaking suspicion bikes are at least a small factor in bike races.

For the rest of the stage race, Ben was working for me. He was a huge help, but it wasn't quite enough to move up to the podium. I would have been second overall if I hadn't lost all that time the first day. It was still a good result, but the important part was that I'd shown my team that I could be a leader, and it wasn't even on purpose.

I'd barely crossed the finish line at Beauce and I was already looking forward to Cascade coming up two weeks later. I'd been down on myself after a mediocre early season, but it just takes one good day to start thinking: I got fourth in the time trial that time, so I can win the next one, and I'll never go back to being the guy who didn't TT in the top five. Makes sense, right?

BE CAREFUL WITH YOUR HEAD

Cascade was the first stage race as a pro for one of my teammates, a 23-year-old named Spencer, from North Carolina. A web site called Strava "sponsored" our team, organizing a program with Kenda that would let amateurs compete for the pro roster by entering a contest on the site and posting their rides. Strava shared the entry fee with the team, which Thompson expected to raise a significant portion of our budget that year. It was a failure, and the gains came out to a few thousand dollars.

Spencer was the "winner." For his victory, the team rewarded him by throwing Spencer into big races he wasn't prepared for yet, allowing him to put way too much pressure on himself to earn his keep. I knew what it was like to be in over my head, and it was tough to see a nice guy and a talented racer in that situation. I tried to watch out for him, but we didn't do a lot of the same races. Spencer also crashed a lot, much like I had in my first year as a pro.

Stage 1 at Cascade always starts with a bunch of skinny guys shivering at the top of a mountain, followed by 45 minutes of nervous downhill. Halfway to the bottom, someone got a flat and Spencer lost control trying to get around him, crashing onto his head at high speed. He was getting up as I passed, and he looked okay.

Spencer finished the stage, but that evening he announced that he wouldn't start the next day due to a concussion. I didn't say anything, but my initial reaction was that he was making a mistake. This was the last stage race of the year, and there was no way he'd come back to the team if he pulled out now. When I played soccer as a kid, we'd had plenty of head impacts and never treated it like a big deal. I recall a kid who hit his head and walked back to the wrong bench. We all pointed and laughed at him, and he played the next quarter.

That night I walked past the kitchen table at the host house and noticed the remnants of a Bananagrams game between Spencer and the son of the host family. Bananagrams is a fast-paced word game, and Spencer was a college graduate, but he'd lost to a 10-year-old. Upon closer inspection of Spencer's side of the table, a lot of the words in his grid weren't even words. That changed my mind: It didn't seem very important for him to finish the Cascade Classic anymore. Fortunately, he was fine in a few days.

I raced well, narrowly missing the win on both mountaintop stages, but 11th place in the time trial took me out of the running for an overall podium. Bobby rescued our team with a win on the last day and barely had enough time to pee in a cup and make his flight back to Connecticut. Bobby was a full-time engineer at Cannondale that year, and he had to work Monday morning. Between winning the stage and having a real job, he sort of made the rest of us look bad. Also, he stole my flip-flops.

DON'T FORGET TO HAVE FUN

My success at Beauce and Cascade caught the attention of some of the bigger teams, who started asking if I was signed for the next year. I had another year on my contract, but I asked Thompson for a raise, because why the hell not? He gave me the same speech he'd always given, about how he'd never paid himself, he was still putting his own money into the team, the economy is terrible, and I'm a greedy asshole. Soon after, he posted pictures on the Internet of his new Subaru STI, and construction that he was starting on his new deck with a built-in hot tub.

The following week, I flew to Boston with Brad Huff on an all-expense-paid trip for a charity ride that Jeremy Powers had organized called the Grand Fundo. Jeremy had been working his ass off for a long time, both on and off the bike, and he was considered the best American on the cyclocross circuit. In Jeremy's limited spare time, he had set up a foundation to support local road and 'cross riders. The more success Jeremy had, the more generous he became. I resolved to be like that, as soon as I was making enough money to live on.

It was good to get to know Brad Huff better that weekend. He'd gone out of his way to help me when we were teammates on Jelly Belly, but we hadn't spent much time together. He didn't turn professional until age 26 but became a top sprinter in a short time. He told me that he had a VO_2 test with a physiologist when he was 23 and scored terribly. She said he'd never be a pro, but he didn't quit. Years later, he went back the physiologist and told her about all his national championships.

"I don't understand how you did that," she said.

"I've got heart," Brad replied.

After the Fundo there was a barbecue complete with a spit-roasted pig. With the serious racing we do all year, it was good to be reminded what cycling is really about: having a good time, making people suffer on the bike, and eating pig. I'd wondered if the friends I'd made as a pro would compare to my amateur teams. With Jeremy and Brad, I had my answer.

THERE ARE TWO SIDES TO EVERY STORY, SOMETIMES MORE WHEN IT COMES TO DOPING

I flew back to Atlanta and drove straight to a new apartment in Athens. I'd moved my stuff in but hadn't unpacked.

Athens is a college town with a strong cycling scene, thanks to cheap living, good weather, and endless country roads. My new place was right down the street from Dan and Rebecca Larson's new house. They were working on their PhDs at UGA, so I had close friends, plenty of people to train with, and housing so cheap that I could finally afford a garage for all my bikes. Remember Maslow's hierarchy of needs from high school psych class? Me neither, but it went something like: food, shelter, sex, commuter bike, track bike, 'cross bike, mountain bike, road bike, time trial bike, and backup road bike, and I finally had space for all of them. The car stayed outside.

While I was unpacking I made a phone call to a friend in Boulder to catch up on gossip. I'd heard rumors about Tom Zirbel, who'd just had his doping suspension for the steroid DHEA reduced, and I wanted to get to the bottom of it. Zirbel had always claimed innocence on his DHEA positive, and it seemed like most of the peloton believed him. Eventually, the story went quiet. My suspicion is that he had proved in a lab that the supplement was tainted and had sued the company for a pile of cash.

Meanwhile, Phil Zajicek, who'd narrowly avoided suspension for EPO a year before, had now been officially suspended, apparently due to information provided by Zirbel. I learned that my old friend Jon Chodroff was actually a big part of it. Jon had purchased EPO, but it was before he got serious about bike racing. He was probably doing it for crew, his main focus in college. Jon traded boats and needles for bikes, but he couldn't lose the adaptation the EPO gave him, or the skeletons it left in his closet. Jon wasn't caught from a positive test. He was caught from the records of the guy who sold it to him, and Zajicek was on the same list. He'd almost gotten away with it, but when Jon confessed to USADA, Zajicek panicked and got in touch with Jon, demanding to know what he was telling the authorities, threatening Jon, and incriminating himself in the process. Jon was just trying to put everything behind him and didn't want to deal with it anymore, but Zirbel convinced him to talk with USADA about what he'd heard. The authorities were so happy to get Zajicek, they rewarded Zirbel for helping them get the info. Jon's suspension wasn't reduced, but I bet he slept better.

It's interesting when you find out a guy you've been racing for years was cheating. Some have the sense to flee from the sport and start over, like Jon. Others manage to maintain their relationships, and even find jobs in the industry. Some come back to racing, but it would take a lot of balls to show up at a bike race and hang out with a bunch of guys you've been robbing. When Jeremy Powers found out the truth about Zajicek, whom he'd considered a friend, he e-mailed him and said "Fuck you," just to make it clear that they weren't buddies anymore. Don't steal from Jeremy Powers.

While I was catching up on the Boulder gossip, I asked about my old teammate Kiel Reijnen. Kiel had also taken Jeremy's advice and left Jelly Belly. He was making good money that year (for a bike racer, anyway) riding for Team Type 1, but he'd contracted some sort of weird illness and didn't race once. I was worried that he'd been sitting home alone starving himself because he couldn't ride, stressing about his future, but I learned that he was patiently letting his body heal, and had distracted himself by restoring an old motorcycle. Kiel was going to be just fine.

CLIMBERS SHOULD STAY AWAY FROM TEAM PURSUITS

The theme of the rest of my summer was "all kitted up and nowhere to go." With Kenda left out of the Tours of Colorado and Utah, and just a few big crits in the budget for the rest of the season, my only remaining team race wasn't until November. Once again in need of a goal, I turned to elite track nationals. I floundered and barely hung on, but my team finished second in the team pursuit. On the podium, I tried a trick that Chad Hartley had taught me: poking the asshole of whoever had finished ahead of me. In the photos, you couldn't tell what my hand was doing, but the facial expression on the victim was priceless.

After the races, I headed to San Diego to visit JC. He was still beating me at chess, but it was great to ride along the ocean again. If you never manage to watch the sunset over Torrey Pines, you've made a big mistake.

YOU CAN SAY NO

The season was mostly over when Thompson sent an e-mail to the whole team announcing our invitation to a one-day race in Taiwan in November. I'm a sucker for bike races, so I told him I'd go if he needed me, but I'd learned my lesson about late-season trips to Asia. I said that it made a lot more sense for the newer guys to go. We had a handful of riders like Jim Stemper and Pat Lemieux who hadn't raced a ton that year; they would train their butts off for a chance to go to a UCI race, and would love the opportunity to go somewhere exotic, one of the few perks we get in this sport. It was a small race, and no one would care or even notice if we won or lost.

Thompson's response didn't surprise me. "No. This is an A-team race. You, Ben, Shawn, Luca, Isaac, and Roman. We NEED to win this." To him, every race was the most important race of the year, even the ones nobody was watching.

A few weeks before we left, I saw our roster for Taiwan: me, Luca, Roman, Isaac, and Chris Monteleone. I called Frankie immediately.

"What happened to Ben and Shawn?" I asked, wondering how our star riders got out of their obligation.

"They said no," was the obvious reply.

It took me a second to wrap my head around that. "Wait! You can say no?" It was our job to race, after all.

"Sure," Frankie explained, like I should have known. "No one's going to force you to go to a race in Taiwan in November."

"Can I say no now?" I asked, ready to call it a season.

"Well, okay, now we have to force you. It's too late to change the ticket."

My teammates and their appetizers. *From left:* Isaac Howe, Luca Damiani, Chris Monteleone, me, and Will Swan, the mechanic.

AVOID THE SPICY BROTH

Five of us showed up early, headed to the southwest part of the island where Kenda's factory was located, to join the sponsors for a ride celebrating the company's 48th anniversary. I shared a room with Luca, who gave me the usual intro: "Phil, when you roommate with me—"

"Yeah, yeah, I know! I flush everything." Once again, I left a daily shit in the toilet to punish Luca, and they were messier on Taiwanese food.

We had great hospitality from the sponsors all week, and lots of amazing meals, some of which were even edible for Americans. Our translator would order for us and then explain what we were getting.

"The starfruit is native to Taiwan. This is the only place in the world you can find it," he explained.

"I get those at the Hannaford in Burlington," Isaac whispered.

One night we went to a restaurant that specialized in soup. We were told to select a broth and then load up at a buffet filled with meats and veggies to cook ourselves as the pot boiled at the table. Isaac chose the spiciest broth they had, and then volunteered to drink the rest of the giant pot if we each chipped in 10 bucks. It took him awhile, but he did it. We all felt bad for Chris, his roommate, that night.

The next morning we asked Isaac how his night was, assuming he spent most of it sweating on the toilet, but he said he was fine. We couldn't believe it, but Chris just looked at us and shrugged confirmation. Isaac must have had an iron stomach. Huge disappointment.

Three hours later we were riding around Sun Moon Lake, and Isaac got a funny look on his face. "Guys! I have to stop! Now!" He dropped his bike and scrambled into the woods. He said it was like boiling water coming out of his ass.

Luca at Sun Moon Lake.

We took a tour of the tire factory that afternoon (I was the only one who'd seen it before), where we watched the tire- and tube-making process from beginning to end. When we left, the guide wouldn't give us anything, not even a tube. I was pissed. We should have gone home with boxes of tires and tubes. They could just make more, after all. If anyone has a factory that makes anything, they should give me some. This includes Stefano Barberi, with his family's yacht factory. They could just make another one, right? I'll find a place to park it.

I would never have considered Taiwan as a spot for tourism or cycling, but the rides there were some of the best I'd ever done. There are bike lanes everywhere, and in the countryside bike-specific roads connect all the small towns. Even the gas stations had floor pumps sitting outside, with basic tools. My first thought was, "How has that pump not been stolen?" And then my second thought was what my first thought said about America, where that pump wouldn't have lasted an hour.

My favorite ride took us through a series of tight, barely paved paths. We'd rip a few miles, stop for photos at a Buddhist temple in the middle of the jungle, and then start rolling again. Isaac was always scared of cobras on the smaller roads, but we didn't see any snakes, pandas, or even monkeys. I found a straw farmer's hat in the road and wore it on my back for the next 80 miles. When we reached the top of the mountain, two elderly men were seated on a bench. They looked at us in a way that said, "Well? What did you think of the climb?"

"BLAAAAARRRGG," I said, bending over as if I was vomiting. The old men laughed. Vomit sound is a universal language.

When the riding was done, we had nothing to do but wander around the city, getting into mischief. We explored a sex shop, got haircuts, did laundry (full service with wash and fold was $3), and had a war with bubble tea, a cold drink available at any restaurant or convenience store, with little balls of jelly floating around in liquid. If you got a jelly ball into your straw, you could blow it out at high speeds like a dart gun. The hotel, built with a courtyard in the middle, had open hallways to the rooms with a clear view to the rooms on the other side. I walked out of the elevator after breakfast one morning and saw Luca and Chris waiting in ambush, with loaded bubble tea straws. I took off toward my room, barely outrunning the "BLAT BLAT BLAT" sounds of jelly exploding on the wall behind me.

The four of us bonded on that trip, partly because we were all so homesick. We were enjoying the riding, but when we asked the translator to order dessert at dinner one night, a bowl of fruit greeted us. "I want a fucking donut," Isaac sighed. We went to McDonald's the next day.

After a week of tourism, sponsor obligations, and killing time, there was finally a bike race. Frankie and Roman had arrived the day before. They'd wanted more time at home with their loved ones, but

Dead end.

they'd missed out on all the fun in the factory town. We took a train to the race hotel with a few other teams, and a white man approached me, speaking English. He seemed a little old and overweight, but he said he was racing and told me some of the teams he'd ridden for. I suspected he was exaggerating, so I stopped him when he mentioned his years on Motorola. "Oh! Did you know Frankie Andreu?"

"Sure, I knew Frankie. We got along pretty well. Still stay in touch."

He walked right into it.

"Well, hey! There's your old buddy!" I pointed, as Frankie, with perfect timing, stepped onto the train. The guy's face turned white, caught in a lie, as he found an excuse to run to another car. At the hotel the next day I pointed him out to Frankie, who said he'd never seen him before. I wondered how many years the guy had been claiming he rode with Lance and Frankie to impress strangers. This sport attracts some real nut jobs. Not me, though. Perfectly sane, right here.

CHECK YOUR BIKE BEFORE YOU GET ON THE AIRPLANE

The day before the race we did a few efforts to warm up our legs. Isaac held onto my seatpost for a free ride on a steep climb, and I still dropped the other guys. My legs were good, but it was November, which meant that my bike had close to 10,000 miles on it. Getting spare parts from the team was close to impossible, because Thompson kept them to sell on eBay at the end of the year. When I asked for a new chain or a set of tires, I half expected him to say, "Sure. If you can suck it out of my ass!" We imagined him swimming in a huge mound of components, tubes, and brake pads, like Scrooge McDuck with his gold coins.

I hadn't been staying on top of basic bike maintenance, and the mechanic was on more of a vacation than a race trip. The day before the race I asked him to replace the chain when I noticed that my gears were skipping. What we didn't count on was that my chainring was destroyed. Those parts wear together, so the new chain and old chainring didn't get along. When the race started, the chain flew off every time I put any power into it. I went back to the car in the neutral section and told Frankie what was going on, but there weren't any spare bikes, and it wasn't the sort of issue you could fix on the road.

"Fuck it. I guess I'm riding in my little ring all day," I decided, almost crashing as I threw the chain again.

"Phil, you can't ride like that. It's dangerous losing your chain every time you sprint. Go back to the hotel."

Frankie was right, but I was angry when I got back. I'd flown to the other side of the world and I didn't make it past the first kilometer of the race. I hurled a glass Coke bottle against the wall in the hotel room. The glass didn't even shatter, just dented the wall of the Taiwanese Sheraton. I picked it up and looked at all the lettering and

It was awkward to ride with, but you have to make sacrifices to look cool.

ingredients, and realized that every Coke bottle worldwide probably said the same thing. Someday, when our civilization is over, they can use Coke bottles as a Rosetta Stone. Then I took a nap. I was over it.

I'd been wearing the straw farmer's hat that I found in the road. It was beat-up and dirty, but the spectators loved me for it, and they kept taking photos with me. The president of Giant Bicycles (there as a sponsor) bought me a nice new one, handing it to me in the hotel lobby that afternoon. I made both hats into lamps when I got home.

I was packed up by the time the race was over, and we were soon on a train headed back to Taipei, drinking beer from a 7-Eleven. I chugged a 40-ounce can labeled "The Beer," which was enough to get me loud and belligerent. I tried to pick a fight with some of the Spanish riders, but they didn't understand my insults.

My ire turned to my own teammates. "Are you going to take a break when you get back to Italy?" Chris asked Luca.

"TRAINING?" I interrupted. "You want to talk about training NOW, with the season over? Frankie, is that what you guys did after the Tour? Talk to Lance about training?"

"Oh, yeah," Frankie laughed. "Hey, Lance. What are you doing with Dr. Ferrari next week?" I was drunk, but I'll never forget that line.

ALL WORK AND NO PLAY

I had the team book my flight home from Taipei a week later, so I could visit a manufacturer in China for my clothing company. All I'd need to pay for was a short round-trip flight to get from Taipei to Guangzhou. Already homesick, I'd be in China for another week, this time with no friends or teammates to keep me company, but after a rough year, it was nice to work on something outside of racing. Besides, I had bills to pay, and bikes weren't getting it done.

We'd expanded our selection, so the goal of the trip was to improve our cuts, fabrics, and patterns. We'd tried American manufacturers, but there were only a few, and their prices would have put us out of business immediately. After months of negotiations I'd selected the best manufacturer I could find in China, done my homework to make sure it treated its employees well, and negotiated pricing and order quantities. All week I had a personal driver, translator, and pattern engineer. We went item by item, choosing the right fabrics for every panel, and the best grippers and zippers for nearly a hundred different items. It took four full days, with breaks every three hours in which the whole factory would stop for traditional tea service.

On the last day, while the engineers worked on samples of the new designs, the translator took me on a tour of Guangzhou. We saw the famous radio tower, the second-tallest building in the world. All the signs called it the tallest, with no mention of the mile-high complex in Dubai that was finished nearly a year before. The translator had never heard of Dubai's tower, and she insisted that theirs was the best. I didn't ask if she'd heard of the Tiananmen Square massacre.

The race was a bust, but the good times in Taiwan and the productive business trip in China made it a successful Asian campaign. I'd run into plenty of Americans during my business travels who got their passports stamped and ate at Outback Steakhouses in one city after another, and never experienced anything like I had. They never saw the starfruit growing on the trees, or the temples on the hillsides. My teammates and I saw the places between the tourist attractions. We stopped at cafés where the locals relaxed, places that don't sell postcards. We felt the air and smelled the smells. It made me understand how lucky I was to experience life from a bike. My wallet was light, but I'd seen more of the world at 25 than anyone I knew.

7
GET SERIOUS
‗‗

I spent my off-season working hard on the business, socializing with the Larsons in my spare time. They weren't riding as much as they used to, so they weren't in shape to train with me anymore. When I met Dan and Rebecca, I'd joined the college cycling team to make friends, and I was barely able to stay in the group. Years later, I'd gotten too strong to train with those same folks, and I had to do my hard rides alone. The sport that once gave me a social life had now isolated me, but since we couldn't ride together, we often went bowling. Bowling is a great equalizer. There's something great about a sport where a 4-year-old can sit on the floor, push the ball forward, and get a strike, and a professional can roll it into the gutter.

I joined a local gym that fall, replacing plyometrics with a more standard weight routine. Jim Stemper was working construction to make ends meet in the off-season. I felt bad for him until I realized that I had just signed up to pay $40/month to lift things and put them back down while he was paid by the hour for the same task.

Jeremy Powers came to visit for a week in December. He was preparing for the Cyclocross National Championships and wanted to do everything right after losing in an upset the previous year. Jeremy flew in with his coach, Rick Crawford, and I was in awe of their focus. They went out for long rides in the cold, with Jeremy pacing behind Rick on a scooter. Rick drove through dirt and gravel areas, forcing Jeremy to dismount and remount, working on his technique and skills. We watched video from his last few races, looking for mistakes and places where Jeremy's rivals had gained on him. Even if Jeremy won, he was open to heavy scrutiny.

This was Jeremy's first time seeing where I lived, and he was angry. I'd been living off of my team salary and my side jobs for years, still saving for grad school or a rainy day. The reality was that it doesn't get much rainier than $20,000 a year, and I'd gone too far in my sacrifice. Jeremy went through the fridge and cupboards, judging me as only a true friend could.

"What is this? You don't have any food. All you eat is deli meat, sandwiches, and rice cakes. You've got to eat real food!" He was exasperated. "You don't live like an athlete! Look at the thermostat. What's that say, Phil?"

I took a peek at the screen. "61 degrees."

"61 degrees! How can you be fast when you have to wear a jacket in your own house?" he asked. "You can sit here and half-ass this thing, and you'll always make $20,000 a year, or you could do it right, invest in yourself, and make 10 times that. You know you have the talent, so stop being scared! You think I can afford to bring Rick here for a week, rent a car, and everything else I do? Not really. But I want to win nationals, and I'm going for it." Rick nodded. Jeremy was right.

"And if you don't have the talent to do better than 20K a year," Jeremy added, "you might as well find out now and quit, because it's not worth it if this is how you have to live."

After thinking about Jeremy's advice, I finally accepted that it was time to throw away the graduate school fallback plan and toss all my eggs (and savings) into the cycling basket. With the amount of energy and effort I was putting toward bike racing, I'd already gambled 99 percent of my life on these crazy odds. It only made sense to kick in that last 1 percent; otherwise, my sacrifices would be for nothing.

EAT BETTER

He'd already given me plenty to think about, but soon Jeremy realized that part of the reason there wasn't much food in my fridge was because I was watching my weight and trying to stay skinny—too skinny. If I'd heard that a climber I'd raced against had starved to death, I'd have been impressed by his self-control. Worst of all, I didn't eat or drink enough when I was training.

Jeremy caught me weighing myself, which earned me another dose of tough love. "Phil, it's December! You don't need to be worrying about your weight right now. You need to eat when you train and get that power up. Feed the beast! Take that scale out again and we'll see what your front teeth weigh! It's time to get serious!"

I started training with drink mix in my bottles (never plain water), and all sorts of bars and sandwiches on the bike. As it turned out, the more I ate, the more I burned on the ride. My weight stayed the same, but I was riding longer and harder.

For dinner one night Jeremy made liver and onions, salad, and rice. I offered him a cookie, and he declined.

"Why not?" I asked. "You said I need to eat more."

"Because I'm trying to win a national championship. I didn't mean you should eat more crap. Muscles aren't made out of cookies."

Oh.

Two weeks later, I watched on my computer as Jeremy crushed his rivals at nationals. His girlfriend rushed through the crowd and hugged him at the finish line, both of them crying. You could tell that the tears were more than joy: They represented six years of team-work. Emily had put up with lots of weekends that Jeremy couldn't be home, with liver and onions stinking up the house. And Jeremy must have sat through plenty of chick flicks because he knew he owed her. I felt like I'd won just for playing a small part in his success, and I'm sure half of Massachusetts felt the same. I never liked asking people for help, but the tears in my eyes when I saw Jeremy on the podium made me realize the value of embracing your friends, and involving others in the process. The next time we spoke, I told Jer-emy that he needed to put a ring on Emily's finger. He knew that already. Jeremy doesn't miss a beat.

I wasn't a successful athlete yet, but I decided to start imperson-ating one. As Kurt Vonnegut said, "You are who you pretend to be." I started with the little things: I turned the thermostat up, bought a few bags of organic groceries, and made a weekly massage appoint-ment. I treated every training ride like a race, timing my breakfast to maximize my energy, with a recovery meal when I finished and as much sleep as I could get. I also started looking at foreclosures nearby to spend my savings on. Renting made sense as a way to save money, but it was also a form of avoiding commitment. If I was going to be a pro athlete, it was time to embrace it.

FIND A GOOD TRAINING PARTNER

In January, Pat Lemieux showed up to stay for a few months. We'd been teammates for a year but hadn't gone to any of the same races, so I'd barely spoken to him since yelling that he should "Shut the fuck up and pull" at Nature Valley two years prior. He'd e-mailed the team looking for a warmer place to stay for the winter, so I offered him a room in Athens.

Pat had ridden for Kenda for no salary the previous year. He was signed again for the same, but he'd recently finished his college degree, so this was the year he needed to step up his training. If he didn't get the results that would earn him a paycheck, he'd have to find something else to do. Pat dove into the deep end, moving in with someone he could learn from, and I was impressed by that. Of course, he had no idea how clueless I was.

STICK TO A ROUTINE

Having Pat in my house forced me to be more like Jeremy, and aim to set an example for a guy who'd come to improve himself. Pat was motivated to lose weight and put in some hard training, and we got into a good pattern together. We'd go to the mountains once or twice a week, stopping at the same place for breakfast on the way. We had fewer cookies and more salads, and we pushed each other on the bike.

Pat is a rare person—I would call him unique—and having him around made my winter much more enjoyable. He refused to use public restrooms for number two, and after he went at home, he'd have to take a shower, no matter what.

"All right, Pat, are you ready to get on the bike?"

"Phil, I just need to use the bathroom real fast, and then I gotta take a quick rinse." How could I criticize when he was so cute about it?

John Murphy visited from Asheville one weekend for a famous Athens Winter Bike League ride. The WBL is a weekly ride organized by an eccentric lawyer in Athens. The winner receives $200 in prize money and the legendary "victory box," a cardboard box filled with magazines, beer, a cigar, and various other silly items that were donated or found that week. The ride draws crowds from all over the Southeast thanks to a well-organized point competition and structured "attack zones," which make for a civil atmosphere and quality training.

John Murphy had ridden for BMC the previous year, arguably the best team in the world at the time, and now he was signed to Kenda with me. I was worried that he'd be unmotivated after such a step down, but that wasn't the case at all. In fact, John was burned out on all the crappy races he'd been doing in Europe. He was excited to live in the United States again and ride for a team that would have some fun, despite the steep pay cut. I wanted to hear more about his old team.

"What's Cadel Evans like?" I asked.

"Well, he's a Tour de France champion." John didn't want to say it outright, but I understood that Cadel was meticulous, detail-oriented, demanding, and all the other traits required to win the hardest event in the world, none of which made him easy to get along with. It's hard to wrap your head around the idea of being "the best." If you're capable of a certain level of achievement, it almost seems like you belong to it, like you have a debt to your own gift, or you owe something to those who don't have it. If you can do something others can't, they think you should want to. They don't have the option, and the pressure could easily be overwhelming. It's probably that way with anything. A great writer can work all day on five pages only to throw them in the trash the next morning. Maybe you have to be tortured to be the best. I guess that would be better than being tortured and coming in ninth.

When the attack zone started with 12 miles left in the ride, I was glad that John Murphy was on my side. After a few hard efforts, we were able to get rid of everyone but Oscar Clark, a local amateur I'd been training with. We had 8 miles to the finish, so Oscar was inevitably going to lose, but he took a lot of blows before he finally cracked, and he never gave up. He was like the kid on the soccer team who still slides through the dirt to save the ball even when his team is down 10 points. You always feel bad for them, but those kids make good bike racers.

ALL A HOUSE NEEDS IS LIPSTICK AND ROUGE

I closed on a house on my 26th birthday. I'd gone to the gym before the bank opened, so I sat there in sweaty gym shorts and a T-shirt with armpit stains waiting to withdraw my life's savings. The house was an ugly foreclosure, with walls and trim chewed up by the previous owners, who must have had a lot of dogs with a lot of teeth. The steps to the front door were leaning to one side, the roof was patched in several places, and the interior was in serious need of new paint and carpet. It was just a crappy house, but I saw it as a pirate ship. As long as I could keep a roommate or two in there, expenses would be low, and I'd be able to weather a rough year or another bad contract.

I'd hired a realtor to help me with the transaction, but she didn't seem dazzled by the opportunity. During the walk-through, the inspector would point out something that needed attention, and my realtor would promptly downplay it in a thick Mississippi drawl. "This place just needs a little lipstick and rouge," she'd say. That's right, the roof leaks and the windows are cracked, but dressing it up like a whore will solve everything.

At first, I did most of the work myself. When a job was too big or I was too clueless, I'd drive down to Home Depot, look at the crowd of workers out front, and fail to remember my one semester of Spanish in college.

"Tiles?" I'd say. Whoever raised their hands would get in the car, and a few hours later, I had tiles in my kitchen.

As the season got closer, training took priority, so I hired a contractor to finish the work and went to Florida for the usual local races with Pat.

ANGER CAN WIN RACES

I arrived for the first race angry and not thinking clearly. I had awakened at 4 a.m. with pain in my lower right abdomen so sharp I could barely move. I decided that I had appendicitis, so I snuck out and headed to the emergency room. But it was a false alarm— after a few hours of tests, a CT scan showed that I was fine and offered no explanation for the pain. The doctor suggested that I might have pulled an ab in my sleep. I must have had quite the nightmare.

There was no time for breakfast, so I went straight from the hospital to the race, where Pat and Bobby were waiting. The three of us sat by my car with my stomach growling as I explained how we were going to handle our race tactics.

"Guys," I said—and what followed was a graphic, violent, and disgusting metaphor for what we were going to do to that race. Fortunately, we didn't really need a plan. By the time you turn pro, you know how to win a local crit.

Pat and Bobby tried not to throw up, and we headed to the start.

I attacked from the gun and kept a half-lap lead to the finish. That afternoon I won the 15 km time trial by a good margin. My abdomen still hurt, but the race wins were delicious.

Pat won the criterium the next day, and we went out that night to celebrate our victories with two girls we'd met over the weekend. Pat had a girlfriend, Gwen, but he came along as my wingman. Halfway through dinner, his date started to get the wrong idea, so he began to talk nonstop about Gwen, showing us photos of her on his phone. At every opportunity, Pat would mention that he was in a committed relationship.

"It's been great weather this weekend," my date remarked.

"My girlfriend likes weather!" Pat would say. I couldn't stop laughing.

After dinner, we went out for ice cream to celebrate Pat's win. It was one of those classy places with a slab of marble and all kinds of candy and sauces you could mix in. Remember how I said Pat was unique? He ordered a cup of plain vanilla, no toppings.

SWING FOR THE FENCES

I won a road race the next weekend, and when we talked about the plan for the crit the next day, I told Pat and Bobby to let me attack early.

"I think I can lap the field solo in 30 minutes," I said, setting a goal for myself. I had good legs, and I was having fun with them.

"That's the cockiest thing I've ever heard," said Bobby, who'd wanted a plan that might make him more likely to win.

"It's only cocky if I don't pull it off. When Babe Ruth pointed to the stands and hit the ball there, was that cocky?" Bobby rolled his eyes instead of punching me.

I lapped the field in 32 minutes and worked my way back to the front. My teammates were up there, sitting behind an amateur team whose riders were well-organized and drilling it at the front, clueless that I'd lapped and their efforts were in vain.

I tapped Bobby on the shoulder. "Who are they chasing?" I asked, laughing.

He was surprised to see me. "You're such an asshole!" Bobby sighed.

After the race, I drove further south to visit David Guttenplan in Boca Raton, but I had to leave early because I couldn't stand his girlfriend. I'd told him for years that she was costing him 50 watts.

THE LITTLE THINGS ADD UP

Business was going well. When pro cycling is your job, you have a lot of downtime. My brain would want to train more, to keep working toward my biggest goals, when what I really needed was a distraction. I filled those hours with work, which was stressful at times, but by pecking away at it here and there I made some extra income and accomplished a lot over the years. It never felt like a huge sacrifice. The business made me feel like I was doing something with my life when the bike racing part wasn't going well, and it helped me to push through the winter months at home. I relied heavily on my business partner, Jon. I'd taken him on out of desperation, but he took all the labor out of my hands with the day-to-day stuff and continued to grow the company, often with very little help from me. I was lucky to have him.

My legs were great coming into the season. Maybe it was just the strength you get from another year on a bike. Or maybe it was those months of eating right, keeping the thermostat at 70, weekly massage, and all the other little things that Jeremy had yelled at me about.

The team had training camp in Tucson, which just about killed me with boredom. It was hard to understand why so many bike racers went to Tucson for the winter; the town had only a couple of roads and one long climb to train on. Four times a week we'd ride up and down Mount Lemmon. Maybe some guys are just determined, willing to put up with the limited route options to get the benefits of the warm weather and higher altitude. Or maybe they're dumb enough that it doesn't get monotonous, like a goldfish doing laps around an aquarium, thinking "look at that pretty rock" every time they come back around.

Thanks to Florida, my legs were already in race shape, and I danced away on the climbs. When we rode up Madera Pass I left my teammates far behind, and Frankie drove up to me in a switchback.

"They're gaining on you," he lied, trying to make me go harder.

"No, they're not," I smiled. Frankie started laughing. We both knew it was going to be a good year. Big wins, yellow jerseys, podium girls . . . it all seems possible, every February.

The only guy who made me earn it was a first-year pro named Curtis Winsor. Curtis was signed as a "ghost rider," just to fulfill the requirement that pro teams have to hire a certain number of young guys, but the team wasn't planning to send him to many races. Curtis knew where he stood, and he showed up at camp ready to prove himself, digging deep on the climbs, and coming in ahead of everyone but me. Curtis earned himself a few race starts and a bigger role on the team. It was fun to watch a guy who had the same kind of fire I did when I showed up at my first training camp, but make him feel like part of the team and be able to give him all the friendly advice I never had on Jelly Belly.

Of course, the highlight of camp was the male bonding. It was nice to be vulgar and offensive with all the guys again. One of my teammates was trying to get his girlfriend to try anal sex, but "every time we start, she cries!"

"So does her father," I informed him.

With all the pent-up testosterone in a house full of men, we always hit on women when we had the chance. I was talking to a cute brunette at a gas station when Chad Hartley came up to me and held my hand. It became a running joke, and we all ruined each other's chances as much as possible.

One night we had a lecture from Arizona State University about social media and sponsor representation. Everyone yawned and fidgeted. If we were good at listening to lectures and watching PowerPoint slides, we'd have real jobs.

Professor: "Topics like politics, religion, anything divisive like that, you should go ahead and avoid entirely. You'll only alienate people."

Shawn Milne: "What about doping? Can we comment on that?"

Professor: "No, I'd avoid that, too."

Frankie Andreu: "Well, wait a minute. What if they want to comment on a recent story or discuss doping's effect on cycling?"

Me: "Just keep letting your wife do it for you, Frankie."

When it comes to doping, Frankie and his wife, Betsy, had done more for the sport and riders like myself than anyone. Frankie knew where I stood, so I was safe to tease him, but a lot of the guys were new and may have thought I'd get fired for that remark. There was a collective sigh of relief when they heard Frankie laugh.

On our last day in Tucson we "raced" up to a spot on Mount Lemmon called Windy Point, often used by locals as a fitness benchmark. The record was just over 53 minutes, set by Marc de Maar at United Healthcare's training camp a year before. My legs were tired from a few big days of riding in the desert, but I finished in 51:20. Francisco Mancebo was in town the following week. He bragged about making it to Windy Point in the high 53s, and it burst his bubble when someone told him my time.

YOU HAVE TO TAKE CHARGE

All the work was finished on my house after camp, so I finished unpacking, spent four nights there, and then left it to Pat and Luca, who'd be staying with me until summer.

I'd done my best to outsource the heavy lifting, but moving was still a lot of stress and labor for a few days before a big race. I worried that my fitness would suffer, but in the San Dimas uphill time trial, I caught and passed everyone who'd started less than three minutes ahead of me. I was Pac-Man and these guys were dots: my only sustenance. I won the TT by 14 seconds, a huge gap for a short course.

At the team meeting, I assumed the plan would be the same as the previous year, when we won it with Ben Day, but before I knew it, the guys had decided that we didn't want to try to control the race. The plan was to put someone in the early break so another team would have to chase. It was an odd gamble. I was confused and frustrated. Did they not trust me to hold on to a 14-second lead in a stage that I'd won two years before? When Ben wore yellow, there was no debate about the plan. It was all for Ben, beginning to end. Somehow, after two years and a big win, I hadn't earned the same respect from my team.

That night, while my teammates studied the race bible, I tried to distract myself from the pressure of the yellow jersey. Sure, if you don't know what the course is like, you don't have your head in the game. But I didn't see how they could keep reading it over and over, analyzing everything in a race they'd all done before. Bike racing just isn't that complicated. Our hosts had an Xbox, and Hartley put in a skateboarding game. We had no interest in scoring points or doing tricks, so we spent several hours intentionally knocking our characters off of ledges, into walls, and under moving vehicles. We both cried from laughter. It might be more responsible for the yellow jersey to focus on the race, but it's also more stressful, and I thought I'd race better if I was having fun.

Andy Jacques-Maynes, a new addition to the team, made it into the break in the road race, so my strongest teammate was in no position to help, and an Exergy rider in the break with him was the new leader on the road, higher than Andy on GC. With cold rain pouring, and no radios or team caravans, it was hard to tell what was going on. On the second lap, we lost two guys to a crash, but my three remaining teammates brought the break down to one minute with three laps to go, so I was still confident in my chances of defending yellow. And then my tire went flat. The team slowed the field to let me catch back on, and the gap went back to three minutes, with 18 miles left.

Nate English was sitting fourth on GC, so we left him out of the rotation, but that was a mistake. It's pretty simple math that to catch a break of four, you just need five guys chasing, but we rode another lap with only two. The gap stayed the same, and when we came through with one to go, it was down to just me and Nate to chase at the front of the field. I gave it everything to catch the leaders, and we got damn close, but I lost a few seconds over the climb and lost yellow. It was hard to reconcile that miserable day with a course that I'd once associated with success, cruising in off the back on the same corners that I'd relived in my head over and over, remembering my first big stage win with Jelly Belly.

Andy came in second on the stage, earning him the GC lead after officials gave a time penalty to the Exergy rider, who apparently used a car to chase back after a flat tire. Chasing on with a car is technically illegal but still standard practice, so it was bizarre and lucky for us that the call went in our favor. If there had been a bumper to draft when I was chasing back to the field after my flat, I'd have used it out of instinct, legal or not.

I tried to hide my anger at the meeting that night. The guys were proud that we had yellow, and they didn't want to admit that we'd lucked into it with a time penalty. The truth was that we had a faulty plan, bad execution, and worse communication. Someone blamed my flat tire. "It's called Murphy's Law. If something can go wrong, it will." I thought the flat tire was a copout excuse, and we'd gambled the race long before I stopped for a wheel. Gaimon's Law: If you send your strongest guy into the breakaway and don't chase like you mean it, you lose.

Andy held onto yellow; I took home the KOM jersey as a consolation. It was a great result for the team, but we were like a blind rat that found some cheese, and we wouldn't win again if we kept it up. Personally, I felt like I'd lost the race at the team meeting, in a weird form of indirect, collective betrayal, or at least lack of faith. I wanted another crack at it.

YOU ALWAYS GET ANOTHER CHANCE

Redlands was mostly the same squad for Kenda, with the addition of Jim Stemper. At the last minute, Jim was told he'd be taking the place of one the guys who crashed in San Dimas, and he drove all night from Berkeley to make the start. If a team had eight guys with a heart like Jim's, they'd win everything.

Our wheel sponsor was making a lighter disc wheel, but the team only had two of them, so I removed the stickers from a Zipp I had at home and brought it with me, just to make sure I didn't get screwed and end up with a heavy one from the previous year. My result, my responsibility.

I put all of Ben Day's advice to work in the Redlands time trial. When I crossed the line at the top of the hill, there were 40 riders left to go, but I knew I'd nailed it and no one would beat my time. It was my first NRC victory, and I teared up in my aero helmet as I coasted through the neighborhoods to get back to the start.

With three days of longer stages to defend, I was nervous for the meeting that night. My teammates were looking at the stage and GC results from the past few years of the Redlands Classic, noticing that the first road race was hard to defend and the yellow jersey had often changed hands.

Hartley called me that evening on his way home to Milwaukee. I'd borrowed his rain jacket for the San Dimas criterium, and I threw it into somebody's yard when it got too hot. He was angry that I'd lost it. Oblivious and distracted, I started complaining about my situation.

"I can see the guys in the living room right now. Frankie's not there, but they're plotting against me. They're all convincing each other that we shouldn't defend my yellow jersey, that we should put a guy in the break again."

"You won the race today," he said. "You have the right to be in charge, so do it. If you're going to be a leader, you have to lead. You're in yellow now. You're the boss. Tell them what to do." Hartley was right. I still owe him a jacket.

When the meeting started, I told everyone how it was going to be.

"I don't want to see anyone covering an early break. I want all of you to stay with me, from start to finish, and I want the strongest guys to be freshest at the end."

I never would have had the courage to say that without Hartley's pep talk. Frankie and Shawn Milne convinced the guys that we were stronger than the teams who'd messed up the Beaumont stage and lost yellow in the past. They'd all wasted energy, setting a hard pace too early, and we wouldn't make that mistake.

The plan worked like a charm. Attacks flew, and the field sucked them back. Our competition jumped around like ping-pong balls in a giant washing machine, but nothing dangerous ever got up the road. An hour into the stage, I called my first-ever NRC pee break, per the tradition for the yellow jersey. There'd been a pileup at the back of the field, so it seemed like an appropriate time since it would let everyone rejoin the group. I learned later that we had been within Beaumont city limits and that 40 riders were fined for public urination (somehow, I wasn't one of them).

Kenda came to the front with 50 miles left, setting tempo to keep the pace high and positioning me at the front. Mancebo attacked on every climb, but he never shook me off his wheel, and I always jumped him over the top, just to let him know that he hadn't hurt me. The field came right back to us on the downhill, led by the Kenda–5-Hour Energy train.

In previous years with one lap to go, the GC leader was without teammates, yellow jersey in jeopardy, doomed to cover attacks for the last 25 miles. But my team rolled through the start/finish on the final lap with all eight guys on the front. I'd never been more proud, and for the first time, I believed I could win the stage race. Every day that I was in yellow, I woke up wondering "How can I do this?" And then I went out and did it. That must be good practice for something.

After Beaumont, the crit the next day was cake. I sat behind the rotation and encouraged the guys, learning another element of being a leader. I'd keep an eye on the time gaps, telling the guys to speed up or slow down. I'd tell them when to sit out of the rotation for a few laps. Andy sat behind me and defended my wheel, and we'd shout "left" or "right" to warn of upcoming attacks, like I'd learned racing crits with Jelly Belly. At one point, Ben Jacques-Maynes— Andy's identical twin brother—fought his way to the front and knocked me off of Roman's wheel.

"Don't fucking let him do that, Phil!" Andy screamed. Talk about sibling rivalry.

There was one time bonus up for grabs at the midpoint of the crit. The year before, I'd watched in awe as Mancebo went to the front with a lap to go, took the corners like a crazy man, and rode so fast that no one even tried to outsprint him. After Mancebo's constant attacks at Beaumont, I knew he'd go for the midpoint bonus again, so we needed someone to beat him (yours truly didn't even pretend). Leading into the bonus lap, we had two sprinters on Mancebo's wheel when he started to go, but they were helpless, and he still took the bonus. At the end of the crit, Mancebo was sitting 11th overall, still 18 seconds behind me. But with the Sunset circuits looming, I knew the rest of the race would be between the two of us.

DON'T FORGET YOUR CLEAR LENSES

The Sunset stage at Redlands is always the big one. The circuits are nonstop turning, climbing, and descending. If your legs go bad or you need to rest for a minute, you never see the front again.

It was cold and pouring rain at the start. With a time bonus available 6 miles into the race, attacks were on from the gun. Mancebo won that bonus, too, chipping away at my lead. I was third, with Andy Jacques-Maynes, my own teammate, beating me for second. When Andy joined the team nobody knew I'd be strong enough to win big races, and we all thought he'd be team leader. Andy signed a contract for less than he was worth, thinking that he would get a few wins (like San Dimas) and earn his full value the following year. If he sacrificed himself for me, Andy's career could have been over. I couldn't blame him for looking out for himself, but I didn't know if I could keep yellow at Redlands if he continued to race against me.

After the time bonus, my GC lead was 16 seconds, and I was the only one who could follow Mancebo's attacks on the climbs. I'd practiced my glare in the mirror, and I wore clear lenses in my sunglasses. I wanted him to see my eyes.

Every couple of laps we'd lose a guy from the chase effort. I was often isolated in the harder sections, but just as I started to panic, outnumbered with no teammates in the group, my boys would come grinding up the hill, led by Jim Stemper and Paul Mach.

I never touched the wind until the last lap of the big circuit, when the field was down to only 20. Mancebo attacked on the KOM as usual, but this time he shook me off his wheel and got a 20-second gap.

He'd outsprinted me for the first time bonus, but Andy had seen me respond to all of Mancebo's attacks that day, and when I really needed him, he accepted that I was the leader and he gave me everything he had for the rest of the lap. He flew down the descent and back to downtown Redlands, where the rain-soaked crowds were waiting. With 20 km to go, Mancebo still had 20 seconds, Andy was finished, and it was all up to me to finish the chase.

The course was all downhill for 5 km, but Mancebo had barely been losing time, riding through the wet corners faster than I could. Getting beat on a descent is like a bad dream. If you try to go harder

Suffering to keep that jersey on the final stage of Redlands.

or faster, you only make mistakes and then lose time correcting them. Or you hit the pavement and lose everything. I had to be patient, keep the gap steady, and make time where I could.

I didn't think I'd be able to do it alone, and my teammates were gone, so I flicked my elbow, indicating that whoever was behind me needed to pull through.

"You've got to help," I said to Optum's Alex Candelario. "Just roll through and pull right off."

That wasn't his job, though, and we both knew it. A sprinter with a good chance at the stage win, he'd be letting down his own team if he wasted his legs to help me, but Candelario contributed in his own way.

"Don't fucking give up, Phil!" he yelled. "If you want to win this race, you've got to earn it, right now. You've got this!"

I don't know how many times he said it, but the words rang through my head as I chased, and I don't remember much else from the minutes that followed.

I'd been getting a lot of subtle encouragement from guys like Candelario, his teammate Mike Creed, and their director, Jonas Carney. Jonas had grown the old Kelly Benefits team into a big-budget Optum/Kelly Benefits powerhouse, complete with a women's team, and he had too much respect for the sport to hire dirty riders. They didn't have a dog in the GC fight anymore, and nobody wanted to see Francisco Mancebo win again, but it meant a lot from guys I'd always competed with, on a team I admired. Stefano Barberi—friend and former teammate—and his fiancée cheered from under an umbrella on the side of the road. He'd DNFed and could have gone home an hour earlier, but he wanted to see me win. Ben Day was off racing in Europe with his new team, but he'd been in touch every day with advice. I'd also gotten a half-dozen e-mails from former racers I'd never even met. They'd raced clean against guys like Mancebo, they were tired of seeing him on top, and they wanted the guy with the CLEAN tattoo to knock him down a peg. I could feel my friends and family reading the live updates on the Internet, crossing their fingers and biting their nails.

I thought about those people, and I knew that if I won, they would all feel their own sense of victory, like I had when Jeremy Powers crossed the line at cyclocross nationals. It wasn't Kenda versus Competitive Cyclist, or even me versus Mancebo. It was good versus evil. I put my head down and dug a little deeper.

In two previous attempts I'd never even made it to the finishing circuits at Redlands, but now I was gaining on Mancebo as we entered the finishing circuits. When I first hit the front, 20 guys remained in the field. I didn't look behind me until I caught him with

Wet bro hug with my teammates at the finish.

two short laps of the crit course to go. I assumed my group would have been caught by a few chasers by then, and I was looking forward to resting in the pack. When I peered over my shoulder there were only five guys left, and BISSELL's Paddy Bevin took off. Bevin had won two sprint stages already, but he was 30 seconds behind after a bad time trial, so I let him go and watched Mancebo. We rode cat-and-mouse for a couple laps, and I could see a BISSELL kit just up the road, so I thought I was safe from Bevin taking too much time.

A lap later, I learned that BISSELL jersey belonged to Ben Jacques-Maynes, who was a lap down, and Bevin was way up the road, trying to steal the stage race from me in the last two minutes. We came through with one lap to go, and Frankie was screaming at me from the sidewalk. "Phil you gotta go or Bevin is going win!" I stopped worrying about Mancebo and put in the fastest lap I could on the tight-cornered finishing circuit, keeping the GC lead by two seconds over Bevin, with Mancebo another second behind in third. Frankie had saved my ass.

Roman, John Murphy, and Bobby Sweeting were waiting at the finish. I hugged them as hard as I could. Someone took a photo of that moment, which is now framed and comes with me to every race. That was the day I grew up.

When the endorphins wore off, I collapsed into the passenger seat of the team car in a fetal position, all the heat vents aimed at my shivering body. Stefano knocked on the window to shake my hand and congratulate me. I couldn't speak for close to an hour. I'd never been in so much pain in my life.

My teammates were back at the host house by the time I stood on the podium, and I hated that they couldn't be there with me. It wasn't fair that I was the one holding the flowers; they'd played as big a role as I had. In most sports, the whole team wins. The headline was never "The Leading Scorer Won the Game." It would make sense for cycling to be treated like other team sports, and I bet it would take a big dent out of the doping problem. All I could do to show my appreciation that day was share my joy and buy the beers that night for my team.

Frankie talked to his wife about the race, and Betsy was skeptical at my big improvement from 2011. "He'd better not be doping!" she told him. Then Frankie told her about my tattoo, and she immediately trusted me. The little bar of soap was working.

SQUIRRELS DON'T GIVE A SHIT WHO WON REDLANDS

It took a while to sink in that I was leading the NRC. I'd never cracked the top 30, but I was a changed man now that I had a win under my belt. If you can do something once, you are never incapable again. Getting stronger each year was the easy part; now I knew how to win. It took me six years, but I'd figured out bike racing. I was proud of that at first, but then I finished reading *The Making of the Atomic Bomb* on the flight home. The Manhattan Project only took four.

Riding a high from the great result, I wondered how long it would take to wear off. When would I get jaded and cynical again? When competition is your job, it's hard to not tie your happiness to how your last race went. But you can't live if you beat yourself up every time you don't win, and it's hard to keep things in perspective when you do. Jonathan Vaughters had congratulated me in an e-mail, so I was half-convinced I'd be riding for his Garmin team in 2013. The win was getting to my head, but I didn't fight it, because being a champion means going into every race feeling like a winner, not wondering whether you can do it.

When I got home, I even noticed a change in Pat and Luca. Our friendships were the same as ever, but they looked at me differently. By then, my teammates had been living in my house for much longer than I had. I had to ask Luca which drawer the spoons were in.

I'd made it home on a Monday night, and I could barely get out of bed Tuesday. Two weeks of heavy breathing in polluted air, several days of racing in cold rain, and pushing my body beyond its limits had all added up to a headache and fever. When I blew my nose, what came out looked like a fetus. I slouched at the kitchen table with a bowl of oatmeal, and Luca decided that this was a good time to inform me that there was a squirrel living in my attic.

My parents had just gone through a struggle with a squirrel of their own. Every time I'd spoken to my mother, I tried not to tune her out as she talked about squirrel traps, poisons, reinforced gutters and flashing, and the $5,000 they spent to finally get rid of it. Now I had vermin in my attic, but I didn't have $5,000. I lifted my weak, feverish body up the creaky ladder, spotted the rodent in a corner, and shot him right between the eyes with a pellet gun.

He fell between the two-by-fours, still alive, thrashing around in the insulation. I stepped carefully, but my foot slipped and smashed through the ceiling as I pumped more rounds at the animal. I grabbed a rafter to keep my whole body from bursting through, and heard Pat and Luca laughing through the hole.

"Please tell me that's a closet I just kicked my way into," I begged.

"No!" yelled an Italian accent. "Is right over my bed! Is a mess here now!"

The squirrel was dead, but my exhaustion was now compounded by insulation in my lungs, 20 minutes of crouching and sweating in a hot attic, and the knowledge that I had a ceiling to patch. I carried a warm, deceased mammal out to the yard, and went back inside for a nap.

Luca didn't handle the incident very well. He was reminded of his pet guinea pigs back home in Italy. When his favorite pet died during a race the year before, Luca had cried all night in his room. Hartley had heard the sobbing and knocked on his door.

"Luca? Is everything okay?"

"My guinea pig died!" Luca moaned, bawling. No one knew how to console him.

CHECK YOURSELF FOR LACTOSE INTOLERANCE

My win in the first race on the NRC calendar landed me on the cover of *Road* magazine. When Luca showed off how shiny his bike was after he cleaned it, Pat shot him down. "Your bike is clean. So what? Phil won Redlands!"

An astronaut came on TV, and Luca said, "He walk on the moon? Big deal! Phil beat Mancebo!"

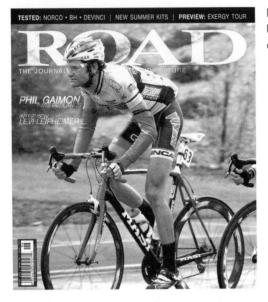

Never has anyone looked more miserable on a magazine cover.

It took a week until I was ready to train again. Redlands was nearly forgotten, and my new job was to win the NRC overall, which meant I'd need a good result at the upcoming Tour of the Battenkill. I was on form too early, and my head cold didn't help. It was frustrating to have goals and be unable to work to achieve them, so I called the team doctor to ask him if there was anything he could think of in my diet or lifestyle that might help me improve. Dr. Brayley suggested I cut out lactose. Notice he didn't say a word about EPO, asthma, or anything against the rules. Not that kind of doctor. I sent him one of the yellow jerseys from Redlands that week.

A few days later, Brayley called to ask how I was feeling with lactose out of my diet.

"I don't know," I said. "I don't think I got any faster. How can I tell if it's helping?"

"How's your digestion? Any pain or gas?"

A lightbulb went off at his last word. "Holy shit. I haven't farted in days!" That meant that my digestion and general health would improve. I did miss farting, though.

That weekend Pat and Luca helped me win a local race near Atlanta, and we spent the prize money racing go-karts on the way back to Athens. I'd never been before, but I beat Luca's best time by two seconds and set the fastest lap of the day. When your legs are good, everything goes better.

EQUIPMENT MATTERS

By an odd coincidence, half of the guys on Kenda's roster were Jewish. The Tour of the Battenkill was on a Saturday, so we decided that if we made the break, we would refuse to pull through. You're not supposed to work on the Sabbath.

My form was still strong that weekend, but the team wasn't running on all cylinders. When we opened the trailer on Friday, bikes hadn't been washed since Redlands, and all the wheels had 23c tires, too narrow for dirt roads. Tennyson, the new full-time mechanic, had set everything up at training camp, but we'd used a local guy at Redlands who apparently considered his job finished when the race ended. Tennyson was left to pick up the pieces.

There wasn't much point racing 23c tires on a dirt course, but it was too late to start gluing new tubulars. The eight of us got 11 flats during the race, more than double any other team. Three of those were mine. John Murphy made it into the early break, and I felt great in the first half of the race, leading the field over climbs and the tougher dirt sections. After three hard chase efforts and two stops at the car to fix mechanicals, though, I was barely hanging on. I made the front selection when Mancebo attacked over a climb, but my front derailleur slipped, leaving me stuck in an easy gear as we blasted across to the break. I couldn't spin my little ring fast enough to stay with Mancebo on the flats, but I managed to catch back on when the road went uphill. I finally got the bike fixed when the team car came up, but at that point I was exhausted, so I worked for John Murphy, who didn't make it over the climb near the end. Guess who won?

I'd noticed Mancebo getting better every day at Redlands, and his form was still on the way up. Had things gone smoothly, I thought I could have beaten him, but my team's poor organization cost me a result. You just have to trust your team to take care of certain things, hire the right staff, and have the right equipment ready. I couldn't show up with my own tires and wheels every weekend, but I had no hope of winning with what the team provided. I found myself in a Catch-22: I needed to be on a better team, but I couldn't get hired by a better team without results at races like Battenkill.

I slipped in the NRC standings, so my days of basking in NRC leader glory were over. When I told Pat that a friend had lost his GPS computer somewhere on the dirt roads in upstate New York, he had a good idea.

"Tell him to keep an eye out for your NRC lead when he's looking for it."

I stopped getting all the attention in the media, and it was a relief.

Summary of life as an athlete: You're training and miserable, you're lonely, you're training and miserable, you won something, everyone loves you, it's over.

YOU CAN'T HOLD FORM ALL YEAR

It wasn't a team-supported race, but some of the West Coast guys got together to race the Sea Otter Cycling Classic after Battenkill.

Andy won, but not without drama. When he flatted during the last stage, the sportsmanlike thing to do would have been to let Andy get back into the race and then continue attacking him, but Exergy's director made them go to the front and set a hard pace, trying to keep Andy from rejoining.

One of the Exergy riders approached me a week later to explain himself. "We wanted to wait for Andy, but the boss said we'd get fired if we didn't ride."

"They made me do it" didn't work at Nuremburg, I thought, and he must have read my mind.

"And I know that the Nazis said the same thing, but we really didn't have a choice—"

"It's over, and Andy still won," I said. It was a bad move on Exergy's part, but not Hitler-bad. The thing about racing is that it all comes back around, and you can't stay mad at someone you see every weekend. For all you know, you could be teammates a year later. I always say that if someone chops your wheel by accident, there's no need to apologize unless somebody crashes. And if you make a mistake in the heat of a race but nothing comes of it, you say you're sorry and then we can all pretend it never happened.

My next event, the Joe Martin Stage Race, started with an uphill time trial. After my uphill victories at San Dimas and Redlands, everyone assumed I would win again, myself included. I wasn't sure if my fitness was where it had been a few weeks before, but I was shocked to finish eighth. I would have been ecstatic with that result a year before. It was funny how quickly my expectations had changed. Now that I'd won a couple races, a top 10 meant nothing.

Shawn Milne won the next stage, which pushed him up to second overall, so we spent the week defending his lead, using me to put pressure on Mancebo's team. I attacked in the hilly crit and got up to a 30-second lead, glad to see that my legs still had their moments. For a minute I thought I might win the stage race, but I couldn't hold onto it. When the field caught me on the last lap, I fell off the back, tumbling from eighth overall to 40th. Mancebo won the stage race, which killed any hope I had of taking back the NRC lead.

DON'T SHOW UP AT GILA IF YOU'RE NOT ACCLIMATED

If my legs were barely holding onto form in Arkansas, they lost it entirely by the time we got to New Mexico for the Tour of the Gila a few days later. Between general fatigue, the 6,000-foot altitude change, and the slightly stronger field, I was pack fodder. Frankie had found host housing just outside of town, so at least we weren't staying at the gym again.

The final stage was the usual "Gila Monster" course, so the sprinters' jobs were done. Frankie told Jim to go for the early break and me and Nate to attack late if we could. When Luca asked about his own job, Frankie didn't even pretend that our poor sprinter had any chance of finishing.

"Just ride around," he said, laughing.

Luca took it well. "Guys, if you need bottle, I'll be the one with the lollipop and the red balloon."

Rory Sutherland won the GC, and he made it look easy. He'd won a ton of U.S. stage races earlier in his career, and when he moved to Europe, Mancebo and his Competitive Cyclist team were like the neighborhood bully of the NRC, beating up on the little kids while big brother Rory was out of town. I'd beaten Mancebo at Redlands, but only by the skin of my teeth. It was refreshing to watch Rory put him in his place.

DON'T COUNT YOUR CHICKENS UNTIL THEY HATCH, OR TRAIN FOR RACES YOU'RE NOT INVITED TO YET

When I was gearing up for the second half of the season, Chad Thompson told me that our invitations were confirmed for the Tours of Utah and Colorado, so those became my targets for the rest of the year. I had plenty of time to recover from the first half of the season and get back into shape, and I knew that if I brought my A game, a result at one of the bigger events could catapult me onto a European team for 2013. To prepare for the altitude, I accepted a friend's offer of his parents' 7,000-foot high vacation home in Big Bear, California. They say that two weeks at altitude is the minimum you need to acclimate, but I gave it a full month, topping it off with the Cascade Classic as my final prep.

When I got to Big Bear, in true Rocky Balboa fashion I got up at 6 a.m. each day, cooked all my meals, and had no fun whatsoever. I ate my veggies and I skipped dessert. Aside from a few rides with locals and a three-day visit from Stefano and his fiancée, I did all my training alone, with tons of five- and six-hour rides, climbing, dirt roads, and heat. On easy days, I rode laps around Big Bear Lake. On hard days, I could descend for two hours all the way into Redlands, and then climb back into town the long way: 8,400 vertical feet over Onyx Pass. The sun fried my skin at that altitude no matter how much sunscreen I wore, and in the valleys, the temperature would rarely dip below 105 degrees. With no gas stations for miles, I often had to hydrate like a deer, sipping from streams in the state forest. I thought I finally saw a bear after a few weeks, but he was shitting behind a Dumpster, and bears shit in the woods, so I must have been mistaken.

It was a lonely life that got difficult after a few weeks. When I thanked the bagger at the grocery store, I realized those were the first words I'd spoken in days. I started listening to talk radio and podcasts while I trained just to hear some conversation.

On weekends, I drove down the mountain for local races or group rides in Los Angeles or San Diego, to mix speed work with all the endurance and climbing I'd been doing. My bathroom scale and the power meter on my bike both reported good news, and I'd never been more optimistic or motivated. Then I learned that Thompson was wrong, and we weren't invited to the big races after all.

IF YOU MUST BITE THE HAND, AT LEAST WAIT UNTIL AFTER IT FEEDS YOU

The selection procedures for races like the Tours of Colorado and Utah are always difficult for smaller teams like Kenda, but getting invited was important to sponsors and riders alike. I could never tell what went into the decision, but after our poor performance the year before at the Tour of California, I wasn't surprised that Kenda had been left out of the big events in 2012.

Thompson blasted the races' organizer, Medalist Sports, all over the media. Medalist was in charge of all three major UCI races in the United States, and his campaign could only have a terrible backlash; we couldn't afford to make enemies if we wanted to be invited to races. Our team was looking for a date, and Medalist was the only girl in a small town. When she turns you down, you have to go back to the drawing board: Hit the gym, get a new car, and make sure you're more appealing when you ask again. Instead, my boss opted to walk down Main Street with a megaphone, calling her a whore at the top of his lungs.

We deserved a spot in the races, but by no means were we entitled or guaranteed. When it comes to selecting domestic teams for UCI races, the Tour of Utah cares about as much as the squirrel in my attic as about who won Redlands, because domestic teams are alike in their eyes: pack fodder. They choose the teams that are sexiest, with the most big-name riders, the coolest clothing and gear, and the biggest fan base. Kenda didn't have those things, so I didn't blame the organizers for choosing Optum, BISSELL, and Livestrong over us, even if we had a slightly better chance of good results than they did. In the eyes of the decision makers, we were the team that always missed the break at the Tour of California, with riders nobody had heard of, in a beat-up rental RV.

I'd been in touch with a number of European teams during the season, and they all noted my early results. "Let's see what you can do at Utah and Colorado," said Jonathan Vaughters, whose team had just won the Giro d'Italia. Now, with those races gone, my hopes of joining them the following year were dashed.

Thanks to Thompson's bizarre public relations campaign, it didn't look like Kenda would ever get to start one of Medalist's races again, so with Europe off the table, it was time to find a new domestic team to ride for the next year. I sent e-mails to BISSELL, Optum, and Exergy. They'd all been invited to California, Utah, and Colorado, and they were all interested in me. Some of the lower-level teams actually contacted me out of the blue. I asked for a salary of $45,000. It was still less than your garbage man makes, but triple what I got with Kenda. I was a champion now, remember?

DON'T LOSE THE GC TO WIN THE STAGE, AND CERTAINLY DON'T DO IT TO FINISH THIRD

My first offer was from Exergy. I met the team's boss at a coffee shop in Bend the day before the Cascade Classic prologue. Exergy was a growing team with a sponsor that had been throwing money all over the sport; it had a women's team, too, and supported a handful of races. All it needed was a shuffled roster and another year of development and it would be the best team in the country. Exergy's offer was $35,000, less than I thought I deserved but still a big step up.

My biggest concern was the team's roster. Its marquee rider was a washed-up sprinter from the doping era. He was still getting results, but I knew he was taking a lot of the salary budget. The team could easily have afforded three solid younger guys instead. Beyond that, I didn't trust a couple of the riders.

Based on rumors I'd been hearing, I wasn't alone in those suspicions, so I figured that if Exergy was planning to improve the following year, it would be getting rid of the guys who concerned me. I asked Exergy's director who he was looking to keep for 2013. "Well, I know we're signing . . ." And then he listed every name I didn't want to hear.

He talked for another few minutes, but it sounded like Charlie Brown's teacher in my ear. It was 2012; good sponsors were hard to find, and the sport was past that. I kept my mouth shut because it was good to have an offer, but there was no way I'd ride for him.

My training in Big Bear wasn't all for naught, because I arrived at Cascade in great form. My weak prologue proved that I didn't quite have the high-end speed yet, but with two mountaintop finishes to drop the time trialists, and a long time trial to get a few seconds on Mancebo, I thought I had a real shot at a GC win.

Frankie was away providing commentary at the Tour de France, so we had a guest director for the week. He did a good job, but he didn't know how to end a meeting, and the guys could go on for hours if you let them. Two guys looked at wind patterns to explain their mediocre time trial results, while Andy calculated what place he would be overall if he lapped the field in the criterium. I finally got fed up. "All right, guys. Here's the plan," I said. "I'm going to crash."

Bobby tried to shut me up. "Phil! Don't say that!" Pro cyclists are a superstitious bunch.

"Nope, nope. That's what I'm doing. I'm going to eat shit. Hard." Bobby cringed. "I'm going to drag my face on the ground like a cheese grater."

"Phil! Shut up! You're going to crash just because you joked about it!"

"Guys, I'm going to lose teeth."

The meeting ended. You can clear a room fast with that sort of thing.

I attacked on the first stage, as soon as the course kicked up with 3 km to go. When I looked back, Mancebo was giving it everything at the front. I had plenty of gas left, and I watched him give up, swinging off the front and motioning for someone else to take over. I didn't stay away to the finish, but I'd cracked Francisco Mancebo on a climb.

Stage 2 was the time trial, and my chance to snag the race lead. I'd beaten Mancebo at Beauce a year before, and this was a flatter course. It should have favored me since I had 5 to 10 pounds on my main rivals. This time I was actually riding my own bike, and although I hadn't done much specific training on it, I expected to do better than I had the year before. I felt good in the race but just didn't go that fast. I lost time to Mancebo.

On the next mountaintop stage, I attacked with 600 meters to go and almost got it, but the Livestrong team chased me down at 50 meters to go, and three of them squeaked by before the line, sweeping the podium. I was fourth. The Trek-Livestrong team was one of a few professional development teams that had started up in the past few years, just as I had grown too old to ride for them. Trek-Livestrong had a big budget thanks to affiliations with Team RadioShack; they picked up the top young Americans every year, giving them a living wage and the support they needed to race well. The ones who made it often went over to Europe, while those who struggled would find their way onto a domestic team like mine, usually with a steep pay cut. I was a little jealous of their opportunities until I saw them celebrating the win and high-fiving each other. I had nothing against those guys, and they'd raced perfectly, but they'd had so many of the sport's sharp edges rounded off for them that they almost didn't look like real bike racers to me. They had no lines in their faces. These kids never had to get in their fucking cars.

I finished fourth overall at Cascade. I was happy enough with the result and the fact that I was the best climber in the field, but it only made it harder that I wouldn't be racing in Utah or Colorado. I had to watch all of the guys I'd been dropping struggle on TV.

AN OFFER ISN'T WORTH ANYTHING IF IT COMES FROM THE WRONG PLACE

I finally returned home in Athens after over a month away, and it was hard to adjust. I had lots of friends in town, but I always had to call them to meet up. It wasn't their fault. I'd been away so much I'd trained them not to invite me. That's one of the hardest things about being a pro athlete: When you're gone for extended periods, you're removed from peoples' routines, and when you get back, it takes a while to insert yourself back in.

Paychecks from Kenda had been coming later and later. When one arrived, I'd immediately jump in my car and head to the bank hoping to get the check processed before it bounced, sure that everyone else on the team was doing the same.

BISSELL gave me an offer of exactly the $45,000 I'd asked for. It was the only team always invited to top-tier domestic races, thanks to a long history of results and a solid, professional organization. BISSELL was also one of the few teams to pay riders a living wage. Technically, I owed it to my current team to let it match the offer first, but things weren't looking good for Kenda: our paychecks were over a month late, and I didn't think the sponsors were secure for the next year. I signed with BISSELL, deciding to keep quiet about it and wait for Kenda to fold, which would avoid another haggling session with Chad Thompson.

The day after I put my BISSELL contract in the mail, Thompson called my cell phone while I was at the airport on my way to the Tour of Elk Grove. He had merged our team with the Competitive Cyclist team for 2013, and proudly informed me that next year I would be teammates with Francisco Mancebo. I looked for an opening to tell him that I was already gone, but he never stopped talking.

"We're keeping half our team, so you, Shawn, Jim, Nate, Andy, and Bobby," he said.

"What about Roman and the other guys?" I asked. "Roman's been a great teammate. We need guys like him."

Thompson glossed over my friends getting fired. "They're gone," he said. "You can't tell them," he added quickly. "Roman's too old. But you and Mancebo are going to win everything, and listen, don't think you'll be working for him all year. Mancebo respects you, and you'd get plenty of chances to lead."

This was a ridiculous argument. No amount of money would make me work for Mancebo for a second without a gun to my head.

"I'm sorry," I said. "I already signed to BISSELL. They asked me what I wanted, and then they gave it to me. I couldn't say no. I didn't think we'd even have a team next year."

"Okay. Well, I have right of first refusal," Thompson said. "It's in the contract." It wasn't. "I'm going to beat their offer, and you're going to flick them. Will you be open to that if we can give you a better deal?"

"Well, sure." I wasn't lying, necessarily. Thompson said that the new budget would be $1.2 million after the merger, four times what we'd been working with. That was easily enough to do a few races in Europe, so it wouldn't matter that he'd alienated Medalist Sports and ruined our shot at the Tour of California. I didn't like the idea of going back on my word with BISSELL, but every man has a price.

"Let me talk to the Competitive Cyclist guys," he said. "We'll get you an offer next week."

That same day, he informed the team that our next paychecks would be a few more weeks late.

My last race with Kenda was the Tour of Elk Grove. I crashed out in a wet corner, my first fall since planting my chin into the pavement in Korea almost two years before. When I finally slid to a stop, I noticed some empty beer cans on the side of the road. I pictured the guy who drank those beers, perched on the back of a truck with his buddies after a hard day's work. Where did I go wrong in my life that a guy who probably didn't go to college or train his butt off to become a pro athlete could drink a beer and toss the can in the street without a care in the world, whereas I was about to limp to CVS to spend $25 on bandages? I bet his paycheck came on time, too.

I watched from the sidelines for the rest of the weekend with an ice pack on my thigh. John Murphy finished second overall. He could have had a spot on the merged Kenda-Competitive squad if he wanted it, but John was ready to move on, and he already had an offer from United Healthcare (UHC) for the following year. Eight months before, when John was dropped by BMC, he told me about how excited he was to race in the United States, and it had made me question if I really wanted to get to Europe. It only took one season with Kenda for John to remember why he crossed the Atlantic in the first place, and UHC was his ticket back.

Tennyson was the team mechanic at Elk Grove. As a fellow southerner, I'd been providing him with fresh-brewed sweet tea each day. In return, now that the team's last race of the year was finished, he gave me five minutes alone in the equipment trailer with a backpack. I loaded up on all the sponsor-provided chains, tires, tubes, bar tape, and cables that Thompson had been stingy with, and shared my wealth with the guys. I don't want him to get in trouble, but Tennyson said I could tell this story as long as I mentioned his rogue good looks and charm. Tenny, you're beautiful, and I love you.

Frankie brought his family out to the race that weekend, so I finally got to meet Betsy. She shared a few embarrassing stories about Frankie, like how when they met she thought he was gay. I wanted to thank her for saving my sport, but how do you casually bring that up?

It was the last race of the year, and the riders all accepted that the band was breaking up. Our reaction: alcohol. The night ended with no one picking up any women, Isaac smashing a glass bottle in the driveway at the host house, and Shawn Milne wandering off into the distance. I called to ask what he was doing. "I'm walking to sobriety," he slurred. He found his way back.

DON'T TRUST A BUSINESSMAN

Thompson hadn't given up on signing me to the 2013 Competitive Cyclist–Kenda team, and I was sick of his phone calls. Just so he'd turn me down and the discussion could be over, I demanded $80,000, citing Mancebo as the reason.

I try not to have rivals or enemies in the sport. I think anger is a good way to get you off the couch and get started toward your goal, but it doesn't make great fuel for long-term success. Still, I thought about Mancebo a lot. I understand why he did what he probably did, and I don't blame him for it, but a handful of riders like Mancebo created a toxic atmosphere in the sport, which led to sponsorship woes and fewer opportunities for riders of my generation, and I'd lived a lot of lean years as a result. Five years before, the winner of Redlands had been making six figures.

Why did the bosses at Competitive Cyclist hire Mancebo in the first place? I asked them about it, and they said that they were businessmen. I took that to mean that Mancebo rides well, so it's easy to overlook the impact on a sport that's trying to move on from a bad era. I would argue that Jonathan Vaughters is also a businessman with his clean team, and he's better at it.

"You two would be co-leaders," Thompson assured me. "But there's no way we could pay you that much. Mancebo only gets 55K."

"Mancebo gets $90,000," I told him. I'd done my homework, and I was starting to enjoy this. Negotiating is fun if you don't want the job.

"Okay, you're right. He makes more than 55K. But you don't have the name recognition he does. You didn't finish top five at the Tour. We just can't pay you the same."

I screamed into the phone, "I ALSO NEVER GOT PULLED OUT OF THE TOUR FOR OPERACIÓN PUERTO! DOES THAT COUNT FOR ANYTHING?" Osama bin Laden had great name recognition. Would he be getting a generous offer? I took a deep breath. "Fine. I'm riding for BISSELL, and that's that." I hung up.

If I'd promised to race for a dime, he would have offered nine cents. I ignored a slew of insults in text messages, happy that another bridge worth burning was sinking to the bottom of the river, and I could look forward to a year with a new team.

KEEP YOUR FRIENDS NEARBY

When I got back to Athens, the Larsons had moved to Oklahoma for new jobs, but my good friends Morgan Patton and Thomas Brown had rented out the Larsons' house. They were another bike racing couple, letting me continue to be a third wheel in familiar surroundings. I joined Morgan and Thomas that weekend for a half-marathon. I hate running, but with all the stress from the long season and a team that was now two months late with my paycheck, I needed a distraction. I would have said yes to anything. "Phil, want to come join a hate group with us?" "Whatever! Let me find some sheets!"

I ran exactly seven times in preparation for the event, but I loved the challenge of trying something different, just because I didn't know if I could do it. I was secretly hoping to win so I could drop this dumb bike racing business, but after 13.1 miles of suffering on trails and slopping through muddy creeks, I wasn't even close.

SAVE YOUR MONEY

Fall 2012 was a bad time to be a pro cyclist. Lance Armstrong's misdeeds finally caught up to him. Tyler Hamilton came out with a tell-all book to cash in on his crimes. Sponsors fled the sport. Tyler's book made the *New York Times* best-sellers list, and he'll probably grab another few million dollars with a movie deal, but at least the Andreus were finally vindicated. I sent Frankie a message to see what he was up to. He said he'd been doing a lot of reading.

Jeremy Powers asked if I wanted to get together in the winter to train again.

"Just you, or Rick as well?" I asked.

"I've learned some things about Rick's past," Jeremy said, vaguely. "Rick Crawford is no longer part of the Jeremy Powers family." Oh, shit!

A few weeks later, Rick admitted to doping some of his coaching clients years before he'd started working with Jeremy. It was scary how close some of the fallout was getting to my friends.

My teammates and I never got those late paychecks. The team spent the remainder of the budget sending us to races. USA Cycling keeps two months of salary in an escrow account, so at least that came at the end. Thompson insisted that we all send our bikes back; in return, he promised that he'd sell them and other inventory to pay the debt he owed us. Everything was sold on eBay over the next few months, but the riders never got our cut. Know what's harder than living off of $20,000 a year? Budgeting for that and only getting $15,000.

When we complained, our boss blamed sponsors for not paying and Lance Armstrong for ruining pro cycling with a drug scandal. Thompson was always the unapologetic victim, lamenting that he'd never paid himself from the team and that we had never given him a share of the prize money. His lawyer explained over the phone that all the contracts and legal options were flushed down the toilet, as the LLC behind the team would be filing for bankruptcy.

"Moral bankruptcy?" I asked.

The reality was that at our level of the sport, money was slim. Managers would approach riders and say, "We've got the sponsors, we just need you to join the team," and then turn to sponsors and say, "We've got the best riders, we just need your cash." Over the years, Thompson had committed to more than the team could afford, sponsors had given less than they'd promised, and when it all caught up to us, the riders were left high and dry.

We had an intense e-mail exchange when I figured everything out. It's not that Thompson stole anything, and I'm sure he came out with a loss, but he misled us all along to save more for himself, and for all that I told him what I thought of him. I wonder if he took down my framed yellow jersey from Redlands.

Meanwhile, the merged Competitive Cyclist–Kenda team was still on track for the next year. Normally, when a team folds, the riders receive the bank guarantee to get whatever is left of the budget, and that's the final nail in the team's coffin. The budget was nowhere near the projected $1.2 million, but with the merger, Thompson had found a way to keep his team and his house of cards somewhat intact. When the merger was final, I wouldn't have been surprised if the other owners had paid him to go away. But I'd probably throw up if I found out how much.

For months, my schadenfreude at watching Thompson struggle was at war with pity for my teammates, many of whom still had to sign for the 2013 team.

Isaac, John Murphy, and I were safe, with contracts signed elsewhere before the bottom fell out of the market, but Jim Stemper was left out. I knew Jim's potential, and I felt that I owed him for his three years of working for me. I spent an hour trying to convince BISSELL to take him, but ultimately, I couldn't repay him for all his sweat and blood. Jim finally signed with Kenda, along with Shawn, Bobby, and Nate, at pathetic salaries. As always, the selfless team players got the short end of the stick. Even Frankie went along to the merged team. I don't think he loved the idea of directing Mancebo, but he had three kids and a wife to feed. Frankie was selling out his principles in a way, but he'd done enough for principles when he stood up to Lance, and his family needed the security.

Also with a wife and baby to support, Paul Mach quit the team and took a software job. While I was building my business in my spare time between races, Paul had been working on a PhD. I thought about the scene in *Good Will Hunting* when Ben Affleck's character tells Matt Damon's character that he'd be glad if Damon's character disappeared someday. He knows he's too good for this life, and he wants him to move on, even if it means he never gets to see his friend again. That's how I felt when Paul retired. At least I got to shake his hand before he left.

Pat Lemieux had an offer to stay with Kenda, but his girlfriend wanted him to spend the year with her. Gwen was a pro triathlete who had just finished second at ITU World Championships, and she raced better with Pat there for support. I told Pat I'd kill him if he didn't take a pretty girl's offer over Thompson's, because some things are more important than bike racing. He obeyed. They're doing great.

Luca had interest from a few American teams, but none that made it worthwhile to leave his fiancée in Italy for another year.

I asked if he'd be able to find a job there. "In Italy, you learn trade in high school. I am a licensed plumber," he assured me. I graduated from college and still didn't have any useful skills. Luca went back to playing with the family ram and raising guinea pigs, and soon he'd be paid to make sure that everyone in town could flush everything, rather than just reminding his teammates to do it.

Roman began work at a law firm, and other guys found spots on smaller teams. Andy Jacques-Maynes talked to all the American teams, holding firm in a demand for a $50,000 salary, but he didn't get any takers. He had a college degree and a brain, so of course he deserved to be paid reasonably. But in that market no team would want Andy that badly, and deep down I think he knew it. A lot of guys end their careers that way. They ask for more money than they're worth, and act surprised when they don't get it. It's a way of quitting while leaving the final decision to someone else. Maybe he wasn't emotionally ready to make it himself, or admit it to others.

Racing together makes you close, but going through those months of financial turmoil made our squad particularly tight. When the paychecks were officially over, everyone was out thousands of dollars. All we had left were a few bikes and parts that Thompson had forgotten about. Rather than just sell what we had piecemeal, we pooled the goods, sold it together, calculated who was owed the most, and distributed the leftover cash equitably. It was going to be a tough winter for all of us, but it was beautiful how we came together. I spoke with all the guys when it was over. I wanted them to know that even if we didn't talk for a while, there was no need to be a stranger. If they ever needed a place to stay, a friend to talk to, or a kidney transplant, they had my number.

FIND A COACH WHO UNDERSTANDS YOU

Colby Pearce had been my coach for four years. I was happy with my progress, but I thought it might be a mistake to spend my whole career with the same coach. To stir things up I hired Matt Koschara, my director from Sakonnet. He was the man who'd told me to get in my fucking car five years before. On his advice, I'd driven alone to the big NRC stage races, which allowed me to make the leap from amateur to professional at the end of 2008. Maybe I could make a similar leap in 2013 with his help, this time to Europe. Matt was excited to help me accomplish what the dopers had taken away from him, and his outside-the-box thinking might find the little boost I needed. When he e-mailed my training, it would say things like, "First interval: time trial pace; second interval: all out; third interval: chariots of fire."

8

YOU GOTTA BELIEVE

T he upside of Kenda's abridged season was that I suddenly had a lot of free time. I breezed through the rest of the reading list I'd made at the end of 2008 and started putting my years of rambling notes into my own book. I finished a first draft by the end of the year and sent it out to a few publishers.

I made up for Kenda's missing paychecks that fall by appearing as a "pro ride leader" for charity events. They didn't pay much when you factored in the travel expenses, but every little bit helped, and my company sold clothing at the events. Tom Danielson and Frankie Andreu were the other leaders for a ride in Florida in December. Tom had recently confessed to doping as part of the Lance testimony and was serving his suspension over the winter. He remembered when I attacked during the pee break and called him "Christian" at the Tour of California, but he didn't seem all bad when we chatted.

I assumed that Tom had noticed my CLEAN tattoo, but I was careful to avoid that touchy subject. When we were talking about diet and nutrition, I mentioned that I was thinking about buying a juicer.

"Do you juice? Are the Euro guys into that?" I asked.

Tom eased off the pedals and stared at me, his expression suddenly changed.

It took me a second to figure out why, and I clarified in a panic. "No. No! Like beets and apples! Jack LaLanne juicing! Not Sammy Sosa!"

During the ride Tom did his best to make me suffer, and I did my best to prove he couldn't, always matching his pulls and never letting up the pace. We finished the hundred miles in well under four hours, and Tom was impressed.

Frankie and I grabbed a few beers at the hotel. We talked about Kenda and the state of pro cycling. There were 12 pro teams racing in the United States when I started; in 2013 that number would drop to five. Even Exergy, a team that had looked like an up-and-comer, had folded. I was climbing a ladder, but it seemed like another rung was removed beneath me every year. I was barely going fast enough to stay above ground.

BEING RIGHT DOESN'T ALWAYS MEAN YOU WIN

When a team goes down the drain like Kenda had, you assume that USA Cycling will take care of you, but it was shocking how little protection and oversight was in place. The organization wouldn't even help us find an attorney, and the ones I spoke to said that it wasn't worth suing Thompson. They wanted to sue the new team, not because those guys had done anything wrong, but because that's where the money was. It made me happy I didn't go to law school.

I couldn't sue a team that my friends were riding for, so I finally gave up. I needed to focus on racing, and trying to beat Thompson was a waste of time and energy. Accepting failure—even though it meant that the bad guy won the war—was probably an important life lesson. I've noticed that the more valuable the lesson, the more it hurts.

NUDITY IS GOOD FOR YOU

In December I flew to Tucson to train with Jeremy Powers and his new coach, old friend, and former Barn resident, Al Donahue. We stayed at the top of Mount Lemmon, which meant a lot of digging out of the snow and driving down 5,000 feet for our training rides, but it was great to catch up with them.

Brad Huff canceled at the last minute, but he made up for it by sending us a link to a research study that showed that if your testicles got a few hours of direct sunlight every day, it would increase your

Huff with his new tattoo.

testosterone levels. I asked him how he sunned his balls without getting arrested, so he sent pictures of his crotch, basking in the sunlight in various places. Jeremy and I reciprocated, and balls went back and forth, in a grotesque, hairy tennis match. Testicle photos are a funny thing because they're not really intimate. The balls and penis are close geographically, but miles apart emotionally. Of course, we were all teammates back in 2009, so we'd seen each other's wangs, too.

Huff also sent me a picture of his new CLEAN tattoo. That made nine riders so far who'd joined the club.

TRAIN WITH PEOPLE WHO CAN BEAT YOU

It seemed like every pro in the country was in Tucson doing intervals on Mount Lemmon that winter. We joked that USADA should test the sand at the base of the mountain since that's where everyone relieved themselves. Al always played God when he peed in the desert. "All right! Which one of you guys wants some precipitation today?" he'd bellow over the plants cowering beneath him. "I decide who may thrive!"

Danielson was in town, so I climbed Lemmon with him one day. I hung on for dear life as I stared at the skinny ass of one of the best riders in the world, and I couldn't finish his workout. I'd trained hard in the past, but in all my years no one had dropped me on a hill like that.

Tom had been spending his winters in Tucson for a long time, and I took him up on his offer to come back in January. My first monthly paycheck from BISSELL had arrived, for $3,750. I wasn't rich, but I was liberated, and I could afford to live and train as I'd always wanted. For years my standard breakfast was eggs and oatmeal, and dinner was eggs and rice. I needed calories, so vegetables

Hiding in Tom Danielson's draft.

were a luxury, empty vitamins I couldn't afford. With $3,750 coming in every month, I could finally have a salad. I ordered the juicer I'd had my eye on, and crammed it with kale and organic beets.

The juicer traveled with me when I drove to Tucson, where I stayed with former Kenda teammates Isaac Howe and Gregg Brandt at the same house where we had held training camp the year before. I reluctantly left the home I'd just settled into in Athens. It was shocking to realize that I could still pack for a six-month trip in 15 minutes and fit everything I needed in the Toyota.

I rented out my house in Georgia to the Mountain Khakis team (formerly Time Pro Cycling) at a steep discount, a favor to repay them for letting me out of that contract four years before; my pirate ship was still full of needy bike racers. I found out that one of those guys was on food stamps. You're eligible in Georgia if you make less than $1,300 a month. Why the hell hadn't I thought of that?

In Tucson I rode with Tom every day for close to a month. His workouts were simple: Day One was three sets of 20-minute intervals up Mount Lemmon, followed by easy climbing for a total of five hours; Day Two was three sets of 45-minute intervals up Mount Lemmon; Day Three was off, or long and easy. Then we'd repeat Day One.

Within a couple weeks, I could finish the whole ride. I was even able to ride next to Tom occasionally rather than hide in his draft. I thought I'd trained hard before, but those weeks gave training a whole new meaning. Riding the same climb over and over was monotonous, but it allowed for more consistent effort and better power.

After the rides, I'd collapse onto the floor in the shower, lacking the energy to stand. If I ate too much or not enough the night before, I would feel it on the bike in the morning. I hadn't known it was possible to focus even harder that I had before, but now I was doing it. On rest days, I cooked huge meals to reheat later in the week. Before bed I measured out my oatmeal for breakfast and left two pieces of bread waiting in the toaster. Watching my improvement over such a short period, Tom said I was ready to race in Europe, and he'd try to help make it happen. Whatever you say, weirdo.

Danielson and I finally talked about doping. He said that it was still a dirty era when he first spoke to Jonathan Vaughters about riding for Slipstream. Tom was told he'd be paid well, but he'd have to be clean, 100 percent. At the time, racing clean sounded like a death sentence for his career. Tom was afraid he'd DNF every race and never get another job, but he took the risk and signed on. For the first couple years, results for Slipstream were slim, but eventually, more guys got caught, more teams caught on to Vaughters's business model of clean racing, and the team started to win. Whaddaya know?

One night we gathered around the TV and watched Lance Armstrong spill his guts to Oprah. I wanted to forgive him, but he still couldn't admit that Frankie and Betsy were telling the truth. I like them too much to let that go. Afterward, Betsy was a guest on Anderson Cooper's news show. No one else got a word in as she tore Lance apart. You could see tears in her eyes.

DON'T SHOOT WITHIN CITY LIMITS

Tucson wasn't without some fun and mischief, of course. Early one morning a woodpecker attacked the side of the house just inches from my ear. I donned my bathrobe, grabbed a BB gun from the garage, and took my best shot. With a puff of feathers, a "pop" sound replaced the hammering, and the woodpecker fell to the ground with a thud. Don't fuck with my sleep.

Two women taking a walk spotted a man in a bathrobe marching back to the house with what looked like a rifle. Minutes later, police burst through the door. They'd found the air rifle in the garage, so their real guns were back in the holsters.

"My name is Phil," I told one officer, handing him my driver's license as he stared at my face.

"Phil the Thrill?" He asked. The cop recognized me from my humor column in *Velo* magazine, and I got off with a warning.

Isaac joined the CLEAN tattoo club that week after a series of bitter fights with his girlfriend. She was against tattoos in general and argued that she'd have to look at it 20 years from now, when bike racing and Phil would be long gone.

"If anything," Isaac pointed out, "Phil will still be here in 20 years, and you won't."

At the tattoo parlor, I asked the artist if anyone had ever gotten notches and numbers on their upper thigh, to measure the temperature by how much their testicles sagged in the dry Arizona heat. He said he'd never heard that one before. I'll do it someday.

MONEY CAN'T BUY HAPPINESS

Danielson was good friends with the actor Patrick Dempsey. They'd started a charity focused on getting people outside to ride their bikes, and the first event was in Tucson. Isaac and I were invited to have dinner with the sponsors (including Dempsey) in a private room at an Indian casino on the edge of town. We sat with local businessmen, lawyers, Danielson, and Dempsey, joined by the owner of the casino, who looked awfully white for a guy who was supposed to be Native American.

I estimated that everyone at the table made at least 10 times my salary, but for a few hours Isaac and I were able to set aside our rice and eggs in favor of king crab and caviar, and no one noticed that we didn't know which forks to use.

It was funny to hang out with Tom. I'm not sure how much money he made, but it was enough to have a nice house in Boulder with a dirt track for his motorbikes, a house in Tucson for the winter, and a place in Spain for the racing season. Tom always picked up the check when we had dinner, and my friends were angry with me for enjoying his "ill-gotten fortune." They felt that his money was stolen because he had doped.

I had a hard time accepting Tom's generosity at first, but I know that conscience can be a powerful enemy; even if it looks like a guy got away with something, he's still paying for it in his dreams, his self-esteem, and in other indirect ways. For example, Tom tweeted me a few times, and I saw some of the replies. He had close to 50,000 followers, and there was a lot of hate in some of those messages. I'd been through it with my blog, but nothing close to the vitriol Tom was facing, and I could tell it was hard for him. Tom's charity work with Dempsey was a form of penance, and I realized that his friendship and time with me was another means of giving back to the sport on a smaller, more personal scale.

It's true that Tom's six-month suspension was lenient—especially because he was allowed to serve it in the off-season—but it's hard to say what he deserved. Judging the fairness of Tom's sentence isn't up to me, and it's clear that former dopers won't be kicked out and sent to the glue factory like used-up racehorses. If I want to get to Europe, it will be a few years until all the guys who ever doped are out of the sport, and I'll have to coexist with them peacefully. Cycling is hard enough without making enemies.

What's the difference between Tom Danielson and Francisco Mancebo? It's hard to put into words without sounding like a hypocrite, and there's a lot of gray area. But here goes. First, Tom confessed and helped kick Lance out of the sport, a huge weight off of cycling's shoulders. Another big difference is that Tom was racing in Europe against a lot of guys with similar backgrounds. Overall, though, as I realized with Jon Chodroff, you have to look at a person's full body of work before you judge him. Frankie Andreu doped, and I couldn't have asked for a better friend or mentor. Jonathan Vaughters doped, and then brought cycling back from the edge of a cliff. Tom hadn't made up for his doping yet, but I'd seen him pull over to help a stranger change a flat tire, and I could tell that he was just another normal guy who did something wrong. I also believe that the world is a meritocracy, and everything will turn out right at the end, so it doesn't matter how I feel about it.

When we left the "rags-to-riches experience" at the casino, Isaac and I both involuntarily doubled over to catch our breath. We couldn't go back to the house right away, so we explored the surrounding neighborhood by foot. Remember how Shawn Milne had to walk to sobriety a few months earlier at the Tour of Elk Grove? Isaac and I walked to poverty.

LOCAL RACES ARE GOOD FOR SELF-ESTEEM

With BISSELL's training camp approaching, I left Tucson and headed to Stefano's new place in Thousand Oaks, California, for a week. It was hard to be confident in my fitness with Danielson constantly beating me up, but a local race with Stefano restored my faith. It started with a long climb, and I attacked from the gun. Half an hour later the race official approached on his motorcycle. "You have two minutes on the field, but there's one rider bridging at a minute and a half. He says to wait, and you know who he is."

Of course it was Stefano. I laughed and pulled over to pee.

"You're actually going to stop?" the official asked, surprised.

"I'm staying at his house," I explained. "And he's my ride home." Besides, I had 60 miles to go, so I liked the idea of drafting. We stayed away, and I got the win.

Training camp with the BISSELL team started a few days later in Santa Rosa, California. I was afraid that Jason McCartney would still be angry about our shouting match in Greenville two years before, but he and all the other guys were great to hang out with. BISSELL's organization, staff, equipment, and teammates were everything I could have hoped for—especially compared to Kenda, which had paid for exactly one dinner in three years. Back then, we had stayed in hotels at training camp, and I'd learned to travel with an electric

Stefano (*left*) and I, post-local-race smashing.

burner, small pots, dishes, and silverware so I wouldn't go broke eating out every meal. My new teammates laughed when they saw my travel kitchen. They were used to decent hotels, plenty of staff, everything on a schedule, and all expenses paid. I learned that the team was actually owned by the vacuum company that sponsored us, rather than some behind-the-scenes manager trying to squeeze out a profit by spending less than his budget. I should have tried harder to beg my way onto BISSELL years before. I'm sure the team would have taken me for $5,000 instead of the $15,000 I was getting from Kenda. It would have been hard to make up that $10,000 in the short term, but I bet I would have developed a year or two faster.

On team rides, I was the strongest every time the road turned uphill. I never attacked—it was just training camp, after all—but guys would ride at the front and push the pace, and thanks to Danielson, I could always maintain it when they cracked. Levi Leipheimer (who'd just retired after admitting his role in the Lance-era doping scandal) lived and trained around Santa Rosa. We'd been riding hard for a few days, but I still beat his record up one of his favorite climbs.

IF YOU'RE IN SHAPE, JUST GO TO THE RACE

BISSELL usually finished training camp with the Merco Classic, a well-attended four-day stage race in northern California. The team couldn't start the whole roster, so a few guys opted out to head home. Predicting that I'd be sick of traveling after a month on the road, I volunteered to skip it, but when Paddy Bevin crashed on a ride, I was quickly subbed in.

Halfway through the first stage I bridged a gap of nearly three minutes to a 10-man breakaway. On the last lap I attacked the break on the climb. Halfway up, only Ben Jacques-Maynes (now riding for Jamis) was still on my wheel, but I could tell he was hurting when he asked me to ride steady. *Steady* is code for "I don't want to admit it, but I'm about to blow up."

I was open to convincing. "I'll slow down if you'll give me the stage," I offered.

I looked back, but Ben didn't respond. Not responding is code for "I'm going to sit on and beat you in the sprint." I shifted into a harder gear as a warning, and looked back again.

"Say it's my stage, or I have to drop you."

Silence. So I dropped him. I made it over the climb with a 10-second lead and pushed hard on the descent and through the valley, winning by nearly a minute. Bridging a huge gap to the break and then soloing away to victory at the first race of the year is code for "I did my training over the winter, and now I'm awesome."

I only lost a few seconds in the time trial the next day, and with the help of my team I kept my massive GC lead through the end of the stage race.

I couldn't remember anyone dominating a national-level race like I had at Merco. Neither could Jonathan Vaughters, so we traded a few e-mails the following week. JV said that he was interested in me for 2014, that I was clearly the best guy in the United States, but he wasn't sure if I had the legs for Europe yet. To find out, he wanted me to see a physiologist he worked with in Denver. Vaughters was a big believer in lactate threshold (LT) tests for selecting his riders, and he liked to use the same physiologist, lab, and protocol for everyone. I told him I'd make the trip the week after Redlands. It may seem odd to learn that a team manager could base roster decisions on LT numbers, but if you are evaluating talent, LT tests can be used to judge cyclists just like stats are to judge players in Major League Baseball. I wasn't doing the big races with JV's team, so this was his next-best way to see how good I was.

WATCH WHERE YOU'RE GOING

I headed to Big Bear after training camp, having asked my friend's parents if I could stay at their vacation home for the summer. They didn't use it when the ski season was over, so all they wanted for rent was a yellow jersey on the wall. I knew I could deliver one eventually, but I never guessed I'd be able to hang one up from Merco the day I got there.

Shawn Milne arrives with my cruiser to take to breakfast on a weekend trip to warmer weather in San Diego.

Shawn Milne, my former Kenda teammate, flew in to train with me through San Dimas and Redlands, and we fought through the snow together in the high-altitude ski town.

I was ready for the racing season, and it showed when I won the San Dimas time trial by 17 seconds. It was great to wear yellow again at the start of the circuit race the following morning. Over my many years at the race, I'd gone through the entire range of emotions, not only as an athlete but as a human being. I'd worn every jersey, won three stages, and helped teammates win the overall twice, but I had never won the whole thing myself. Halfway through the circuit race, my legs were good, and I bridged to a break on the climb to give my teammates a chance to recover from riding on the front. As we neared the start/finish, I looked back to see if the BIS-SELL jerseys were with me again.

At that point on the course, the road narrows with a fence that comes out from the curb. I'm not sure whether someone bumped into me, or whether I didn't see it, or whether I saw it and had nowhere to go, but the fence caught my handlebars and pulled me right down. About 100 meters from where I'd celebrated my big stage win four years before with Jelly Belly, I was knocked out cold for several minutes in a pool of my own blood while my brain did a full reset. I've heard a rumor that I peed my shorts while I was passed out on the course, but I'm pretty sure that someone made that up. Pretty sure.

I was airlifted to County USC Hospital in Los Angeles, where all the illegal aliens, gang members, bike racers, and drug addicts end up. I regained consciousness briefly in the helicopter. Just in case there is a God and he was listening, I told him that I wanted to live. I should have asked for new furniture, too.

Then I tried to speak to the medic. I never figured out whether he couldn't hear my voice over the helicopter blades, he was ignoring me, or I wasn't actually speaking, but he didn't respond. I concluded that it was an out-of-body experience, that I was dead. I remember thinking I'd had a pretty good run for 27 years. It's nice to know I wasn't afraid.

They say that laughter is the best medicine, but I think medicine is actually the best medicine, specifically morphine. My next memory is speaking to a nurse at the hospital, trying to piece together what happened. I knew I had been in a bike race, but I couldn't remember where. When I tried to move my head to look around, my neck muscles refused to lift my sore noggin from the pillow. I figured my neck was broken, so I grabbed a handful of hair with my left hand and turned my head manually.

They must have cut my clothing off while I was passed out, because I was wearing a hospital gown, and I could see half a pair of BISSELL shorts spilling out of a paper bag in the corner.

"Nurse, did you cut a jersey off, too?" I asked.

"Yes, sir, we did," she confirmed.

"Do you remember what color it was?" I had a hunch that I might have been doing well in the race before I crashed.

She peeked into the paper bag. "It's yellow," she said, removing the bloody, torn race leader's jersey from the bag. As my memory slowly came back, I started to get angry.

"I'm going to need more morphine, please." She must have wondered why I hate yellow so much.

I was kicked out of my bed for a meth addict who'd been stabbed but wouldn't give his name to the police. I couldn't hear much after that over all the hollering. The cycling news sites had reported that I was airlifted from the race, and when BISSELL's director arrived with my phone, I saw I had hundreds of texts, e-mails, and voice-mails from concerned friends and strangers. It was exhausting trying to respond to everyone, so after an hour of that my morphined brain thought it would save time to tweet a photo of myself, shirtless, with cuts and bruises on my chest, and my thumbs up, grinning through a black eye and torn face, to tell the world how well I was doing. That photo filled a full page in the next issue of *Velo*, with all 17 stitches visible in my forehead.

I went to the race the next day as a spectator. I was mangled and bruised, but I wanted to show my face and let my friends and team-

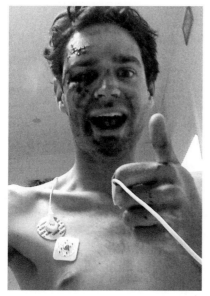

Post-crash selfie.

mates see me alive and walking around. Shawn Milne picked me up after the stage, and we sped out of that town like we were in an action movie.

The following days were miserable. I had horrible pain in my head, neck, shoulders, hands, face, jaw, mouth, head, neck, shoulders, head, and head. Training was out of the question, and the doctor said to avoid TV and computer screens, which slow concussion recovery. I couldn't eat, I didn't have the energy to read—I had nothing to do that week but take narcotics and stare at the wall. Something about the healing process made me crave red meat, so every time I woke up from a nap I demanded that Shawn drive me into town for another burger.

With all that free time in a drugged haze, I got a lot of thinking done. I decided that I had to take responsibility for my crash. If I wanted to credit hard work for success, I couldn't blame bad luck for failure. The first thing I learned when I started riding a bike at 5 years old was to watch where I was going. It was funny to think that 20 years later, I had to relearn that the hard way. Actually, that's not funny at all.

Days before, the season had looked like a breeze. I was going to win every NRC stage race, podium the Tour of California, and it was only a matter of time before I'd be racing in Europe. Now, I'd miss my chance of wearing number one at Redlands, and I'd have to train hard just to be able to start the ToC. I thought about all the hours on Danielson's wheel in Tucson. Was that wasted after two weeks on the sofa? Would I be able to put myself through the training I'd need to get my fitness back? And this time Tom was in Spain, so I'd be on my own.

I had to watch Redlands from the sidelines. The last day, Mancebo put in the same attack I'd shut down the year before. This time it worked, and he won the stage race. I looked at the chasing field, knowing that I was the only one in the country who could have caught him. If I'd had my bike, I probably would have jumped in.

The hardest part was seeing my old teammates riding for Mancebo instead of me, but I felt better after I talked to Shawn about it.

"Know what's nice about working for Mancebo?" he asked. I couldn't imagine. "I really don't care if he wins or not," he said. "Last year was so much more stressful and emotional when you were in yellow. I stared at Twitter to see if you held it after I pulled out the last day. This year, I did my job just the same, but while he was attacking, I took a nap."

The support that came after my crash was the silver lining in a dark cloud. My phone never stopped buzzing, and I even got chocolate chip cookies in the mail. I fell, but friends were there to catch me. I had to make a strong comeback, and luckily the headaches stopped after a few days. For weeks I had trouble remembering names, or why I'd walked into a room, but it got better. I did catch myself making a lot of rude and offensive jokes. Of course, that was also a problem before the crash.

DO WHAT WORKS

Vaughters suspected I had the legs for Europe, and the Tour of California was my best chance to prove it if I wanted a contract for 2014. Now I had a chance to show him that I also had the heart. I was still popping narcotics to ease the pain and soreness, but I needed to start training again, and I couldn't ride if I was all drugged up, feeling like a zombie. I tossed the pills into the toilet and pulled on the BISSELL tights, pain be damned.

The riding I had done with Danielson in Tucson had given me the fitness to win in Merco and San Dimas, so I did the same workouts, this time alone. Every day, I drove to the bottom of Big Bear Mountain and smashed my way up, over and over. I had to sit on the floor of the shower those nights, just like I had in Arizona. Training is no fun when you don't feel good, and I was miserable, but I kept it up, day after day, for the hardest two weeks of my life. At the top of the climb I was distracted from my suffering with a view of the pines and Big Bear Lake, with snow still falling on the peaks nearby. I'm not rich or famous, but the indirect perks of my job were undeniable.

To escape another blizzard in Big Bear, I headed to San Diego to visit JC and Pat Lemieux, who was in town with Gwen for a triathlon. She won, confirming that Pat made the right decision leaving Kenda to stay with her. The next day we all went bowling, and this time we were joined by Chris Glossner (who I'd found on the Internet). JC and I had joked about his double 299 games, but he'd bowled a few 300s since the last time I was in town. Glossner didn't give up, either.

NUMBERS DON'T LIE

I flew to Denver the week before the Tour of the Gila to do my testing for Vaughters. My legs weren't back to where they'd been before the crash, but it was the only week that fit with my race schedule, and the tests went well enough. My power-to-weight ratio put me above average for the European pros, and I tested close to the best in some areas. The physiologist said I would do well at Gila. I laughed at that.

I sent the results to Vaughters, starting what turned out to be a long interview process. How was I healing up from San Dimas? While we're on the subject of crashing, how were my bike-handling skills? Do I get homesick? The process was stressful, but I did my best to give honest answers and make myself look good. The final question was the hardest.

"Why did it take you so long to develop, when most top riders start to peak much younger?"

I talked about my late start to the sport, and my years on smaller teams with limited opportunities. I tried to keep the answer short, because I could write a book about it. Literally.

Vaughters brought up everything except a contract, so I assumed that he wanted to see how I did at the Tour of California. I was nervous, and then I found out that Dan and Rebecca Larson had their baby. Perspective—and faith in humanity—were slightly restored.

I also looked at the results from the Athens Twilight and the crits surrounding it. I could tell that David Guttenplan had finally left his girlfriend, because he was riding well. The Gutt got back those 50 watts that she'd taken from him.

After the testing I stayed with Chris Baldwin in Boulder. I'd never forgotten his kind words to a young amateur when I was first starting out, and it meant a lot to spend time with him years later as a peer.

We joked about how far I'd come and everything I'd learned.

"By the time I finally figure out how to do everything right, I'll be too old to be fast anymore!" I laughed.

Chris was 38. "Welcome to my life," he smiled.

YOU CAN RACE BROKEN

Pain in my hand had started to get worse. I found out that I'd fractured two bones in my wrist when I crashed at San Dimas, and it's common for initial X-rays to miss it. My start at the Tour of the Gila was suddenly looking doubtful, and I was concerned about missing California the week after, along with my shot at a spot on Garmin. The team decided to line me up anyway. If it got worse in New Mexico, I'd drop out and put it in a cast.

I was tired of everyone asking how I was healing. A win on the first stage would have been a great answer, even if I was wearing a wrist brace, but luck was against me. Halfway through the stage someone ran into my derailleur in the feed zone, which meant I had to stop and wait for a neutral bike from SRAM. I made it back to the group, but I was caught behind a crash a few miles later and had to switch bikes again, this time for one set up for a teammate.

While the car and teammate Pat McCarty helped me catch back on again, I couldn't help but think about my first experience on that same course in 2008, where I made a left turn into the parking lot and drove back to San Diego instead of racing up the Mogollon climb to finish the stage. I had a lot more against me this time, with the pain in my body, the two stupid crashes that day, the effort of chasing back into the field twice, the pain in my wrist, and the alien bike I was riding. I turned right.

Jason McCartney on grill duty. The team cooked dinner at the hotel every night.

When the attacks started on the steeper sections, I was the only one able to stay with Janier Acevedo from Jamis, but he cracked me near the top. And that was it; I flew backward to finish seventh. I'd taken the pressure off of Baldwin, though, and he rode to an impressive second place on the day. My broken hand was still bothering me, but it wasn't getting worse.

Carter Jones was my roommate at the hotel that week. He'd had his own share of mechanicals the first day, but with worse timing, and he lost over a minute on the final climb. He couldn't hide his frustration that night.

"Carter," I tried to explain. "You can't tie your happiness to one race. You just have to think about the next one and how you can learn and improve from the experience." When the fuck did I learn that? I got along well with Carter, but it was hard to be his roommate. He was too much like me two years before.

My wrist was killing me. Every bump in the road sent a shock of pain into my hand. I squeezed the bars with white knuckles, counting down the miles until I could cross the finish line and jam my hand into a bucket of ice. My legs, however, were getting better and better. In the time trial, I placed eighth, ahead of all my GC rivals. On the final Gila Monster stage, Acevedo was still in the lead, but he was out of teammates with 60 km and lots of climbing to go. I was on Baldwin's wheel, and he suddenly cracked. Chris was still the team leader, so I started to wait with him. "Come on, Chris!" I urged.

"GO!" he said, gesturing up the road to Acevedo.

I went. The front group was down to six, with only two of them ahead of me on GC.

With 30 km to go, Acevedo was looking tired, and I went on the attack. I built up a one-minute lead as the group shattered behind me, and it looked like I'd win the stage race until Phil Deignan (United Healthcare) and Mancebo broke away from the group and worked together to catch me.

With 5 km to go, I still had 30 seconds, but the race was now among two guys who'd finished in the top 10 at grand tours in Europe chasing one guy who was airlifted after crashing on his face four weeks ago. They caught me 500 meters from the finish, leaving me with second overall. As you've probably noticed, I'm pretty hard on myself, but I'll admit that I was proud of my result. I've seen riders lose entire seasons to head injuries. But second place stings. If I could be happy with second, I wouldn't have made it far to begin with.

BELIEVE IN YOURSELF

Vaughters was following the race reports online, and he criticized my tactics in an e-mail. He said that I rode myself out of the race on the first day when I covered Acevedo's attack to take the pressure off of Baldwin instead of riding my own pace to the finish. In doing that,

I'd lost crucial seconds that eventually cost me the GC. I tried to justify my sacrifice, pointing out that I had no way of knowing I'd be able to contest the overall.

Vaughters's reply was true, and it made me wince. "You've got to believe in yourself," he wrote.

BELIEVE IN THE COLD VIRUS

I had a sore throat and a stuffy nose when I got back to Big Bear, with six days until the start of the Tour of California. With no fever, minor symptoms, and a power meter reading that said my legs were fine, I chalked it up to the high pollen count, loaded up on antihistamines, and crossed my fingers heading into Cali.

FINGER-CROSSING DOESN'T WORK

I wasn't feeling 100 percent, but the first stage at the Tour of California was downright pleasant. After years of fighting for wheels at NRC races, it was refreshing to be among real professionals. American directors always tell their guys to ride at the front of the field, but it's usually just a waste of energy, and that mentality leads to a lot of crashes. There's just not room at the front of the field for everyone. The Europeans, in contrast, don't bother to go up there without good reason, which makes riding conditions very civil in the group. Or did, until we approached the base of a climb. Then it was more like Best Buy when they open the doors on Black Friday.

Stage two was longer and hotter: 126 miles, 114 degrees, and a 20-minute climb to the finish. We could feel the temperature rise as we dropped into Palm Springs, blasting into our faces like we had our noses pressed to a truck exhaust. We soaked ourselves with cold water from our bottles, but volunteers had to catch us before we toppled over when we crossed the line at the top. No one could take another pedal stroke. Friends told me that we looked like torture victims. I finished 15th, behind a handful of domestic guys I'd always beaten on the climbs. Javier Acevedo from Jamis won the stage. I'd killed him in the uphill TT in San Dimas just a couple months before.

I sat in the parking lot for a few minutes to regain my breath. When I stood up, my skin was stained from melted blacktop. The team vehicles were parked at the base of the climb, so we had to coast back down. I barely had the energy to dodge the riders still on the ground who were suffering from heat stroke and surrounded by medics. In the RV, my teammates were already naked. Even socks were too warm after a day like that. I joined them.

Ironically, the heat made my cold worse. The next day, I found myself dropped and riding among the cars every time the road pointed uphill. I lost contact with the group, chased for 80 km, and was finally yanked out with 5 km to go, when officials said I'd missed the time cut. I was sick, and there'd be no finishing that sort of race at 90 percent.

The worst part about a DNF is sitting in the team car following the race. Your legs feel better so quickly that you forget why you were dropped, and you want to get out and rejoin the race. But you can't. After the stage, you're back among your teammates in the hotel rooms, or at the buffet, but nobody looks at you. You wouldn't want them to. You might as well be invisible, or dead.

DON'T BE AFRAID

The team flew me back to Athens the next morning to rest up for nationals in Chattanooga. I coughed all the phlegm and sand out of my lungs and slept for a few nights (and days) in my own bed. My inbox was filled with messages of pity and condolences for the DNF. Everyone thought that a result at the Tour of California was my only shot at Europe for the next year, but my extended e-mail interview with Vaughters continued. He knew that bike racers could get sick, and I still liked my chances.

I wasn't sure if I'd be in shape for Chattanooga even after a week of rest, but I could tell I was having a great day after the first two climbs up Lookout Mountain. Jason McCartney asked how I was feeling, and I hesitated to tell the truth. Asking how your teammate feels is another code, meaning "are you a leader or a worker today?" If I said I felt good, that meant that the guys would ride for me, and it's hard to shoulder that pressure. I hesitated, and heard Vaughters's voice in my head: "Believe in yourself."

"I feel fucking awesome," I told Jason.

My team went to the front and reeled in the breakaway over the next lap, and the group was down to 15 riders after the last time up Lookout. BISSELL had three in the group, but we weren't going to fare well if it came down to a sprint. I attacked alone and got a small gap with 20 miles to go.

My lead grew to over a minute as the chase behind me got organized. I passed through the finish line with one 5 km lap to go, and the crowd roared when they learned that I still had 30 seconds. My arms, legs, and neck were cramping, but I didn't let up, attacking every hill and bombing every corner. I knew that I had a chance to win a national championship, and this could very well be the best day of my life.

I was solo for about 45 minutes. As the gap started to come down in the last 4 km, I thought about my parents and Dan Larson in the crowd, and my friends and supporters watching on their computers, just like I had when I was struggling at Redlands the year before. It helped me dig deeper and suffer more than I ever had before. But it was still 10 against one, and I was caught with 500 meters to go. I was heartbroken. Just like when you DNF, when it's over, you forget how you felt, how much you were hurting. Why didn't I just go harder? Didn't I want to win?

That night the team went out for a Southern barbecue dinner. I'd missed sweet tea and baked beans since I'd left Georgia in January, but it was hard to taste anything but defeat. Freddie Rodriguez from Jelly Belly had won, and he and his team walked in to the same restaurant to celebrate while my team tried to help me forget (there was a lot of beer). Jeremy Powers and Brad Huff skipped the first glass of champagne at their team table. They came over to sit with me.

The following morning I was depressed, a little hung over, and so sore I could barely walk through the airport. After the flight, I sat on the cold, metal edge of the baggage carousel in San Diego and checked my e-mail while I waited for my friend JC to pick me up. Jonathan Vaughters had sent me a contract to join Garmin-Sharp in 2014.

ONCE YOU MAKE IT, YOU CAN TELL PEOPLE WHAT YOU REALLY THINK

It was a modest offer, but I signed without negotiating anything. Making money is easy compared to what I'd been through. Lots of people get rich (somebody got rich off of stuffed-crust pizza), but how many people get to ride for one of the best teams in the world? I wasn't about to risk my shot at Europe because I tried to get a few extra bucks. Besides, how could I be expected to negotiate through tears of joy?

When the news was announced in the media, my phone didn't stop ringing. It felt great to soak it in and to thank everyone who helped me along the way. Finally, though, I had to turn it off and go for a bike ride. That's how I celebrate.

EPILOGUE

It's been eye-opening to look back at what I've put myself through to race a bike. There have been times when I've hated my job, tired of the travel and the financial struggles. I've wanted to drop out in the middle of a race, sure that pro cycling isn't all it's cracked up to be. But overall, the good parts stand out more than the bad. Every career has rough patches to push through and near misses to accept. Everyone's loved and lost, and we all hit our head at some point.

I still don't know if I'll make it in Europe. I'm not even sure what "making it" means exactly, but I have to keep pushing the boulder up the hill, perhaps just to see if it's possible. There will be more crashes, pain, and suffering, and quitting will cross my mind, but I know I can't, because I can also see myself winning races. Silly as it is, I can imagine winning the Tour de France. Of course, maybe everyone who fails felt something similar all along, right up to the moment they gave up. Maybe it's my fate as a man to repeat the mistakes of history.

What about doping? What if racing clean is like bringing a knife to a gunfight? I'm glad that I came up in a generation that didn't have to worry about that. I wouldn't have made it this close to the top if doping were still rampant, and I would have seen it a long time ago. If I'm racing in Europe, to say that the sport isn't clean is to say that no one has more natural talent than I do, and that's silly. We'll always have cheaters, because cheating is a means to money and glory. I believe, though, that it is more the exception than the rule. Cycling is in a bad place now, but sponsors and fans will come back because it is a beautiful sport.

With or without the dopers, I can get what I need out of cycling—and in a lot of ways, I already have. I'll never go back to the overweight, unhappy person I used to be, because I have a respect for my body and a world-class work ethic. Any good idea I've ever had (both of them) came to me on the bike. Thanks to winning Best Young Rider at Univest in 2007 with the sniffles, I'll never have to call in sick to work. Because of the day I chased Francisco Mancebo on the Sunset circuits, I won't buckle under pressure. After all the times I raced with my shorts torn open, and scrubbed gravel out of my flesh in tepid motel showers, I feel pain, but it doesn't bother me; looking around, I always feel like the toughest man in the room. When my doctor takes my pulse and heart rate, he says I'll live forever (I'm always afraid he'll stab me after that, but so far, so good). I've peed over the side of the Golden Gate Bridge, and once, during a training ride, I even caught a glimpse of a unicorn. (It might have been a goat with one horn broken off.) Most important, I've seen the world from my bike and experienced all sorts of adventures and excitement in its climbs and descents.

It won't be easy moving to Europe, competing in races I've only watched on TV, against guys I've always idolized. I feel like I just exited a five-year obstacle course, took a deep breath, and found another one in front of me, but I can't wait to set new goals and see what I can learn. I chatted with Matt Koschara about training one day, and he brought up a big-picture question: With a contract in hand so early, was I still motivated to train for the rest of the season? Would I still race hard now that my big goal was accomplished, without money or a contract at stake? He just wanted me to think about it, but he knew the answer. Of course I could. It's not about the money or the next team I'll join. It's about the feeling of racing a bike. I need it. I spent all that time trying to "get" cycling, and it turned out I had it backward.

I'm 27 years old now. In another 25 years, maybe I'll have a yellow jersey from the 2015 Tour de France hanging in my palatial estate. Or maybe I'll be crammed in traffic on the way to a cubicle. I do know that however I spend the rest of my years, as much of it as possible will be on two skinny tires, going as fast as I can. Bike racing won't look like much on a résumé when it's finished with me, but I can't think of a better way to spend my time. I think about all the intellectual and emotional parts of this sport, the ups and downs, the love and hate, the physical and mental anguish, goal setting, hard work, pressure, teamwork, conquering fear, and overcoming odds. Even if I fail at this mission I'll be more prepared for the next one, because no matter what happens in life, I will already have lived through it on a bike.

So what did I tell the two kids in Tucson who wanted to know what pro cycling was like? Nothing. We ate the pizza, and they didn't bring it up again. Maybe they sensed my fear and had mercy on me. Now that I've thought about it, what I should have said was this:

It's a bitch of a sport, but it's worth a try, because if you accomplish something that you never knew was possible, you'll always have a reason to swing for the fences. On the way, remember that good days don't mean a thing if you haven't had a few bad ones. But if you can make it through all the struggles and pain, the hardest part will be keeping a straight face when you get your paycheck. I don't think I'd recommend anyone try to take my path exactly, but maybe learning from my mistakes will help. Keep in mind that a dream can string you along, and chasing it might mean a sacrifice in security and comfort, and understand that for everyone who made it as far as I did or farther, there are probably a thousand who floundered and failed. And no matter what, wear a helmet, because it still takes some luck, and as great as riding and racing is, cycling isn't something to pin all your hopes on. It's too precarious.

GLOSSARY

Attack: When a rider sprints ahead of the group to break away. We usually just do it to look cool, but sometimes it backfires and you have to be in a breakaway all day.

Bicycle: A transportation device with two wheels, metal, and carbon fiber parts. Some idiot decided to race them, and it could very well ruin your life if you happen to enjoy it.

Breakaway (or break): A rider or group of riders who escapes from the main pack. The break almost always gets caught.

Caravan: Pack of team support cars and officials that follows a race, to ensure that bikes have a negative impact on the environment.

Cassette: Part of the bike attached to the rear wheel, with cogs of different sizes for each gear. Sometimes, they play music from the 1980s.

Category: Racers are split up by experience and ability levels. You start at Cat. V, and as you improve, your number goes down. Cat. I is the highest you can get as an amateur, and it makes you eligible for pro teams. Cat. V is like a game of bumper cars in tights.

Chainring: The part of the bike that's mounted to the crank, with teeth for the chain to ride on, or to dig into your flesh when you crash, which makes a cool scar.

Clipless pedals: Modern racing pedals that allow the shoe to connect to the pedal mechanically, without the traditional toe clip. You twist your foot to get it out, but you'll make an ass of yourself crashing at a stoplight at least once before you get used to it.

Composite team: A team that forms for one race, made up of riders who don't have teams or who normally ride for different teams. You only do it if you're really desperate, and it's never worth the effort.

Criterium: A type of race common in the United States, with lots of laps around a course that's usually less than a mile long. Great for spectators who like to watch crashes. Often abbreviated "crit."

Cyclocross: Different discipline of bike racing, in which riders race laps around a mixture of dirt, pavement, and obstacles, which often requires carrying the bike. It's kind of a combination of road racing, mountain biking, and mud wrestling.

Derailleur: Part of the bike that moves the chain onto a different cog when you hit the shifter button. Also, the hardest part of the bike to spell.

Domestique: A rider whose role is to support others rather than to get results himself. These guys usually get paid shit.

EPO: Erythropomyacin, or something like that. I'm afraid to look it up, because the anti-doping authorities are probably watching my computer. In fact, I could get in trouble just for typing it. DELETE DELETE. Anyway, EPO is a performance-enhancing drug taken via needle. I know a couple former pros who used it back in the day. They said you'd have to get up in the middle of the night to get your blood pumping so you wouldn't have a heart attack, and that's why a few guys died. But if you didn't die, boy could you pedal fast.

Field: A pack of cyclists in a race, not to be confused with a gay pride parade.

Field sprint: When the race doesn't finish in a breakaway, and the whole pack sprints together to the finish, except for the guys who fall down.

GC: Short for *general classification*, a rider's overall placing in a stage race.

Hillclimb: An event that goes up a hill, with all the riders starting in a pack at the bottom. I always did well at these, but there aren't nearly enough of them.

Intermediate sprint: A sprint in the middle of a race for points, time bonuses, or separate prizes. Climbers and GC riders usually get out of the way.

Interval: In training, a certain amount of time to go a specific intensity. Coaches insist that intervals make you faster.

Junior: A rider under 19 years old. Little brats, usually.

KOM: King of the Mountain. Some races have a separate competition, giving points at the top of each climb. Always won by a skinny dude.

Lap the field: In a criterium or track race, escaping the pack and then catching it again from behind. When you lap the field, you feel like a badass.

Meter: Metric measure of distance. It's like a yard. Pretty much the same as a yard.

Motel: A building that allows you to watch TV and sleep, in exchange for a fee and a small amount of your self-esteem.

Motorpace: When a rider drafts a motorized vehicle, in training or in the race caravan. It's good if you like exhaust fumes.

NRC: National Racing Calendar, the traveling circus of professional races in the United States.

Peloton: *See* Field.

Prime (pronounced "preem"): A prize for the winner of a specific lap in a criterium. It's usually a gift certificate for $25 to a nearby bike shop, which I sell for $15 to a local.

Prologue: A short time trial. Often the opening stage of a stage race, it requires guys to fly in a day earlier, carb load, warm up, and ride really hard for less than five minutes, and it never affects the end result of the race.

Pull (or pull through, or take a pull): When a rider takes a turn in the wind, allowing others to draft him. You only do it if you absolutely have to.

Race radio: Walkie-talkie with an earpiece, so the riders can get yelled at by their bosses during the race, instead of after. Most races don't allow radios anymore. Fine by me.

Road race: The traditional type of one-day race, where riders start together in one place and race to a finish line in some other place.

Rotation: Standard rider formation in a race, in which they take quick turns at the front and then move over for the next guy to take a pull. Wind determines whether you rotate clockwise or counter-clockwise, but I always screw it up.

Selection: The front group of a race after a majority of the pack has been dropped. They usually attack each other to show off, and then let the group catch back up.

Soigneur: Staff on a professional team, in charge of massage, bottles, food, etc. If the soigneur likes you, you get a longer massage.

Stage race: Type of race made up of several stages over multiple days. Like they do in France.

Time bonus: In a stage race, the winner of a stage or intermediate sprint often gets a time bonus, which is time subtracted from his overall time. A sneaky way to move up on the general classification.

Time trial (TT): A type of race where riders start on the course individually, and the placings are determined by who finishes in the fastest time. Equipment nerds love this one.

Velodrome: A venue for track racing, with banked corners and seating for spectators. Picture a giant toilet bowl.

ACKNOWLEDGMENTS

Thank you to my friends, family, teammates, coaches, directors, hosts, and everyone who believed in me over the years for enabling me to live this story. Many of the people who were critical to this journey couldn't be properly thanked or mentioned in the text, because this is a book, not an acceptance speech. But whatever happened here, I couldn't have done it without you.

And to Jen Whalen, who'll star in the sequel.

ABOUT THE AUTHOR

Phil Gaimon is a cyclist, writer, and entrepreneur who retired from laziness and computer games in 2004 in favor of riding a bike to lose weight. On a whim, he started racing and soon discovered that he was a natural. Phil advanced rapidly through the amateur ranks and turned professional in his second full year, still ignorant of a century of cycling etiquette. He slowly learned the rules while clawing his way to the top of the American pro ranks, joining Garmin-Sharp in 2014. He maintains a web site, Philthethrill.net, where he chronicles his ceaseless pursuit of the best cookies in America.